HOPE FOR HURTING FAMILIES

Creating Family Justice Centers Across America

DISCARD

CASEY GWINN, JD with GAEL STRACK, JD

VOLCANO
· PRESS ·

Hope for Hurting Families: Creating Family Justice Centers Across America

Copyright © 2006 by Casey Gwinn and Gael Strack

Published 2006 by Volcano Press

Library of Congress Cataloging-in-Publication Data

Gwinn, Casey, 1960–
    Hope for hurting families : creating family justice centers across America / by Casey Gwinn and Gael Strack.
       p.   cm.
    Includes bibliographical references.
    ISBN 1-884244-30-0 (pbk.)
    1. Victims of family violence—Services for—United States. 2. Problem families—Services for—United States. 3. Community-based family services—United States. 4. Family violence—United States—Prevention. I. Strack, Gael, 1958– II. Title.
HV6626.2.G75 2006
362.82'925250973—dc22   2006000276

ISBN 1-884244-30-0

Cover and Interior page design by Jeff Brandenburg
Editing by Marj Stuart

First printing Volcano Press, 2006
Printed in the United States of America

For online catalog and ordering: www.volcanopress.com
For bulk discount information, contact: sales@volcanopress.com

Tel: 209.296.7989
Tel: Orders only: 800.879.9636
Fax: 209.296.4515

Volcano Press
Box 270
Volcano, CA 95689

Contact Volcano Press about the forthcoming manual, *The Family Justice Center Handbook*, on how to create a Family Justice Center in your community.

Contents

Dedication

To Beth
Kelly, Karianne, and Chris

To Jan
Samantha and Taylor

With the hope that you, your children, and your children's children
experience lives filled with affirmation and love . . .
lives free of violence, sexual assault, and abuse . . .

ACKNOWLEDGEMENTS

It is almost impossible to thank all those that have made this book possible. Hundreds of dedicated friends, supporters, colleagues, survivors, and other professionals have played a role in helping us create and share this vision. Special thanks go to Judi Adams, Jan Strack, Beth Gwinn, and Marj Stuart for their tremendous work as editors. Adam and Ruth Gottstein are the best publishers that any author could ever ask for. We are also deeply indebted to so many who toil in the trenches of the San Diego Family Justice Center day in and day out, pouring their souls into the lives of hurting families. Three years ago, so many dedicated staff members in the City Attorney's Office helped make the Center become a reality. And long before the Family Justice Center vision ever became a reality, the groundwork for this movement was laid by advocates and survivors in San Diego, across the country, and around the world who kept advocating for better ways to provides services to victims and their children.

As this vision expands, we have come to be so thankful for the Family Justice Center staff and our national training team including Jim Barker, Diane McGrogan, Kimberly Pearce, Brenda Lugo, Bonnie Pearson, Lyndsay Wolf, Jennifer Bodine, Robert Keetch, George McClane, Charles Wilson, Linda Quinn, Judy Nelson, Judi Adams, Gina Vaughn, Mickey Stone, Alondra Orozco, and so many others who have played powerful roles in helping us run the San Diego Center and support other Family Justice Centers developing in the United States and around the world. Their day to day work has helped shape every chapter of this book.

We must give a special thank you to our city and county elected officials for their courage to do the right thing in the midst of major budget challenges. Despite very limited resources, they kept their priorities straight and made funding this Center and related family violence services one of their highest public safety priorities.

Thanks to so many private foundations and other funders and donors that have provided the financial support necessary to open and operate the Center. And a very special acknowledgement to our wonderful, gifted, and dedicated volunteers—who stick by us despite always being under construction at the Center, including the Family Justice Center Foundation board members who keep investing so much to make the Center and Camp Hope shining beacons of hope to so many in need.

And when it is all said and done . . . we must especially acknowledge the thousands of survivors who have graciously shared their stories with us and invested their lives in us by holding us accountable for meeting their needs and the needs of so many other victims and children that the Center has the opportunity to serve.

FOREWORD

Oprah Made Me Do It

This book is written to offer hope . . . hope for hurting families across America . . . hope embodied in a new approach to providing services to those hurt by verbal, emotional, physical, and sexual abuse in intimate relationships.

Today, victims of domestic violence (violence between adults in intimate relationships) and their children face a gauntlet of agencies and programs when they seek help in virtually every community in the country. In the midst of terror, trauma, shock, and pain, they must navigate a hopelessly complex web of systems, agencies, services, laws, policies, procedures, and regulations. They are forced to go from place to place to get all the help they need and must tell their story over and over again. This book lays out the Family Justice Center (Center) vision as one of the best approaches to solve the frustrating and ineffective system that has evolved.

This book is written to challenge domestic violence advocates, policy makers, elected officials, and caring people to consider a new vision for helping hurting families. The vision is simple and straightforward: specialized "one-stop shop" service centers across America with staff from many agencies coming together in one place to provide convenient, effective, and efficient services to victims of family violence and their children.

This book is also personal. It challenges readers to examine their own views of family violence, their own family histories, and their own experiences in considering the vision presented in this book. No matter how bad the abuse, no matter how long the pattern of violence, no matter how horrific the sexual assault, there is hope for violent and abusive families in America. The cycle can be broken. Healing is possible. Help is available. Now, 30 years into the domestic violence movement, we are beginning to see the path to effective intervention through creative partnerships.

So the question remains. What motivated me to write this book now? What motivated Gael Strack to agree to join me in this journey? What happened that gave me the desire to spend many long hours working on a book? Mindful of the need to keep my sense of humor after 20 years as a man in the feminist-led domestic violence movement, let me answer the question about the genesis of this book.

I am passionately committed to helping stop family violence, but writing a book was not part of the plan. Quite frankly, I'd rather just do the work—prosecute the bad guys, help victims and their kids find help, and dream of new approaches to the difficult challenges of breaking the generational cycle of family violence.

I am a prosecutor, not a writer. I am trained to think like a lawyer, investigate criminal cases, and prosecute cases in a courtroom. So what motivated me to write a book for average Americans, seeking to point the way to effective prevention, intervention, and healing for the hurting families of America? The answer is actually very simple. Oprah made me do it.

In the fall of 2002, the City of San Diego, along with many local community agencies, opened the San Diego Family Justice Center, the most comprehensive service center for victims of domestic violence anywhere in America. During the same time period, the New York Times ran an article discussing the failures of the criminal justice system in dealing with domestic violence. The article quoted a New York University professor, Linda Mills, who condemned the inability of the criminal justice system deal with domestic violence. Oprah Winfrey saw the discord between the goals of the Center and the claims of Linda Mills.

I was invited to be on the Oprah Winfrey Show, and the producer said I would have the opportunity to discuss the vision of the San Diego Center. It seemed natural and obvious that I would talk about San Diego's efforts to help hurting families. But it did not take me long to realize that I was not actually on the show to talk about San Diego's response to family violence. While Oprah did, in fact, air an excellent profile of the Center, I was really on the show to debate the professor. Once taping began, the debate began, and Oprah quickly became the moderator and referee.

I arrived in Chicago on January 23, 2003, to talk to Oprah about our new program in San Diego. But something very different happened. The professor from New York was the main guest, though I had no idea she was the focus until I met her on the set of the show. As the taping unfolded, the professor advocated for the decriminalization of domestic violence in America. She used a wide brush to paint every law enforcement intervention as misguided and counter-productive. She called for the repeal of mandatory arrest laws and reduced focus on criminal prosecution of batterers. She criticized and critiqued our work in San Diego, though she had no personal knowledge of our programs and had never visited the new Center.

I agreed with her on the need for healing for the whole family. I agreed with her that some law enforcement agencies revictimize victims with their uninformed, paternalistic, and condemning approaches. But most of my agreement with the professor stopped there. Resmaa Menakim, who was also on the show that day representing the Tubman Family Alliance in Minnesota, argued for healing men in America. Oprah argued for healing women. I argued for the arrest and prosecution of offenders in order to make the rest of it possible. It was a lively show and the "after show" was even livelier. The experience convinced me that the truth about effective intervention and prevention as embodied in the Center vision needed to be written down in plain language and made available to as many people as possible.

On the way to the airport, I had no doubt about the need. I felt compelled for the first time in my life to put in writing our simple thesis for stopping domestic violence within our lifetimes, a simple organizational structure to bring communities together to stop family violence. Many communities were already headed down the road of co-locating some small number of professionals, but no one was writing about it. No one was articulating the simple, profound power of bringing professionals together into one geographic location and then challenging every segment of the local community to rally around this new living organism until it grew into a powerful haven of safety and a force for change.

The need was for a book for men and women, victims and survivors, cops and prosecutors, pastors and counselors, priests and rabbis, employers and employees, citizens and immigrants, politicians and policy makers, moms and dads, fathers and mothers, grandfathers and grandmothers—a book that would thoughtfully, carefully, and simply challenge the American people to come together and pursue a path toward hope and healing for violent families.

It was a book that could not simply call out a course of conduct, though. It was a book that must recount how to get from point A to B to C to D in order to make the Center vision a reality. The book could not simply tell you what to do at point D. It had to talk openly about what works and what does not. Social change is too complex for a simple approach. No community quickly arrives at successful intervention or prevention of violence and abuse in the home. It is trial and error. At times, the results are mediocre. At other times, the result is failure. It is a long, complicated process.

And let's be honest. Resmaa and I spent the show in the front row of the audience where most of Oprah's quick, brief guests sit these days, not on Oprah's couch. Why? We didn't have a book. San Diego didn't have a book.

We didn't have anything published with any kind of national attention that could point the way. We simply had the arguments of this prosecutor or that advocate. We had a keynote address from time to time at a conference or symposium. The ones who had been doing the work day to day in our community could mount a very passionate appeal for San Diego's co-located services vision. But we were hard-pressed to find it memorialized in print.

Resmaa Menakim and I were just trench workers that day on Oprah. We were the clinicians listening to the "author" and the "academician." The professor had some nice artwork for the cover of her new book and a thesis—a controversial, dangerous thesis—but a thesis, nevertheless, about how to help hurting families caught in the generational cycle of domestic violence. If that was what would spread our humble message across the country, then why not write a book? If that was what would stake out our position in the national debate, then why not do it?

There is a new vision emerging that gives real hope. There is a new consensus emerging that is bringing together diverse professionals and trench workers in the day-to-day grind of providing services. It is a vision and an action plan that must be repeated over and over. It must be disseminated. It must be listened to. Perhaps as never before, we have an opportunity to say, "This works." We have an opportunity to say, "We have one important answer in a very complex movement."

Our answers from San Diego (and now other successful jurisdictions across the country) are not the result of manipulated or misrepresented social science research. They are not held captive to a political ideology or partisan political agenda. The answers we offer from the San Diego experience have been proven in the lives of hurting women, men, and children in our communities. Indeed, many of this book's chapters start with the true stories of heroic women who have escaped abusive relationships. We have seen firsthand the compelling stories of real people who have been helped and healed. Yet this book is more than anecdotes. It includes the feedback, through testimonials and focus group results, of many clients who have now used our Center. It also touches on the trends and patterns and consistent evidence of success emerging in our community now that we are 30 years into a movement that started long before I was involved in the issue.

Those working to stop family violence today must acknowledge their roots. We are all profoundly impacted by the feminist movement in this country. Most of us are products of women who have invested themselves in our communities and our lives. They have shaped our views. Even as we dive into the challenges we face in dealing with family violence, we must acknowledge where we have come from and who we have learned from.

In my views of family violence, I am a product of three feminist advocates who invested their lives in me in 1985. I was born and raised in a conservative, Christian home with loving parents, but professionally speaking, I am a product of the feminist movement. My work and my life have been informed by many advocates and survivors of family violence. It is their love, support, and friendship that help drive me forward day by day even after two decades of dealing with violence, pain, trauma, and heartbreak.

In 1985, I was a new prosecutor in the San Diego City Attorney's Office. As is still true in many prosecutors' offices in America, I was assigned to handle family violence cases. I was junior. I was inexperienced. I would openly admit, I was only marginally competent in any aspect of criminal prosecution, let alone the complex arena of domestic violence. I had graduated from Stanford University in 1982 and UCLA School of Law in 1985, and yet I had never heard the phrase "domestic violence" until going to work in San Diego. I was green and naïve, inexperienced and uninformed.

In the midst of those handicaps, three women came into my life in a matter of days: Ashley Walker, the founder of the first battered women's shelter in San Diego and the Executive Director of the YWCA Battered Women's Services; Joyce Faidley, a rape counselor at the Center for Women's Studies and Services (now the Center for Community Solutions); and Judy Rowland, the Director of the California Crime Victims Legal Clinic. They came to me without being solicited. They were women of substance and passion. They were advocates determined to argue for the needs of battered women and their children.

I was the first prosecutor ever assigned in the San Diego City Attorney's Office to handle domestic violence cases full-time. They had heard of me through the battered women's grapevine and came to see what they had to work with. They didn't declare war. They didn't tell me I was incompetent (though I was). Well, they might have called me an idiot at one point (and I was)! But they came and offered help, expertise, support, and, most importantly, friendship. They invested their lives in me. And neither I nor San Diego will ever be the same because of their decision to connect our lives in a cause bigger than ourselves.

Within two years, our efforts had dramatically expanded to build relationships between agencies and disciplines and among individuals that share a passion for this issue. One of these incredible individuals was Gael Strack. Gael and I met in a courtroom, initially as professional adversaries, but soon joined forces to change the world. Gael was a criminal defense attorney. I was a prosecutor. She was defending a domestic violence offender. I was trying to put him in jail. Though we were adversaries, it was immediately clear to me that this talented, passionate lawyer was a person who could play a powerful role in our emerging vision to provide healing to victims.

And healing victims is what it is all about. It is not about how *we* are going to help *those* people or *those women* who have *this* problem. Domestic violence is not about *that* socioeconomic group or *that* ethnic group. It is not only about those who are married. It is not only about those who live together. It is not about *those* Bible Belt families. It is not about *those* immigrant families. It is not about *those* gay and lesbian couples.

It is about us! It is about our view of women in society. It is about our view of intimate relationships. It is about our views on male privilege. It is about men and women who grew up in unhealthy, abusive homes. It is about a culture dripping in violence, anger, hate, and disrespect for others. It is about straight and gay relationships. It is not only about people of color or the poor or disenfranchised. It is about every ethnic group and every socioeconomic group. It is about how we treat our partners and our spouses. It is about *our* beliefs, *our* choices, and *our* values as a society.

We are also writing this book for men. I want to set an example for other men. I want to set an example for my son, Chris. I want to inspire men and boys—motivate them, challenge them. I speak for many in San Diego when I say we want men to stand up and be counted along with women. We want men to speak out. We want men to lead their communities forward, in partnership with women. We want men to come together with loud voices to hail healthy, equal, honoring relationships characterized by mutual respect and empowerment.

We want men to acknowledge their God-given, unique gifts and abilities. But we want men to respect, serve, and honor women. We want men to stop apologizing for themselves and start becoming who they are destined to be. I am not a "male basher." I am not an emasculated man. I work with determined, focused, driven men who believe passionately that domestic violence will never end until men stand up and, in partnership with women, become a large and powerful part of the solution.

Finally, we are writing this book as a testimony to the *power of we*. By now, you have seen me shift back and forth between "I" and "we." It will happen often in the book. I have written most of the book, but Gael has also written key chapters and played an important role as an editor. The primary reason for "we" throughout the book, though, is to recognize the hundreds of people and businesses that have made the Center a reality in San Diego. In fact, beginning in Chapter 4, you will see quotes from those who work at the Center and those who have benefited from it. We interspersed them as a tribute to victims and survivors, and as a strong statement of respect for the many who work day in and day out at the San Diego Center helping to develop a model that is already traveling around the world.

So we are writing this book for many good reasons. But when I am asked in the quietness of the moment by my children, my wife, or our close friends why I really decided to write a book with such grand goals and aspirations, I look at them thoughtfully, reflect silently for a few moments and then give the real answer: Oprah made me do it.

Casey Gwinn
Co-Founder, San Diego Family Justice Center
March 2006

INTRODUCTION

Finding Hope for Hurting Families

When Tricia came to the Family Justice Center on a sunny San Diego day, it was the first time in her life she had ever set foot in any kind of facility for victims of family violence though she had been victimized since the tender age of 11. She was terrified when she arrived. I saw it on her face as soon as she walked into the reception area. She was afraid of the consequences of disclosure. She was afraid of outside involvement in her family. She feared retaliation, rejection, and isolation. But she was taking the first step toward help.

We did not use the formal intake procedure. She was not ready for that. I agreed to simply sit and talk to her. In the quiet of an interview room, referred to only as the den, with a flower- filled painting on the wall, silk plants, overstuffed chairs, soft lighting, and a warm purple couch, Tricia settled in after shaking my hand. She did not speak. She listened, head down. She did not look at me even after I began to speak. So I just talked. I explained how the criminal justice system works. I explained what would likely happen if she told someone what had happened to her. She wanted my promise that her abuser would not go to jail. I told her I could not make that promise, but I would promise protection and support for her.

She stared at the ground for most of our meeting until I began to tell her about my own family experience with abuse. I was honest and forthright about my dad's father and about the issues I saw and experienced in my family. Only then did Tricia lift her eyes and meet my gaze. For a moment, we had a bond. I felt a small fraction of her pain. I had felt the loneliness and shame of family violence, and for a few brief moments as I shared about my own extended family, she stared directly into my eyes. But as soon as I returned to the procedures and policies of the criminal justice system and the operating protocols of the Center, her eyes returned to her downward stare.

Finally, after an hour of trying to connect with a trapped, traumatized, and deeply withdrawn young woman, I offered Tricia a tour of the Center. In our first sixteen months of operation, we had given tours to thousands of visitors. The Center had generated much excitement with local, national, and international visitors. After I appeared on the Oprah Winfrey Show in February 2003, we hosted visitors from all 50 states and 37 other countries. But that day, a new first happened. I spent an hour giving a tour to a victim of family violence. Though thousands of professionals had walked the halls of our new intervention approach, we had never thought to give our clients a tour of the facility before they received services. Tricia became the first and she helped to teach us about the needs of victims and survivors.

Tricia was simply introduced as a visitor as we walked amiably through the 40,000 square feet of social services, faith-based services, medical services, law enforcement professionals, and prosecutors. I explained what each agency did for clients and why. I showed her our file room that already held information about a number of cases. I treated her as I would any visiting dignitary. She acted poised and professional. She looked like any of the thousands of visiting professionals we have at the Center.

After the tour ended, I thanked Tricia for coming and offered the help of the Center whenever she was ready to come forward. She thanked me and left. I didn't know if my new technique of victim outreach would yield fruit and offer hope to Tricia or not.

Just two days later, I had my answer. Tricia returned and began the long, painful, complicated road to healing. The Center became her new beginning—the birth of hope for Tricia in the company of those who believed her and surrounded her with help and support.

It is for Tricia and millions of other victims of family violence that we write this book. No matter how bad the abuse, no matter how long the pattern of violence, no matter how horrific the sexual assault, there is hope.

We are at the beginning of a movement already being referred to as the Family Justice Center movement. It promises to be one of the most profound steps forward in the domestic violence movement in America in 30 years. It grows out of the shelter movement and the courageous work of many advocates and survivors. The vision is a call for greater coordination, collaboration, and cooperation. It is a call to co-locate all available services for a victim of intimate partner violence in one place. It is also a personal call for more caring Americans to step forward to make a difference in stopping family violence that touches millions and millions of families.

If you have never read a book on family violence, and if you never read another book on the subject, don't put this one down! Learn about the creation of Family Justice Centers across America. Learn how you can help. Come to grips with violence or abuse you may have suffered or may be suffering. If you are not a victim, prepare yourself to assist others. We need you to help us keep moving forward.

So much remains to be done. Many families need the hope that this book can offer. Domestic violence and child abuse have destroyed enough families. This is not only a women's issue. It is *our* problem. It is *our* challenge. It is *our* responsibility to come together to provide hope and healing to hurting families. Professionals, policy makers, and caring community leaders need to know what stops family violence. Beyond partisan politics, beyond debates about scarce resources, beyond the willful ignorance of so many, there is hope. There are answers.

With our eyes set on the hope for violent families this book has four major purposes. First, it sets the table for addressing the issue of domestic violence, child abuse, stalking, and sexual assault in American families. The first few chapters lay out the basics. Why is it so hard for us to listen to battered women in this country? Why is there still so much denial about the prevalence of family violence? When we talk about violence between mom and dad or boyfriend and girlfriend, why don't we want to talk about its impact on the children? Why is there such hostility between the child abuse movement and the domestic violence movement? What is the impact on children when they witness violence in the home? What is the impact when they actually experience abuse and sexual assault? We all need to be on the same page about the problem before we can start talking about one of the most innovative solutions to appear in the last 30 years.

Second, this book recounts the history of the domestic violence movement, particularly as it informs the future of the Family Justice Center movement. To understand why multidisciplinary service centers are an idea whose time has come in healing hurting families, we need to recognize the building blocks that bring communities to the point of being able to develop a Center. Portions of the San Diego story are also included in the book since San Diego is a case study in how to bring a community together to stop family violence and related sexual assault.

Third, this book is a rebuttal to those who would roll back the progress that has been made to date in addressing family violence, particularly in relation to the role of the criminal justice system. It is a defense of approaches that are working and strategies that are effective. It is a clear explanation of how initiatives over the last 20 years are now folding into the Center vision. Today, some are calling for reduced emphasis on criminal justice initiatives to deal with child abuse and domestic violence. By pointing to communities where intervention is failing and victims are being revictimized by institutions seeking to help them, critics are denying the successes of the domestic violence movement. And they are ignoring the opportunity to take the healthy components of our current strategies and meld them together into a unified vision for helping violent families.

Finally, and centrally, this book is a call to a simple straightforward approach to stopping domestic violence through true coordination of services for victims, perpetrators, and their children. Informed by the success of Child Advocacy Centers, which have developed in the last 20 years to deal with victims of child abuse, the National Family Justice Center movement, inspired by San Diego, now seeks to take the concept of one-stop shop services to a whole new level.

There is a premise in this book: In family violence situations, we are sending ambulances to the bottom of the cliff instead of building a fence at the top of the cliff. We are waiting too long to help hurting families. We are waiting too long to help children growing up in violent and abusive homes. We must get involved earlier and with more coordinated resources in order to stop the need to send faster and faster ambulances to the bottom of the cliff. The Center vision is really about building fences. The vision is to get the offender involved with accountability and consequences as early as possible. You will hear the focus on spending money sooner rather than later throughout the book.

The book is organized into chapters that seek to move us forward toward a Family Justice Center approach to dealing with family violence.

Friends have warned that the general public will not be interested in a book about family violence and abuse. It is not the hot topic these days. America's focus on family violence in the mid-1990s has given way to school violence, 9/11, the Iraq conflict, and the global war against terrorism. But we remain undeterred. It is time for this book. Every major conflict on the planet has its roots in failed relationships—between countries, leaders, levels of government, families, relatives, and even between individual men, women, and children. The genesis of most major social ills, in fact, trace back to the family. Homelessness, drug and alcohol abuse, gangs, school shootings, bullying, male privilege and patriarchy, juvenile crime, and adult criminal behavior all have deep connections to family violence.

Why, after decades of initiatives, are we still dealing with the issues of child abuse, domestic violence, and sexual assault in this country? We have laws. We have policies and procedures. We have had public awareness campaigns. We have profiled the issues in movies, television shows, and music videos. So, why aren't we done yet? The answer, we will argue, is that we have not yet reached what has been called "critical mass" or the "tipping point" in social change theory. We have not yet marshaled our forces to get large numbers of communities—rural, suburban, and urban—moving forward with a common vision. We have not yet identified family violence as one of the most persistent and endemic public safety and public health issues in America. Perhaps this book can play a role in helping more people move forward sooner and faster than has been the case in the past.

To be sure, no one should never write a book related to domestic violence with even a pretense of having all the answers. Neither we nor our San Diego community have all the answers. Nor is the Center service delivery model a panacea for all violence in families. Gael Strack and I don't have it all figured out. We still make many mistakes, don't have all the answers, and try to keep constantly learning as we go.

Though much of the philosophical content of the book is written by one author, the book often uses plural pronouns to describe what we have experienced over the 25 years since San Diego, and many other communities around the country, began to focus on family violence issues. It uses we to describe how so many have worked together in San Diego to bring about the Center. It uses we to recognize Gael's role throughout this book. Though her chapters are identified and her specific content pieces are titled, Gael also played a role in editing and providing input throughout the book. The book also uses we to describe the developing National Family Justice Center Initiative in tribute to so many who are now joining this movement on a national level.

This book uses *we* often as well because it is a call to the power of *we*. It is a call to real, meaningful, coordinated community response. It is a call to the power that small groups of individuals can exercise in changing the world as they know it. As Margaret Meade said many years ago, "Never underestimate the ability of a small group of committed individuals to change the world. Indeed, it is the only thing that ever has." It is with deep reverence and respect for so many who have invested so much for so long that this book briefly shares the San Diego experience and advocates for Centers across America and around the world in the context of the national and international domestic violence movement.

Violent families in America and around the world need hope. But we must give it to them. We must give it to them with healthy personal relationships that bring our communities together. These goals will be best accomplished by creating living organisms called Family Justice Centers where hope can be cultivated and then flourish in the lives of hurting families.

We must build relationships that will triumph over turf issues, political battles, and resource debates. We must provide intervention, and then we must be sure that no family is left behind. We cannot fail. Too many generations of marriages, relationships, children, and lives have already been lost. So let's move forward to give hope to hurting families. It is time.

1

I Have a Friend . . .

Mara heard our church was having a sermon on family violence. She usually attended a small church on the other side of San Diego. Her husband was in the Navy and often away from home. Her church had become her support network, especially when her husband shipped out on a six-month deployment. Those were the loneliest times of her life. But they were not her worst problem. It was when her husband was home, not when he was away, that Mara suffered the most pain. Mara's husband, a Navy corpsman, was a batterer. He started hitting her when she became pregnant with their first child. Now, with her daughter nearly four months old, the violence was becoming more severe.

The pastor and I hosted an evening entitled "The Prosecutor Versus the Pastor," and Mara came. It was not an adversarial session. It was the first time in the history of our church that domestic violence was dealt with openly from the pulpit. It was attended by many of our own members, but was even better attended by women from other churches who could not safely come forward for help in their own church.

After the meeting ended, Mara came to the front of the church. She introduced herself by first name only and then said, "I have a friend who needs help." She was shaking and had clearly been crying. I recognized but did not confront her clear misstatement of the situation. I had little doubt that she probably did have friends who also needed help. But I was also sure that I was talking to a woman who was not quite ready to admit her own victimization. Within a week, she would be staying in our home and would begin the long journey toward healing from family violence and regaining health.

I will never forget her time in our home. The first night she was with us, I heard "night terrors"—the blood-curdling screaming of her 10-month-old baby. While every domestic violence shelter staff member in America has heard the crying of a child growing up in the middle of domestic violence, I had never heard such a sound. It is a sound I will never forget. Mara was with us for two weeks. It was an education. She would confront me at the dinner table when I patronized her. She would ask me to explain over breakfast the conduct of her abusive husband. She would cry when talking about how much she still loved him even though she was afraid of him. She would help us understand the honest challenges of a battered woman still in love with her batterer. But I will never forget her first words to me—"I have a friend. . . ."

Over the years, I have lost track of the number of people who learn of my work in the field of family violence and then say, "I have a friend…." It is always the same. "I have a friend who just left her husband because of his alcohol abuse." "I have a friend who gets hit by her boyfriend all the time." "I have a friend who threatened to kill her husband last week, and she ended up getting arrested." "I have a friend who I think is being abused by her live-in boyfriend, but she won't confide in me." "I have a friend who was raped by her husband." The stories vary. The sentences end differently. But the first four words, "I have a friend…," are usually the same.

Everyone reading this book has been affected by domestic violence because people we come in contact with every day have been affected by domestic violence. In fact, everyone reading these words knows someone who is a victim and someone who is a perpetrator. Millions of women, men, and children in this country have been and are being affected. There are no exceptions. Abuse, of course, includes not only physical and sexual assault but also encompasses verbal and emotional abuse. The physical abuse is often pushing, shoving, grabbing, shaking, slapping, punching, and kicking. But it can escalate all the way to homicide. Sexual assault includes unwanted touching, being forced to do things sexually that you don't want to do, all the way to violent intercourse.

As we come to understand the continuum of abuse from verbal abuse to homicide, we can understand how widespread intimate partner abuse is in our culture and around the globe. If you have been abused, you know the pain, the heartbreak. It is not hard for you, after you get out of the situation, to see others who are trapped in the same situation. If you have not been personally abused, you may have more difficulty identifying others who have been abused by a partner. They may never disclose their issues to you, but they are nearby. They live in your neighborhood. They sit with you at your kids' soccer games. They go to your church, synagogue, or mosque. You see them at work. You vacation with them. You send them holiday greeting cards. You see them at the parent-teacher association meeting. You chat at the grocery store. Let me repeat—there are no exceptions. Everyone with their eyes on these words has either been verbally, emotionally, or physically abused by an intimate partner or knows someone who has been abused. There are no exceptions.

While I know most of those I talk to likely do have a friend dealing with violence in an intimate relationship, it is often equally clear that when I hear "I have a friend…," they are talking about themselves. They don't want to disclose what is really going on in their lives. They don't know me. They don't trust me. They have a terrible secret, but they cannot be open and honest with someone they have just met. At times, it is, indeed, blatantly obvious that they are not telling me the truth. Yet I don't confront them for lying to me. I don't sit them down for a counseling session or hand them a brochure. I usually just listen and then offer some humble advice on how to help a friend. No book on domestic violence, even one focused on providing hope for violent families by creating Family Justice Centers across

America and around the world, can begin without touching on the fundamentals of dealing with victims of family violence—not a treatise on the subject, just some simple principles for anyone who "has a friend."

Recently, Elaine Weiss published an excellent book devoted to providing practical advice and support to friends in need.[1] It is a must-read for anyone who wants to provide practical help to others victimized by family violence. But I have a less ambitious goal in this chapter. It is to share my simple, practical, personal view of victims of family violence after 20 years of working through the issue professionally and personally. The views shared here are deeply held by many dealing with intimate partner abuse. The pages that follow are a foundation, if you will, for much of this book. It includes some philosophy, some challenges, and some practical advice for anyone interested in diving into the ultimate goals of this book—to convince caring people across America to support the creation of Centers in their communities.

Some of the advice has been learned by trial and error. Some of the wisdom I hope to impart has been passed on to me from battered women with whom I have worked. And some of it comes from the mountains of research about battered women, battered men, and their children. There are simple, straightforward principles to apply. There are ways to phrase things for victims that do not blame them or revictimize them. I wish someone had sat me down 20 years ago and said "Here is the way to talk to victims of family violence. Here is the way to ask questions. Here is the way to offer help." The primary goal of this chapter is to impart those ideas as simply as possible.

But first, I want to offer some simple questions to ask those in need and some simple words of encouragement to offer. And before that, I need to set the stage. If I don't set the stage and expose the challenges to really helping our friends, you will jump to the formula without understanding the process. If you are now being abused or you are a survivor of abuse, these next few pages may be difficult to read, but I hope they will be encouraging. We all need to be on the same sheet of music before we start talking about Centers.

Every reader of this book should fully understand the philosophy and approach that we must all embrace before we can start talking about creating these Centers in communities across America. This will be difficult for many who just want the answers and not the conscientious learning process that brings us to the answers. Indeed, we all want to jump to the solution before fully understanding a problem, whatever the subject. We need to understand the disease of domestic violence before we understand one of the major cures developing through the vision of Family Justice Centers.

Before we can offer help to our friends, family, and neighbors through the creation of Centers, we must understand what often compromises our ability to help. It is the elephant in the room. It is the reality we don't often talk about in popular culture or even within the domestic violence intervention and prevention movement in this country. It is a powerful social belief system that impacts all of us. If we don't acknowledge the social forces that influence us, we won't be much good to victims of family violence. We may even be counterproductive in our effort to help, driving them back to their abusers. We may, by our ignorance or bias, unwittingly consign them to months, even years of ongoing abuse.

Admitting Our Bias Toward Battered Women

So, what is this bias? What is this powerful social belief? What is so important for every person in America to know about our views about victims of domestic violence—many of whom have also suffered sexual assault? What is our bias? And toward whom are we biased?

Here it is: *Our culture still has a profound bias against battered women.* Even after nearly 30 years of the women's movement and the battered women's movement, we must be honest with each other and with ourselves. Many in our society still don't like battered women. Some professional women who have never been victims say they would never let a man hit them. Some law enforcement professionals are tired of dealing with them. Some pastors, priests, and rabbis see them as spiritually weak and needy. Some medical professionals see them as expensive (and often uninsured).

One colleague of mine has said, "The first time you are hit you are a victim; the second time you are a volunteer"—a provocative but dangerous statement when actually spoken to domestic violence victims in the midst of abuse. It, like so many other views, still leads us invariably toward some form of victim blaming. Oprah Winfrey, who has done so much to help domestic violence victims over the years, called relationships with violence and abuse the "sick dance" when I appeared on her show in 2003. During the show she asked many victims she interviewed what they did to provoke or facilitate the abuse. To be fair, Oprah's questions were designed to stimulate conversation. Oprah has earned the right to ask such questions, and she is a powerful advocate for those who have been abused. But sadly, this type of thinking by others is often society's way of discounting the complexity of victimization and putting the responsibility on the victim.[2]

We don't want to deal with victims of domestic violence. We blame them. We demean them. We criticize them. We refer them. And usually, we end up trying to ignore them. The emergency room doctor wants to refer them to their family physician. The church or synagogue wants the government to deal with them. And when no other professionals are in sight, we have our fallback position—their family should be helping them. It is none of our business. It is not our problem.

Our bias against battered women, in fact, serves us well. It saves us time and energy. We are busy, harried, rushed human beings. We constantly look for a few extra minutes. We regularly try to avoid additional time commitments. So it should come as no surprise that we regularly shortchange battered women and abused men, even if they identify themselves to us. It does not take much to make them go away. And we certainly don't easily welcome them. Why don't we? Why do we welcome them once but not the second, third, or fourth time they seek help? The answer is often unspoken but latent in the hearts of most of us. As a society, we don't want them to come forward. We don't really want to deal with them. Why? Let's be honest! We know what will happen. We have heard the old adage—if you build it, they will come. If we welcome them, we will be deluged. We don't have the resources to deal with the full scope of the problem so we choose to deny it, ignore it, or explain it away.

I remember talking to a nationally known pastor a number of years ago; he said, somewhat matter-of-factly, that he had never preached on the subject of spousal abuse. When I asked him why, his response was chilling—he had never spoken on it because he knew many women would come forward for help, and the church simply did not have the resources to deal with the problem! Studying any battered women's shelter in America proves the truth of that reality. Shelters are still regularly full to overflowing. Shelters provide assistance 24 hours a day, seven days a week, and they are overwhelmed. Any time we create good programs, they always have too many clients and not enough resources.

Yet recent crime data from the Bureau of Justice Statistics in Washington, D.C., has concluded that domestic violence reports are going down across America, so how can I say that the numbers are still overwhelming?[3] If reported cases are dropping, how can we keep saying that the numbers continue to be significant? Lost in the data debate is the reality from the National Crime Victimization Survey, which continues to confirm that most victims of domestic violence do not report the violence to law enforcement agencies, courts, shelters, or even friends.[4] Most victims, men and women, are still not using the systems we have created to address the problem of violence in intimate relationships. Verbal and emotional abuse of an intimate partner is not a crime, though often devastating to the victims. But even if victims of this abuse come forward, we cannot help them with the system approaches we currently use in this country.

Beyond victims of verbal and emotional abuse, the domestic violence shelters offering help to the physically abused deal primarily with those in less advantaged socio-economic groups, and they are still unable to meet the need. Shelters are often full to overflowing. Most communities and most agencies decide not to build systems that will cause victims, in all forms, to come forward in large numbers. Better to have a complicated intervention system than an extremely accessible one. Better to screen people repeatedly than to simply welcome them all without reservation. Better to stay small and sustainable than to grow large and require substantial resources to maintain our operations. Our bias against battered women is evidenced even in the agencies that care the most for victims and their children.

A number of years ago, I talked to an elected sheriff in the Midwest who did not want to do a public awareness campaign on domestic violence. At first, his excuse was that domestic violence was not a major issue in his community. Within 10 minutes, though, the real reason came through: A public awareness campaign would bring more victims, and more victims would raise the crime statistics in his county! Ignorance was bliss. Ignorance was a chance to brag publicly that since his election, violent crime had dropped 27% in his county. Never mind that the drop in domestic violence cases was likely the result of law enforcement officers failing to take reports, not a dramatic drop in actual violence and abuse in intimate relationships. It was more likely that victims did not feel safe enough to come forward than that the crime was not happening in homes in that community. And law enforcement is not alone.

A friend in a service club once told me he did not want to speak on the issue from the podium because too many women and even some men might come forward, and such issues were simply not the responsibility of his service club. They had chosen their priority issues, and family violence was not one of them.

The bias, however, runs even deeper than simply not wanting to take the time to deal with very troubled and dysfunctional victims of domestic violence. If we are honest, in our heart of hearts, most of us think there is something wrong with victims of domestic violence. They made poor decisions. They made bad choices. They are weak, unwilling to leave their abusers. Few of us want to help those we believe are unwilling to help themselves. And it is easy to rationalize our distance from those who are victimized: "She made her bed." "She married him!" "She moved in with him." "What does she do to push his buttons?" "If I was living with her, I'd hit her, too."

Over the years, I have heard it all—from friends, coworkers, neighbors, police officers, judges, prosecutors, pastors, and, at times, even advocates. For those who become victims, such bias usually dissipates. But even those who have experienced abuse can sometimes feel no sympathy for victims who are unable to leave quickly after the abuse begins. The reasoning goes, in the quietness of the heart: "If I left after the first or second incident, why can't she?" Irrespective of the reasons for a lack of sympathy and understanding, for the vast majority of Americans who have never been personally victimized, it is indeed a difficult issue to understand.

On the one hand, our victim blaming is a safety mechanism. If victims are stupid, or ignorant, or culpable in some way, our own responsibility for their plight is diminished. We can always feel less social responsibility for the homeless if we can blame them for being homeless. Likewise, we can always feel less responsible for the battered victim if his or her own choices put them in the mess in which they now find themselves. The classic line from *The Burning Bed,* the well-known 1977 Farrah Fawcett movie about a battered woman and her abusive husband rings true even today. When the wife in the movie goes to her mother for help, her mom delivers our bias with a firm tone, declining to help her and, in fact, telling her to go home to her abusive husband: "You made your bed hard, you lie in it." Sadly, that sentiment is alive and well in the hearts of many, even if it is no longer politically correct to say it out loud in our slowly changing culture.

In 1987, in the early years of my work as a prosecutor, I experienced this reality firsthand. I was in the hallway of the courthouse getting ready to start picking a jury in a domestic violence criminal case. I had subpoenaed the victim to testify in the case. She was not a willing witness. She wanted the charges dropped. I had to explain that she had not filed the charges so she could not drop them. The People of the State of California filed the charges and only I could dismiss them. And I had no intention of dismissing them. Her boyfriend was violent, and the abuse had gone on for four years before she had finally made her first call to the police. By the time I had filed charges in the current case, the victim had called the police three more times, though no charges were filed after the first two calls. The boyfriend refused to accept any responsibility for his violence, and I was going to convict him in front of a jury.

As we stood out in the courthouse hallway, the victim told me she did not want to testify and that I should not proceed with the case. I was adamant in my position as the prosecutor. We did not have specialized advocates back then. I had no support staff at all. In fact, I had just met the victim for the first time in the hallway. It was, by current standards, a terrible way to handle a domestic violence case and its victim.

As she told me of her frustration with the case, the victim became more and more agitated. I was quite paternalistic and uncaring. I was tired and buried in a hundred other cases besides this one. I just wanted to try the case and move on with my other responsibilities. But it was not so simple for the victim. This was her life. And I was, from her perspective, doing nothing to help her deal with the wreckage. After 10 minutes of mounting anger (and fear), the victim finally started shaking her hands in my face and screaming at me, "My blood will be on your hands when he kills me." It was a scene!

As she screamed, I looked around. People were walking by. Everyone was staring. The bailiff even peeked out from inside the courtroom where our case was about to begin. I remember thinking how embarrassing it was for me to have her screaming at me in front of so many people. In my ignorance, I wondered if she knew I was a national domestic violence expert! As if I had anything to teach her, the one living the nightmare, about violence in the family. But I remember thinking, "No wonder she gets hit."

My reaction was not unusual. It revealed my own bias. It relieved me of facing my own responsibility for the way I was handling her case. It let me put her in the "irrational, hysterical victim" box instead of addressing her concerns and, quite frankly, her thoroughly rational and profound fear of dying at the hands of her abuser. Blaming her was easier. I remember telling her she did not understand our system and she did not realize how much we were helping her. At least one of us did not understand domestic violence issues. It was not, however, the terrified victim standing in front of me. It was me. And underlying my ignorance was a very powerful form of victim blaming.

The Question We All Ask

Beyond the obvious bias against, dislike of, and blame toward the victim, however, is a deeper bias. It is rooted in a question that still permeates our culture—"Why does she stay?" It is *the question*. It has been explained and argued about in books, at conferences, and in personal debates and discussions for years across the country. *The question* permeates the mind of the law enforcement first responder, the medical first responder, the social worker, the next-door neighbor, and every other person in our culture dealing with battered women. It may not always be voiced but it is always present. *The question* is always just below the surface, even if we never voice it. We read about a victim in the newspaper and we wonder why she stays. We find out we really do *have a friend* who is struggling with domestic violence, and *the question* colors our advice to her. It is always present and it is insidious. What is the matter with her? If she really is being victimized, why doesn't she leave?

The bias of "Why does she stay?" often appears in the form of other responses. Instead of asking her why she stays, we say, "You need to leave him." Or we phrase it more as a victim blaming question—"Why don't you just leave?" or "Why don't you protect your children?" Whatever the version of *the question*, though, the underlying pathology is evident. We blame her for what has happened. If she had left, this would not have happened. If she had reported the violence the first time it happened, we would not be dealing with 10 years of complicated abuse patterns. Based on research, the fundamental problem with this approach is obvious. It blames the victim for the violence. Her injuries become her fault. The impact of the violence on the children becomes her fault. Because she stayed, now her children are traumatized and damaged. Because she stayed, the violence has escalated. Because she stayed, she now uses alcohol to self-medicate. Our biased question becomes a large neon sign flashing in her face that says, "This is your fault."

Tragically, when victims are blamed by intervention professionals, or even caring, well-meaning neighbors or family members, they are not more likely to get help. They do not suddenly snap to their senses and break out of the abusive situation they are trapped within. They often turn away from the one blaming them. Sadly, they often return to the abuser in the face of blame. The abuser, after all, blames them for everything. If the intervention professional or the loved one now blames them as well, they see no hope to break the cycle of violence. Without a safe place to seek refuge, a return to the abuser seems the only viable alternative for the victim.

The other troubling aspect of *the question* is the assumption that underlies it. In asking, we assume that if she leaves, the violence will stop and she will be safe. Neither assumption has any basis in reality unless a lot of people work together to help her. Indeed, the research is now incontrovertible that when a victim leaves her abuser, she is actually in greater danger than when she stays. Clearly, this danger does dissipate over time for many victims. But when a victim leaves, the violence does not stop. In fact, "...the most severe violence and the greatest threat of fatality may exist when a battered woman leaves,[5] and this threat may exist for months and even years after she has gone.[6] So our assumption is false. What victims have been saying for years is far more accurate than we understood. When a victims said, "I am scared to death of him, but I am staying with him," we thought she was crazy. Now the truth is confirmed—battered women know *instinctively* what we now know statistically; victims are in more danger when they leave than when they stay with their abusive partners.

The reality of the danger to victims when they try to leave should therefore guide everything we do to help them. We should rethink our deep-seated biases, our words, and our unspoken assumptions. And we should eliminate *the question* from our vocabulary. Never again should we be caught asking "Why does she stay?" unless we understand the complexity of the answer. She stays out of fear for her life. She stays out of love for her partner. She stays out of fear for her children. She stays because her options are so limited. She stays for complicated reasons related to dependency, lack of self-worth, lack of resources, and a lack of community support.

Unfortunately, by failing to get educated about the issues, it is easier for us to simply step past battered women we come across. We see them, we blame them, we alienate them, and we move on with our own lives. Or, even more commonly, we live our lives without seeing victims of domestic violence at all. We socialize with friends without ever talking about intimate issues such as violence and abuse. And if we never get that deep with our friends, we will never have to find out that during an argument last week, they pushed each other. We will never have to know that he slapped her twice in the last two months.

I was reminded of this just a few months ago at a restaurant in San Diego. My wife Beth and I had gone out with friends for dinner. It was a very nice steakhouse and the manager was a dynamic, energetic Latina woman who came regularly to our table to check on us throughout the course of the evening. The talk was mostly focused on the food and the atmosphere. But I was fresh from a tough day at the Center and was reflecting on my interactions with a very traumatized mother we had dealt with that very day. As we talked to Eva, the steakhouse manager, I decided to delve a little deeper into her life. How long had she been at the steakhouse? Had she worked her way up to manager, or did she start in another position? Did she have children? How many? How old were they? How did she juggle being a mom and a professional in such a tough working environment, with long hours and constant personnel challenges?

It did not take long to get a picture of Eva. She was a single mom with four kids. She worked long hours and struggled to make ends meet. Her oldest was 17 and her youngest was 10. Her husband was only around sporadically, and she was thankful for that. I asked her if she feared for her safety if her husband did return to the picture. Her eyes flashed a knowing look directly into mine. She had never been asked the question, certainly not at work. But she answered quietly and softly, "Yes." There it was. I told her how courageous she was and offered words of affirmation. In a high-end steakhouse in San Diego, California, I was able to express support and encouragement for a survivor of domestic violence who still faced the fear and danger of her abusive husband, even though they were separated. It did not take long to go deeper with Eva. It did not ruin our dinner, and I believe it encouraged her to know of our support even as strangers.

My interaction with Eva is not common for most of us, though. In general, we don't go very deep with most people. In virtually every venue of our lives, we keep our interactions on a surface level. Such strategies protect us from subjecting ourselves to levels of intimacy that take considerable time and energy to develop and maintain. We maintain our privacy and we let others maintain theirs. Everyone can smile and say hi, and we don't have to deal with the messy, dysfunctional parts of our lives. It is extremely utilitarian. It saves time at work. It saves time in the neighborhood. It saves time at our parish, synagogue, or mosque. It saves time in our recreational and sporting activities. But it is deadly for those who suffer silently at the hands of an abuser.

When it comes to the issue of domestic violence, a guarded and standoffish approach is particularly tragic for those who need our support, affirmation, love, and encouragement. All around us are hurting women, men, and children living "lives of quiet desperation." But their lives are worse than simply loneliness and monotony. They are infected by violence and abuse and no one knows; therefore, in their view of reality, no one cares.

We don't know what others struggle with though they are all around us. We see the employee who is chronically late and we simply fire her. Then one day we find out she was dealing with an abusive partner and traumatized children every day before she came to work. The employee we fired ends up on page A-1 above the fold in the local newspaper because her husband shot and killed her after she filed for a restraining order. We see the child who has behavior problems in school, and we send him to the principal's office. Then one day we find out that child was regularly watching and listening to mom and dad fight until late into the night. The child is arrested for vandalizing the school with his new gang friends, and now we have a whole new set of problems to deal with. We see the angry, bitter coworker and we choose to avoid him. Then one day he brings a gun to work and opens fire.

Sadly, even when the research has pointed out the issues to us, we don't want to deal with them. In 1994, the National Safe Working Place Institute released a report that studied hundreds of workplace homicides. They found that over 40% of the shooters were men with a history of violence against women in their lives. While some employers now assertively address the issue of family violence with their employees, most employers still ignore or minimize the issue, but don't deal with it. This is the common response of many throughout our culture when dealing with intimate partner violence.

It is a familiar story. Domestic violence murders happen regularly. Murder-suicides often dot the pages of newspapers across America—"Domestic Dispute Results in Death of Woman" is the headline in the local paper. "Domestic dispute results in death…"? What an absurd statement! A domestic dispute occurs when my wife and I cannot agree where to go for dinner. No one dies in a domestic dispute. But the phrase still populates media accounts of domestic violence murders.

My theory for such inaccurate media reporting is this: It is our way to minimize the violence, blame the victim, and even minimize the killing itself. If it is a marital spat, it is the fault of the disputants. If it is a *domestic dispute*, it is not something we need to spend a lot of time reviewing. It's *only a domestic dispute*. It is not as if a stranger killed an innocent woman. This woman is part of the problem. This is a woman who "made her bed hard" and became part of such a "sick-dance" relationship. It is easy for us to move on after reading about deaths from domestic disputes. If the headline read, "Loving Wife and Devoted Mother Murdered by Cold-Blooded Killer," that would trouble us, wouldn't it? Why did she deserve to die if she was a loving person? Why was he not stopped before he killed her? Who let him avoid accountability? How could someone possibly kill someone in cold blood? What could we have done to stop him? If that were the headline, we would have far too much personal and professional work to do. If that were the headline, we as a local community might have to get involved.

It is played out on the pages of our lives day after day. Women die in domestic violence homicides. Children die. Sometimes men die at the hands of their children. The problem, of course, is that we don't know most of those who were killed. And if the story is about some juvenile who has committed a serious crime, we simply condemn the juvenile criminal and bemoan what is happening in our culture. We don't look into his background. We don't end up visiting the 13year-old in juvenile hall who vandalized the auditorium at the middle school. We don't sit down with him and find out he has been witnessing violence in his home for the last 10 years. We don't actually employ the woman who ends up dead from a *domestic dispute*. Though millions of women and children are victimized each year in this country, we don't usually interact with many of them. They are TV stories, they are newspaper articles, they are statistics—they are not our friends and family members.

Sadly, as we distance ourselves from the actual family violence going on all around us, we don't have to engage in the debate. After all, most of us are not police officers, prosecutors, judges, or emergency room doctors. We are not experts in family violence. We don't really understand the issue, and, therefore, we feel little reason to get involved. And even if we do work in the field as I do, we still don't talk about it often enough or specifically enough with those around us.

And the risk of confronting those we love is always profound. Will I sacrifice my relationship with my sister if I push this issue? Will I lose a friendship if I "pry" or "butt in" to my friend's life? Is the risk of losing the friendship really worth it? We may not verbally articulate our mental processes, but the processes operate and lead us to the path of least resistance very quickly.

A number of years ago, I was having breakfast with a friend from church. My wife and I had socialized with him and his wife. We had been in each other's homes. Our children were about the same age. He and I were both heavily involved in athletics. And as we sat at breakfast one morning enjoying a time of fellowship, he asked me, "So tell me more about your work prosecuting guys who hit their wives."

I was thrilled to tell him about the specialized prosecution unit I was running at the time. I explained our policies and procedures. I explained the sentence for most first-time offenders and the longer sentences for second- and third-time offenders. He was intrigued and asked very specific questions.

His next question caught me off-guard. "Now, when you talk about domestic violence you are not talking about a husband and wife who argue and end up pushing each other around, are you? You are not saying that the regular fights that all couples have are domestic violence, are you?" He asked the question almost assuming an answer in the negative. I said, "Yes, Phil, I am. When a man or woman lays a finger on their spouse, that is not done in love—that is domestic violence." He was quiet and thoughtful. Our eyes met for a brief moment. Then when the silence was too much for him, he said firmly, "Well, I am not saying my wife and I have ever pushed each other like that."

Perhaps I should have let it go, sensing that he was not ready to talk about it. But I pressed forward. "Phil, have you ever laid a finger on Terry that was not done in love?" He shut down on me, "No, of course not. Why would you say such a thing? Are you accusing me of being one of your defendants?" I did not need to accuse him. The truth was flashing like a neon sign in the booth where we sat.

I wish I could say the outcome was positive from my conversation with my friend, but it was not. We never socialized again. He never confided in me again. By gently and thoughtfully asking about the truth, I had lost a friendship. Not by my choice, but by the choice of a man who had issues with interpersonal violence and aggression and was not, in any way, ready to talk about it. I have replayed that conversation in my mind over and over as the years have passed. We still see each other from time to time, but Phil and I did not remain close friends. Perhaps I confronted him too soon in our relationship. Perhaps my tone or body language was too strong. But I have remained committed to asking the hard questions of those I care about many times since, and to confronting men in my life who appear to have violence and abuse issues with women, even if it has meant risking a friendship in the process.

Sometimes if you have gone on record with those close to you about the issue of family violence, they will come to you instead of you having to go to them. After I appeared on the Oprah Winfrey Show in February, 2003, many friends who I had never talked to about my work against domestic violence finally raised the subject with me. Usually, the sentence began, "I have a friend...." It could have been me raising the subject with them. After all, I have worked in the domestic violence movement for nearly 20 years. I have spoken at conferences in all 50 states. I have trained in Canada, Australia, and a host of other countries around the globe. Yet I never talked with many of my friends about my work except in the most general of terms. But after they saw the topic discussed and debated on Oprah, they were motivated to get involved, to speak about the issue with me, and to ask what they should be doing to help.

If we acknowledge how prevalent family violence really is in our communities, we will begin to look for solutions. If we even begin to broach the subject with our friends at church or our co-workers, we will meet victims of family violence. If we talk about it at our service clubs or community organizations, victims and survivors will come out of the woodwork. If we slow down enough to really ask our friends and family members about their personal relationships, we will see the telltale signs of physical, verbal, and emotional abuse in the lives of those we care about. We will see the stunning prevalence of family violence in American homes.

In an adult class I teach at my church, I took a few minutes one Sunday morning simply to raise the subject of family violence. Amazingly, nearly half the class had been touched by it. They simply needed to be asked about it in a thoughtful and sensitive way. Once they were asked, a dialogue and discourse could begin. Once they started talking, it was amazing to see how many in the class got excited about playing some small part in the effort to stop family violence. It was, in fact, that class at our church that provided most of the volunteer help to build the first specialized wake boarding, waterskiing camp for battered women and their children in the country, now known as Camp Hope (www.sdcamphope.org). We talk later in the book about Camp Hope.

The product of our openness is obvious. Once we start talking, we will find victims and survivors, but we will also find volunteers for the movement. We will find supporters. We will find opponents as well, a subject we will address later. But most importantly, we will find those in need of help who have not yet come forward. People will indeed start saying, regularly, "I have a friend...."

But Then What?

What do we do when we meet those touched by family violence? How should we respond? Do we simply refer them to professionals? What should we say? How should we treat them? How can we help them? What should we do? Will getting involved put us in harm's way? Will actually trying to help deal with the issue expose our own families to things we do not want our children exposed to? How can we really make a difference? What if our community does not have the kinds of resources that victims and abusers really need to get help? Before we can talk about the exciting movement toward Centers across America, we need to understand how to talk to those experiencing family violence.

Five Simple Questions for Those We Know

The longer I live the more convinced I become that questions are more important than answers. Listening is more important than talking. And helping others to find solutions is more important than unloading my dump truck full of answers to their problems.

So first let me give you five questions to ask when you have opportunities to open doors for those you love to share the hurting they may be experiencing in their lives. This is not a call for every American to become a pop psychologist or peer counselor. It is not a call for us to force our way into the intimate corners of the lives of others. But it is a call to create opportunities, and it is the foundation for the simple, caring statements below that do need to be delivered to all those who "have a friend."

1. Are you ever afraid of your partner? Why?

2. What do you wish you could say to your partner that you have never been able to say?

3. Are you ever afraid for your children when your partner gets upset?

4. Have you ever been forced to do something sexually with your partner?

5. Has one of you ever laid a finger on the other that was not done in friendship or love?

These questions are only a start, and the depth of a friendship or relationship may dictate which of these questions you can ask and when you can ask them. But the questions are still good ones to store away for future reference. Most victims of domestic violence don't consider themselves victims. Most victims don't think of themselves as battered women or battered men. With that in mind, the challenge in responding to those who have a friend or need a friend is sometimes difficult. I have asked some version of each of these questions to many women in my life over the years and some version of three of these questions to a number of male friends in my life. With my male friends, I will often ask if they have ever done anything to hurt their wives or girlfriends, and I will not define *hurt*. In the intimacy of a deeper friendship, I will ask if he has ever laid a finger on his wife or girlfriend that was not done in love. Usually, sharing my own frustrations and challenges is a good starting point. And the moment and mood must be right. The need for and the importance of this conversation with our friends can never be underestimated.

Beyond asking questions, though, I have also found that planting seeds in the lives of those I care about and suspect of being victimized will often yield fruit. Phil did in fact change his behavior pattern with his wife in the years after I confronted him and impacted our friendship negatively because of my stance with him. Even if the questions are not answered in the affirmative, I can still share with those I care about what concerns me, what I fear could be happening, and why my concern is so real for them.

Five Simple Things to Say to Victims of Family Violence

I have spent a great deal of time with victims and survivors of domestic violence (good idea). My wife and I have housed them (bad idea). We have helped fund housing for them (good idea). I have tried to lecture them (bad idea). They have lectured me (good idea). I have often failed to let them say all they need to say (bad idea). And I have brainstormed with them about options for their lives (good idea). I have chased them down street while their batterer is hitting them (bad idea). But most importantly, I have decided to accept them and support them—no strings attached (good idea).

Out of those many interactions, I have begun to learn how to talk to victims who come forward. I have also been immensely aided in my steep learning curve by professionals in the field of family violence intervention. Heroic, powerful women like Sarah Buel, Ellen Pence, Barbara Hart, Debby Tucker, and many others have challenged me in how I talk to victims of domestic violence.

Perhaps Sarah Buel, a nationally recognized prosecutor, advocate, trainer, and survivor, has contributed the most to the five simple statements that should roll off the tongue of every caring person who is talking to a victim of domestic violence. And I credit Sarah with much of the wording behind each of these statements. I have also developed statements to make to children of domestic violence homes who will reveal themselves as we open a dialogue with children in our communities. I share those in a later chapter of this book.

I have slightly modified each of the statements I have heard over the years and have added a few of my own. They are statements you can use to begin the journey with a victim of domestic violence, once she identifies herself. So let's take a shot at five simple things to say to adult victims of family violence as a starting point.

I am afraid for your safety.

Most victims of domestic violence know when they are in danger.[7] My friend Gavin de Becker, in his New York Times bestseller, *The Gift of Fear*, identified the problem that often occurs with domestic violence victims and others who know instinctively when they are in danger. They ignore their instincts. They let other mental processes overcome their fears. Victims of domestic violence, specifically, deal with so many complex emotions that they do not pay adequate attention to their fears. Many times they have lived with the fear for so long that it is normative.

They need to be validated. They need an objective third party to express concern for their safety. They do not need to be blamed. They do not need someone to minimize the past violence or threat of future violence. Victims minimize on their own, without any help from others. They need someone to speak honestly, personally, and lovingly. They need someone to validate the intense fear that obsesses the recesses of their mind but is often buried beneath immediate life needs. They need food and shelter. They need money. Their children are acting out. They need to find a job. They miss their abuser. They love their abuser. They believe he will change and that they can help change him.

When we say, "I am afraid for your safety," we dig through the immediate needs. We reach into the recesses of the victim's mind and find the raw fear that is there. It helps her bring questions that lie dormant to the forefront of her mind. Will he hit me again? Will he escalate the violence next time? Will the injuries be more serious next time? Will he kill me? If someone else is scared for my safety, then maybe my fear is rational. Maybe his apologies are not a guarantee of future safety. The simple fact is that if he has hit in the past, he is likely to hit again. One simple statement can begin many profound and powerful thought processes in the mind of a victim. Coupled with encouragement to talk to a domestic violence professional about her fears, it can be the beginning of planning for her safety. Those thought processes can help her to rationally and thoughtfully, with professional assistance, think through the issues that need to be addressed in order to provide for her own safety.

One of the complex issues is that fear often motivates her to stay, however, rather than leave. Over 10 years ago, domestic violence experts identified fear of her batterer's retaliatory violence as the number two reason a woman stays.[8] The number one reason was she hoped her partner would change.[9] Women in one early study listed fear of retaliation, along with the following, as the reasons for staying that ring as true today as they did over 20 years ago:

He kept seeking me out and finding me.

I felt other people would die if I left.

He was suicidal; I feared he would come after me.

I have left before and still can't get away from the abuse, threats, and fears.

I remember feeling afraid to go and afraid to stay. The very real fear of revenge is such a powerful deterrent to doing anything. . . .[10]

But helping a victim articulate those fears is still a powerful first step in encouraging her to seek professional help for planning her safety if she chooses to leave. At the San Diego Center, our advocates often develop safety plans with victims, once they come forward for help. Whether the victim is still with the abuser or has left the abuser, professionally trained advocates now know how to help victims plan for their safety.

The challenge is to connect emotionally with the victim's profound level of fear. Even if we have never been victimized personally, we all understand a victim's fear if we reflect back to some of those scary dreams we had as children or adults. Have you ever had one? Most people have—that dream where someone is after you and you get to a point where you are so scared you cannot scream, you cannot move; you are paralyzed with fear. Put yourself in it. That is what victims of domestic violence feel constantly.

Caring family members and friends should not substitute themselves for experienced domestic violence advocates who know how to help a victim plan for her safety, but we should all know that such safety plans often mean the difference between safety and further violence, between life and death. Safety planning is complex and involved, and should be done in a specialized domestic violence program setting in a shelter, in a prosecutor's office, or in a Center. But it is extremely helpful to know that once a victim starts focusing on her own safety, it is easier to get her to seek the help of trained professionals who can help her to be safe.

I am afraid for the safety of your children.

Working with battered women and years of research and evaluation have confirmed something that many in the domestic violence movement have known for years: Women are more likely to leave their abusers when they realize the impact of the violence on their children. Battered women do not intentionally put their children in harm's way. They do not intentionally ignore the profound impact on their children. (We discuss this in detail in Chapter 8.) But they minimize the impact. They ignore the impact. They choose to believe their children are resilient and protected from the impact. Those working in the movement now know that is not true. Some children are resilient and do bounce back quickly from witnessing violence, but most children are profoundly impacted. Children who witness violence between adults carry it with them for the rest of their lives. And children in domestic violence homes are often physically and sexually abused themselves. So the challenge is to focus the adult victim, usually a woman, on the effect family violence has on her children.

Telling a victim that you fear for the safety of her children is tricky work because a slight, even subtle, variation in this theme of expressing fear for her children's safety can become victim blaming. We can quite unknowingly point the finger at the victim, as we discussed earlier in the chapter. "Why aren't you protecting your kids?" "Do you see what you are doing to your kids by leaving them in this violent situation?" It does not take much. Suddenly, it is her fault. You are not on her side. You see her as a bad mother. You see her as part of the problem. And instantly you have lost an opportunity to build a bridge with someone desperately in need of your help and support.

However, the statement, "I am afraid for the safety of your children," is neutral. It does not blame her. In fact, it likely validates her. Again, at some level, she knows that her children are caught in the cross fire. She knows that her children are experiencing the pain and the trauma. But she does not want to believe it. She is trying to save her marriage. Her children become secondary. She wants them to have a father. She is focused on her primary relationship, and it needs major attention.

But when a caring friend says, "I am afraid for the safety of your children," it focuses her on the honest concern of another for her children's well being. The victim of domestic violence quickly begins to focus there as well. And when she does, her deep love for her children helps her begin to evaluate objectively the costs and benefits of being in an abusive relationship. As she weighs the pros and cons of staying with her abuser or leaving, she begins to factor in what he is doing to her children and what he may still do to them if she stays. Expressing concern for the safety of her children may plant a seed in a victim's mind, even though she has returned to her abuser over and over in the past. It may begin to help her see why she must seek help and why her abuser must be held accountable for his conduct.

You do not deserve to be treated like this.

Perhaps the greatest struggle for victims of family violence is the tendency to blame themselves and to believe the abuser's verbal and emotional abuse which, even more powerfully than the violence, demeans them, ridicules them, and puts them down. Counselors, advocates, and therapists working with battered women identify low levels of self-esteem in any clinical assessment. After months, years, and even decades of verbal, emotional, and physical abuse, victims believe they deserve to be treated badly. They must deserve it, or so they reason, or they would not have been treated like this. Indeed, many batterers tell their partners they deserve it. The children too come to think and talk like their father and mother over time.

I witnessed the power of a batterer's words in my own family with a friend of my oldest daughter, Kelly. One of Kelly's friends in high school grew up in an abusive home. Though we never knew all the details, there was clearly verbal and emotional abuse coupled with alcohol abuse. I strongly suspected that there was also domestic violence. Donald would often spend time at our home. He was, and is, an incredible young man. Though haunted by many demons from his home, he is bright, articulate, and compassionate. He is fun-loving and thoughtful. But there it was…in my own living room. I saw the generational cycle from Donald's past playing out in my own home.

Donald came over to our house one evening and was just "hanging out." He and Kelly watched a little TV, sat and talked, had a little ice cream, and made a few phone calls to friends. I was frittering around, engaging with them from time to time, but generally doing my own stuff. But as is often true when our kids have friends over, I stayed close enough to watch their interaction. What I saw was nearly imperceptible. It was not malicious. In fact, it was often in the form of sarcasm or humor. But it was the voice of an abuser speaking through the mouth of his son. I heard it first as Donald laughed and teased Kelly about her essay for one of her advanced placement classes. "You are such a loser," he said. I gave it little thought the first time I heard it.

Teenagers say unkind things to each other. They joke and mess around and use a vocabulary that I have long since lost track of in my aged state. Ten minutes later, though, I heard it again. Kelly was talking about something she had done poorly at water polo practice that day, and Donald said it again, laughing, "You're such a loser." Now I was starting to pay attention. My wife Beth and I have a philosophy in our home. We believe parenting is about two basic principles—affirmation and accountability. We believe that as parents, we can and will cover a multitude of sins with love and affirmation. We always try to build our kids up. We praise them. We affirm them. We encourage them. We do not put them down, ever. I have never called one of my children a loser, and I never will. So Donald's words seemed foreign in our home. They were an uninvited guest. Before the evening was over, I heard him call my daughter a loser or stupid five times, each in jest or with laughter or sarcasm attached.

The next day, I raised the issue with Kelly. I asked if she noticed what I had noticed the night before. She knew of Donald's family situation because we had talked openly about it with them as they became more interested in each other over a period of months. I was intrigued. Did my daughter, raised in a nonviolent, nonabusive household, notice the foreign substance introduced into our home? Did she care? Was her personal interest in him blinding her to the issues? I was careful in asking Kelly about it and did not identify the name-calling the night before. I simply asked whether she had noticed anything about the way he talked to her. She did. In fact, she slowly and carefully responded that she had noticed. She did not know how many times he had called her a loser, but she heard it. It was unwelcome and unpleasant for her. She had certainly never been called a loser in her own home before. When I told her he had called her a loser or stupid five times, she was deeply troubled. She was starting to like Donald, and for the first time she saw up close and personal the potential risks of dating a young man who had grown up in an abusive home.

I also realized that night what many know who work in the field of domestic violence. Victims of family violence become emotionally prepared for it. Verbal and emotional abuse often precede the first violent episode in an abusive relationship. Over a long period of time, many victims come to believe they deserve the abuse they experience. They are called names. They are ridiculed. They are belittled. And over time they do indeed come to think they deserve the physical abuse they experience. They come to believe they are part of the problem—they are partly to blame—they said the wrong thing—they did the wrong thing—they acted the wrong way. And when a friend has an opportunity, the message can be powerful and effective: You do not deserve to be treated like this!

There is help available.

Few other messages are as important today for those caught in the web of family violence and relationship abuse. Not only do many victims become isolated and hopeless, but many do not realize how much help is available. Thousands of community organizations and caring professionals exist to deal with the aftermath of family violence. Specialists abound. Police officers and prosecutors are specializing in family violence prosecution. Advocates and attorneys are specially trained to meet the needs of family violence victims. Doctors, nurses, therapists, teachers, and even many judges, now have significant knowledge and training about issues related to abuse in the home. Pastors, priests, and rabbis are becoming educated and available to help.

There is help available, and every American should be prepared to deliver that message when she comes in contact with those in need. Simply offering victims the phone number for the National Domestic Violence Hotline gives them a sense of the help available: (800) 799-SAFE. Memorize it! Then be prepared to offer it to anyone in need. Virtually every community also has a local hotline that you can find in the phone book. You can obtain brochures from the local domestic violence shelter and distribute them in your business, school, or place of worship.[11]

I am here for you no matter what.

Now the platitudes about loving our neighbor and caring for our fellow man end. Now the moment of truth arrives. If we are going to engage in the high calling of caring about the abused and terrorized in the homes of America, we need to be there for them. We need to deliver the statements here with passion and commitment even if victims choose to return to the abusive situation over and over. When we come in contact with a friend or loved one in need, and offer help and they do not accept it, what are we going to do? When we explain the conduct they are tolerating is a crime and they return to their criminal abuser anyway, what are we going to do? When they tell us to "butt out," what are we going to do?

The right answer for those who want to do the right thing is to deliver this simple message: I am here for you no matter what and whenever you want my help. There should be no judgment. There should be no ultimatums. There should be no emotional or financial manipulation. There should be no victim blaming. The research tells us that many victims of family violence leave three to five times before they leave for the last time.

Victims are emotionally invested in the abusive relationship. They believe they can change their partners. They believe love can conquer all and that their love can transform evil to good. They are financially committed to the abusive relationship. They, like all of us, want to make their relationship work. They don't want to give up. They want an intact family. They want the violence to stop. They want their partner to get help. But they may not accept the help of outsiders initially. They may leave and return. They may get angry when others try to intervene. They may even view interveners as the enemy. But we must remain available for that moment when they are ready for help. We must remain ready no matter how many times it takes and no matter how many times we have to offer the same words of encouragement.

Conclusion

There is much more to do if we are going to provide true hope for hurting and violent families. We must overcome our bias against them, our unwillingness to deal with them, our tendencies to blame them, and insistence on focusing on their difficulties in leaving their abusers. We need to talk far more openly about the issue of family violence with those we are around, we need to engage others in helping to address the problem, and we need to learn what to say to those being abused. We need to ask the right questions, and we need to offer thoughtful, compassionate responses to their answers.

It is with these thoughts firmly in mind that we should use the next few chapters to understand the history of efforts in this country to help domestic violence victims, and absorb from the rest of the book hope for violent families offered in the powerful, growing movement toward Family Justice Centers. I guarantee only one thing now that you have read the Introduction and Chapter 1: Even if you are not personally touched by family violence, you will begin to see the impacts and the need more readily if you take to heart the principles here. You will not be able to avoid it if you start talking with those you love about family violence. And others will become more open as well. So as you read on, I dare you to start asking your friends, start talking about the issue in polite company, and you will hear the words that come more and more often from those I come in contact with—"I have a friend. . . ."

Endnotes

1. Elaine Weiss, *Family and Friends Guide to Domestic Violence,* Volcano Press, Volcano, CA, 2003.

2. Gavin DeBecker, *The Gift of Fear,* Little, Brown and Co., Boston, 1997.

3. See www.ojp.usdoj.gov/bja.

4. Lawrence Greenfeld, Director, Bureau of Justice Statistics, United States Department of Justice. Presentation to National Advisory Committee, Washington, D.C., November 14, 2005. For further data go to www.ojp.usdoj.gov/bja.

5. M. Mahoney, "Legal Images of Battered Women: Redefining the Issue of Separation," *Michigan Law Review* 30, 1991, pp. 97-102.

?. J. Ptacek, "The Tactics of Men Who Batter: Testimony From Women Seeking Restraining Orders," in *Violence Between Intimate Partners: Patterns, Causes and Effects,* A. Cardarelli (ed.), Allyn and Bacon, Boston, 1997, pp. 104-23.

6. M. Wilson and M. Daly, "Spousal Homicide Risk and Estrangement," *Violence and Victims,* 1993, 9, pp. 3-16.

7. H. Eigenberg, "Woman Battering in the United States: Till Death Do Us Part," Chapter Three, *Explaining Battering* Waveland Press, Inc., Long Grove, IL, 2001, p. 134.

8. Ola W. Barnett and Alyce D. La Violette. *It Could Happen to Anyone: Why Battered Women Stay*, Sage Publications, Thousand Oaks, CA, 1993, p. 48.

9. Ibid., p. 48-9.

10. Ibid.

11. *A Community Checklist: Important Steps To End Violence Against Women*, United States Department of Justice, Advisory Council on Violence Against Women, 1995.

2

Looking Back Before We Look Forward

Mabel married Gardner soon after his first wife died during childbirth. She had never been married, but she was taken with this young widower with two small children. He was a businessman with dreams and aspirations—and a broken heart after the death of his first wife. He courted Mabel; they fell in love and soon married. Mabel wanted to care for Gardner and his sons, but she also wanted her own children. Within two years, she was pregnant. Over the course of the next 12 years, she gave birth to six children of her own.

Gardner was not abusive with Mabel at first. He was a firm disciplinarian with the children, but he did not raise a hand toward her until later in their marriage. His anger and rage were potent. No child ever wanted to cross him. The consequences were swift and unequivocal. Later, the adult children recalled his tongue lashings, name calling, and physical abuse. One child much later recalled ushering her younger brother out of the room when mom and dad began to argue. The youngest child remembered dad throwing things at his mother. One daughter remembered the radio being turned up so the children could not hear the arguments. And each of them remembered, like it was yesterday, their father saying over and over, "Quit your crying or I'll give you something to cry about." The youngest child mastered the strategy and used it later in life, like many other parents in his generation, on his own children.

The children grew up not knowing that healthy families did not function like the family ruled by Gardner. They grew up thinking their family was like all others. They lived through the many experiences of a home with varying levels of emotional, verbal, and physical abuse, even as America came to grips with the ugly secrets of a patriarchal, male-dominated society where abusive conduct was used systematically to control both women and children. And sorting it out was never simple. Gardner was not a monster. He was not always abusive. He taught his children the value of hard work. His firmness was balanced by love and care from their mother. Gardner had a strong faith and deeply held beliefs about family, commitment, and perseverance that later took his children far in life.

The details of Gardner's abusive ways have never been fully documented. Mabel took her eyewitness accounts to the grave and never disclosed what she endured. The children did not even begin to discuss the potential impacts until the suspected suicide of one of the brothers. As one of the older sons' spent his last days in hospice care (at age 81), he disclosed for the first time to his youngest brother their father's verbal and emotional abuse that he had carried with him his whole life. His mother had died giving birth to him. Throughout his entire life, his father blamed him for his mother's death. It was a deep, deep wound. The youngest boy later acknowledged actions of his father that today would be prosecuted. But even he hesitated to call it violence or hitting. It was a painful admission that he needed to minimize and rationalize, even as the "junk in the trunk" that each child carried into adulthood, out of Gardner and Mabel's home, slowly came out over the years.

And as noted, the baggage was not all bad. There was faith in Gardner and Mabel's home. Gardner taught the boys the value of perseverance and determination. He taught them to play tennis, to garden, to be handy around the house, and to make a goal and pursue it. He was a successful businessman and church leader. Mabel was a towering woman of prayer and faith who passed on to her children a strong commitment to serving the needy and putting their faith into action in the face of great difficulty. Surely such good things should not be ignored or the family shamed by disclosing the ugly underside of verbally, emotionally, and physically abusive conduct in the home.

But the story of Gardner and Mabel is an important story—first, because they raised those children and sent them off to raise children of their own during the budding feminist movement of the 1940s, 1950s, and 1960s. Second, they are important because they remind us how gray family violence can be. It is not always black and white. The bad guys are many times also good guys. The families with ugly secrets and unhealthy, dysfunctional behavior often have many positive, redeeming attributes. Finally, Gardner and Mabel are important because they are my grandparents. The youngest boy in that home was my dad.

My family story is a fitting introduction to our look back into the history of the domestic violence movement. We cannot know where to go until we have carefully reviewed where we have been. And we cannot fully engage in developing solutions for those people who struggle with family violence until we admit that we are all those people. Those victims and those women are our families, our relatives, our friends. We are all part of the history of family violence and the powerful social change movement that is ever so slowly beginning to impact that violence. Mindful of the complexity of this history, let's look at a brief history of where we've been. For those of you not interested in the nitty-gritty details of the history of the battered women's movement, read the next two paragraphs and move on to Chapter 3. For the brave, the determined, and the domestic violence professional, read the whole chapter!

Thumbnail History of the Domestic Violence Movement

For thousands of years we have tolerated violence against women. It has been ignored, condoned, and sometimes even glorified. No one did anything about it until the last few hundred years. And only in the last 50 years, with the development of the battered women's movement, has any real progress been made. In the 1960s and 1970s, the battered women's movement evolved out of the women's movement and focused on providing shelter to women and their children fleeing abusive and violent men. Then the battered women's movement realized domestic violence would never stop without the help of the criminal justice system because the criminal justice system is the way we stop people who do really bad things to others. In the 1980s and 1990s, the battered women's movement focused most of its energy on passing laws, training law enforcement professionals, and demanding that the criminal justice system stop batterers.

I am a product of that effort. I have been a prosecutor for 20 years while the battered women's movement has sought to shape the criminal justice system into a tool to stop male domestic violence offenders. During this profound period of social change, the battered women's movement has also worked to recruit public policy makers, elected officials, doctors, nurses, attorneys, business leaders, and many others in the struggle to stop violence against women. This powerful social change movement resulted in the creation of more resources to help victims and their children than at any other time in human history. In the process, it has also created some major problems. First, battered women have been arrested and prosecuted for defending themselves by the very criminal justice system that the movement recruited to help stop batterers. Second, the large increase in funding for programs to help victims has created way too many places and way too many systems where victims have to go to get help.

A Longer History of the Domestic Violence Movement

Thousands of women have lost their lives in past decades and centuries, and thousands more have devoted every fiber of their being to founding, developing, shaping, and leading the powerful social change movement that now forms the foundation for the potential development of specialized Family Justice Centers. It is worth the time to remember our history and honor those who have come before us.

Recently, I heard an elected official describing his work to address domestic violence issues. His ego far eclipsed the size of his contribution to the work of stopping family violence. But to listen to him, you would have thought he invented the domestic violence movement. He appeared to have no understanding of what came before him. He did not understand his very, very, very small role in a massive social change movement that has been evolving for centuries. In my mind, he became far more dangerous in his noble goal of helping victims because of his ignorance of the past.

The problem of family violence, of course, is as old as Cain and Abel. Throughout the centuries, violence in intimate relationships has been normative in most cultures around the world. We will touch more on this later in the book. But the movement to respond to domestic violence is far more recent.

In 1982, Susan Schecter did an excellent job of looking at the history of the domestic violence movement in the 1960s and 1970s.[1] But the history goes back much further than the modern development of the battered women's movement.[2] In 1868, the legal doctrine of *family privacy* was articulated by courts in North Carolina and across the country with the following statement: "However great are the evils of ill temper, quarrels, and even personal conflicts inflicting only temporary pain, they are not comparable with the evils which would result from raising the curtain and exposing to public curiosity and criticism the nursery and the bed chamber."[3]

Ellen Pence cites research looking back as early as 1640 for the genesis of the struggle against *wife beating* and the call for the government to play a role in providing protection for abused women.[4] Pence writes:

> *The suffrage and progressive social reform movements of the late 19th century produced legislative changes, ending more than 200 years of regulating wife beating, and criminalized the practice regardless of the woman's behavior. By 1911, laws forbidding wife beating had been passed in every state. Because no infrastructure of local efforts existed to advocate for implementation of the new laws, they were noted in law books and shelved until 70 years later, when the next wave of feminism gained momentum and activists insisted on their enforcement.[5]*

In the 1960s, the women's movement began to call on male-dominated institutions throughout our culture to start paying attention to violence against women. Violence in intimate relationships was only one of many issues addressed by the women's movement, but it soon became a very identifiable movement in and of itself. The focus on culturally acceptable violence against women was new in the 1960s. Indeed, one of the first major legal decisions in America to address the new awareness of the issue was not published until 1964 when the North Carolina Supreme Court said it was better to "forgive and forget," but acknowledged the reality that some violence in the home had to be criminalized when it rose to such a level that serious injury or death occurred.[6]

In the 1970s, the battered women's movement began to grow out of the much larger women's movement and included the anti-rape movement. The battered women's movement was a loosely arranged group of survivors of family violence and feminist advocates who began to organize survivors into an identifiable group of activists. The movement grew slowly at first, but then more quickly as private shelters and privately funded social service programs developed. Although it was made up primarily of women, small numbers of progressive men supported the movement even in the late 1970s and early 1980s. And though the movement was distinct from other powerful social change movements developing in America, it found common allies in the civil rights movement and later in the child abuse movement.

In the 1980s, feminist advocates began demanding legal protections for battered women. Del Martin's seminal book, published in 1980, became a clarion call for caring people across America to step forward and act to stop family violence.[7] Class-action and individual lawsuits were filed by victims and survivors attempting to treat violence against women as a civil rights issue under state and federal law. One of the most famous lawsuits was litigated and became a published court decision in 1983 when Tracy Thurman successfully sued the City of Torrington, Connecticut, for violating her civil rights by failing to protect her from her violent and abusive husband, Buck Thurman.[8] As Joan Zorza points out, the effect of this one case was dramatic, not only because a federal jury awarded Tracy and her son $2.3 million, but it "was widely reported in popular press and in academic journals. It graphically confirmed the extreme financial penalty that could be imposed on police departments when they abjectly fail to perform their duties. In addition, it confirmed that in appropriate cases these massive liability awards would be upheld."[9]

The Tracy Thurman story became a movie years later and educated many about the terror and trauma of domestic violence. Many individual victims began using civil litigation to demand monetary compensation from law enforcement agencies that failed to protect them from their abusers. Mandatory arrest laws, restraining order laws, pro-prosecution policies, and a host of legal mandates came forward in legislatures across the country. Specialized police officers, advocates, and prosecutors sprang up in jurisdictions across the nation as we began to realize the difficulty of dealing with domestic violence cases in the criminal justice system.

In 1984, then-Attorney General Edwin Meese created the first national task force on domestic violence issues with the support of President Ronald Reagan. For the first time, the federal government looked at the broad nature of family violence issues. Still today, the *Task Force Report* is an excellent primer on the complex history of family violence issues in America. It also yielded a powerful set of recommendations that helped launch many initiatives in the mid-1980s.

As the newly established domestic violence intervention movement developed political power, more and more policy makers and elected officials began to advocate for resources, legislation, and policy changes related to America's response to violence in the home. Nationally and internationally, more and more attention was being given to the issue of domestic violence.

In the 1990s, the mainstreaming of a feminist view of domestic violence (violence as a power and control behavior exercised through male privilege) continued. Specially trained police officers, prosecutors, and judges, all products of the feminist movement, began advocating their views within the criminal justice system itself. In 1991, the National College of District Attorneys held its first ever national conference on the prosecution of domestic violence. Judges, prosecutors, police officers, and advocates from across the country came together for the first time.

Prosecutors attending the first and subsequent conferences of the National College of District Attorneys learned how to prosecute cases even if the victim did not want to "press charges." Evidence-based prosecution, first advocated by law enforcement agencies in Minnesota in the early 1980s, was endorsed by the National College of District Attorneys as the best approach to victim safety and abuser accountability. Simply put, evidence-based prosecution was the strategy to prosecute a batterer even if the victim refused to press charges or testify. Jurisdictions such as San Diego, California; Quincy, Massachusetts; and Baltimore, Maryland, led the way in training prosecutors in newly developed prosecution techniques. For the first time anywhere in America, the responsibility for law enforcement intervention in family violence cases was slowly removed from the shoulders of victims and placed squarely on the criminal justice system itself. Advocates, police officers, prosecutors, and judges began working together cooperatively to develop coordinated approaches to deal with the long-neglected crime of domestic violence. While controversy swirled around so-called "mandatory arrest" laws and "no-drop" prosecution policies, more and more jurisdictions began treating domestic violence as seriously as any other major crime.

Though the issue remains somewhat controversial in some jurisdictions, the thesis of aggressive prosecution with or without victim participation is simple. If we don't ask victims of other serious crimes if they want to press charges, why should we ask domestic violence victims? If someone robs a bank, no one asks the bank teller if she wants to press charges. Why? Because bank robbery has been defined as a serious crime in this country and bank robbers get held accountable whether or not the teller in the bank wants to testify, or "prosecute"! Slowly, jurisdictions began applying the same principle to both misdemeanor and felony domestic violence cases.

As the change process evolved, judges from across the country began joining in the criminal justice focus on domestic violence. In 1992, the first-ever National Judges Conference on Domestic Violence was funded by the State Justice Institute and organized by the National Council of Juvenile and Family Court Judges. The Chief Justice of each state Supreme Court named a delegation that attended the conference and worked on statewide plans to train judges, educate court personnel, and revise court policies and procedures to better protect the rights of domestic violence victims. The conference, held in San Francisco, California, became a catalyst for organizing efforts in court systems across the nation and inspired many of the specialized domestic violence courts that have developed.

Without question, the 1990s saw an ongoing expansion of laws related to domestic violence, child custody issues, child support issues, and other related legal issues that impact families torn apart by violence. Policy-based legislation was only one part of the national legislative focus. The first major federal funding for domestic violence initiatives in American history finally occurred in 1994. The Violence Against Women Act (VAWA) became a landmark piece of legislation. Passed by Congress and signed by President Bill Clinton, VAWA created federal criminal offenses related to domestic violence,[10] mandated legal protections for battered women,[11] and authorized funding for shelters, tribal communities, law enforcement agencies, prosecutors, and a variety of intervention initiatives in every state. VAWA was a far-reaching, historic, bipartisan step forward in the effort in the United States to address domestic violence issues. Within a similar time frame, laws were being passed and funding was being made available in Canada, Australia, and many other countries in the Western world.

The O.J. Simpson Case

In June 1994, the O.J. Simpson case focused America and much of the Western world on domestic violence issues as never before. International, national, and local media became captivated by the terror and tragedy of domestic violence. As the case developed and later went to trial, it was covered worldwide. Simpson's acquittal in the criminal case, though stunning to many, did nothing to dampen the public fervor to seek justice for victims of family violence.

The media saturation about the O.J. Simpson case caused widespread public awareness. In 1996, *Newsweek* reported that 96% of Americans deemed domestic violence to be a major social problem in need of attention.[12] More laws were passed, more specialized services were created, and more funding was allocated as public interest skyrocketed. The chilling 911 tapes and other evidence of prior violence by O.J. Simpson that preceded Nicole Brown Simpson's murder caused many to question whether the Los Angeles intervention system had failed to protect Nicole when she was in obvious danger. ABC, NBC, CBS, CNN, Court TV, and other networks produced hundreds of stories on issues surrounding family violence. Print media as well devoted thousands of column inches to telling the stories of domestic violence victims, abusers, and system responses to such violence in jurisdictions across the country.

It is fair to say that during the 1990s, America focused on domestic violence issues as never before. Task forces formed in local communities and at the state and federal level. Arrest and prosecution became standard procedure in family violence incidents. Counseling and support groups for victims proliferated. Batterer intervention programs multiplied across the country. More specialized resources were devoted to family violence than at any time in our history. And some of the first major public awareness campaigns were launched at the local, state, and national level.

The result of this major focus on family violence was predictable. Mandatory arrest and pro-prosecution policies deluged the criminal justice system with domestic violence cases. Court dockets became clogged and personal attention to individual cases was often sacrificed in favor of "one-size-fits-all" policies for arrest, prosecution, probation, and counseling. Filing policies were refined to find reasons not to file charges, cases were reduced to lesser offenses to relieve jail overcrowding, and the criminal and civil justice systems adapted to survive the massive shift from ignoring family violence to viewing criminal justice as a major part of the solution.

Supporters and opponents of the burgeoning intervention movement could be found throughout the media and popular culture. Many men decried the criminalization of domestic violence as "male bashing." Backlash movements developed as more and more fathers began losing child custody rights in the wake of domestic violence incidents and subsequent divorce actions. Screening for and analysis of domestic violence issues became commonplace in divorce actions, medical venues, and employment situations.

Within 20 years, the civil and criminal justice systems in America went from seeing few, if any, domestic violence cases to seeing hundreds of thousands across the country. Law enforcement agencies went from briefly responding to family violence calls and leaving without writing reports or taking action to arresting many offenders and conducting on-scene investigations to facilitate prosecution. The hidden crime was hidden no more. The silent victims were silent no more. And America was, at long last, talking about the carnage of family violence. The dirty little family secret was coming out of the closet. Just as sexual assault in the late 1970s and child abuse in the 1980s, domestic violence was now front and center in the late 1990s. In many ways, the culmination of over a century of social change—the power of the domestic violence movement—was being felt at every level of society.[13]

Signs of Progress in Reducing Homicides

And the results were initially promising. Domestic violence homicides began to decline. Indeed, a 20-year retrospective from the Centers for Disease Control published in 1999 confirmed a significant decline in intimate partner homicides across America since the early 1980s. Stories of reformed abusers began to trickle into public view. Victims were finally able to get restraining orders, and judges were more likely to enforce them. Fewer criminal offenders were getting custody of their children after documented cases of domestic violence. And police officers were starting to treat domestic violence like a serious crime. To be sure, there were many problems and gaps in the services provided to victims, but the trend toward culture-wide awareness and action was encouraging to many.

Statistics seem to bear out the perception that progress was and is being made. Recent analysis by the Bureau of Justice Statistics demonstrates that reported cases of family violence have declined across the country. Intimate partner homicides involving men and women of color have dramatically declined in the last 20 years.

The positive impact of increased local, state, and federal government resources has been found in research over and over.[14]

While few ever thought the criminal justice system alone would end domestic violence, many thought that we had reached "critical mass" in social change theory by the late 1990s. In the words of Malcolm Gladwell, we thought the "tipping point" had been reached.[15] Surely massive reductions in violence would be evident soon. Surely abusers would stop the violence when faced with arrest and possibly even prosecution. Surely public funding for shelters would provide the needed beds for victims to be housed in the short run, and job training, public assistance, and advocacy would provide victims the needed resources to get out of abusive relationships in the long run. And surely, with the resources available, victims would not stay with their abusers; they would leave as soon as they had a safe opportunity to do so.

But a funny thing happened on the way to ending family violence in our lifetime. Adequate resources to address the problem never fully materialized. National media attention faded after the Simpson civil case concluded. The national frenzy about domestic violence subsided. School shootings, juvenile crime, and a plethora of other major social issues took over the airwaves. The criminal justice system had been mandated and directed to treat domestic violence as a serious crime, but in many jurisdictions very little was done other than arrest. Prosecutions had increased, but even if prosecution happened, there was little accountability for offenders and few resources for victims and their children. Judges ordered offenders into counseling programs, but there were virtually no consequences if they did not attend. While billions of dollars poured into the criminal and civil justice systems, only hundreds of millions ever materialized to focus on family violence. Health and human service funding to address family violence as a public health problem initially spiked but soon began competing with hundreds of other priorities.

Social science researchers who had been quick to seek out available monies for research on domestic violence in the 1980s and early 1990s began publishing research that questioned the effectiveness of criminal justice responses to family violence. Though much of the research was irresponsible, it clearly slowed the national march toward a "one-size-fits-all" approach. The research demonstrated that people of color and other marginalized groups were, in many ways, being revictimized by poorly implemented criminal justice responses to domestic violence.[16] Within less than five years after the O.J. Simpson criminal case, the national spotlight had dimmed. The movement continued, but the pace and the intensity of the effort was significantly reduced.

Comprehensive trainings, occurring for a decade at regular intervals in every affected profession, slowly surrendered to other pressing priorities. Though homicides had been reduced, women, men, and children were still dying. Though counseling programs for offenders had been created, curriculums varied, and strong evidence indicated that many batterers were not being "cured." Specially formed task forces languished and lost their way amidst other pressing social priorities.

No one can dispute that tremendous progress was made and is still evident. Indeed, major initiatives continue to develop and unfold even with reduced national emphasis. But budget pressures are currently forcing many jurisdictions to curtail their specialized intervention programs dealing with family violence. While the current efforts to eliminate local funding initiatives provide evidence of the low priority given to family violence intervention today, powerful forces now seek to roll back the successful initiatives developed in the 1990s. Even competition between agencies has begun to increase as available resources decrease, increasing tensions among agencies that should be working as allies.

In the current competitive atmosphere, well-meaning advocates and criminal justice professionals have begun to question one another's programs. Social science researchers with particular policy biases have interjected themselves in the national debate, calling for approaches to intervention that are consistent with their world view for dealing with family violence. The New York Times and other major media outlets have published stories openly questioning an aggressive criminal and civil justice approach to reducing family violence. Collateral consequences of nearly 20 years of legislation and policy implementation are now being debated throughout the country.

Recently, New York State University professor Linda Mills, as noted in the Introduction, called for the decriminalization of domestic violence—less arrest and less prosecution.[17] Mills and others argue that poorly implemented mandatory arrest laws and pro-prosecution policies revictimize victims and fail to deter many violent offenders. The International Women's Forum advocated for repeal of the Violence Against Women Act, rejecting the notion that women should continue to allow others to see them as victims. Others, inside and outside the feminist community, question whether the country is pursuing the right course for ending family violence.

Feminists feel their ideology was distorted and disfigured as it mainstreamed into the criminal and civil justice systems. It is an understandable conclusion. Feminist views go in one end of the criminal justice system and end up looking very different when they come out the other end. Those outside the movement feel a feminist analysis of family violence fails to fully capture the complexities of the issues. In fact, the struggle for the very heart of the domestic violence movement is beginning to emerge into public view as more and more players join the battered women's movement.

Amidst the emerging struggle is a fundamental reality: Some of those now working in the family violence arena have not come from the feminist movement and do not share a feminist view of the issues. Some don't even know the history of social change that has brought us to the issues of the day. Some are now questioning whether the movement has failed to address violence *by* women in intimate relationships in their zeal to stop violence *against* women. Some, coming from a child protection movement perspective, question whether the domestic violence movement adequately acknowledges the impact on children in violent homes in their zeal to protect adult women.

Beyond the debate among ideologies, many other issues are swirling. Some rightly call for more male leadership in national intervention and prevention efforts. Others point to the faith community, the medical community, the judiciary, and other major players as the areas most in need of national attention. While debates and disagreements abound, three major dynamics are clear and generally undisputed: 1) Many victims still do not leave their marriages and relationships even after aggressive community, social service, or law enforcement intervention; 2) many law enforcement agencies, prosecutors, and judges do little to ensure ongoing treatment, monitoring, accountability for and rehabilitation of abusers; and 3) very few places in America create a comprehensive, coordinated, multidisciplinary approach to dealing with every aspect of the violent family in providing long-term healing and hope.

Where To Now?

In the face of these clear dynamics and undisputed realities, critical questions must be asked. Even as we look back and remember where we have come from in addressing domestic violence, we must honestly, openly, and without bias ask some fundamental questions in looking toward the future. Where should we go now? Should we roll back the progress of the last 30 years? Should we minimize the role of the criminal justice system? Should we minimize the role of the government in the intervention processes we have been developing?

Conclusion

We are all products of the battered women's movement. We need to respect the powerful progress it has made and the issues that its progress has created. The Family Justice Center vision, informed by over 20 years of advocacy by the domestic violence movement for coordinated community response and informed police response, is intended to be a personal and corporate call to action in the future, even as we remember the past. It is a call to grab hold of a vision that can move this country forward in breaking the cycle of family violence. Mabel and Gardner's children and grandchildren and millions of others still need our help.

Endnotes

1. Susan Schecter, *Women and Male Violence: The Visions and Struggles of the Battered Women's Movement,* South End Press, Cambridge, MA, 1982.

2. Elizabeth Pleck, *Domestic Tyranny: The Making of Social Policy Against Family Violence From Colonial Times to the Present,* 1987, pp 3-13. [Citing to the Puritans of

Massachusetts Bay Colony being the first to pass laws against family violence during the 1870s.]

3. North Carolina Family Privacy Doctrine, "Breaking the Cycle: A Coordinated Community Response to Domestic Violence." Cited in *Coordinated Community Responses to Family Violence*," presentation by Casey Gwinn. June 1992. Available at www.familyjusticecenter.org/library.

4. Ellen Pence and Melanie Shepard, *Coordinating Community Responses to Domestic Violence: Lessons From Duluth and Beyond,* Sage Publications. Thousand Oaks, CA, 1999, pp. 5-6.

5. Ibid., p. 6. Citing R.E. Dobash and R.P. Dobash, *Women, Violence, and Social Change,* Routledge Kegan Paul, New York, 1992.

6. State v. Oliver, 70 N.C. 44 (1874). See also State v. Rhodes, 61 N.C. 453, 459 (Phil. Law 1868). ["It will be observed that the ground upon which we have put this decision is not that the husband has the right to whip his wife much or little, but that we will not interfere with family government in trifling cases....We will not inflict upon society the greater evil of raising the curtain upon domestic privacy, to punish the lesser evil of trifling violence."]

7. Del Martin, *Battered Wives,* Volcano Press. Volcano, CA, 1976.

8. *Thurman v. City of Torrington.* Conn., 595 F. Supp. 1521 (DC 1984).

9. Joan Zorza. "The Criminal Law of Misdemeanor Domestic Violence, 1970-1990," *J Crim. L & Criminology,* 1992-1993, 83, 46.

10. Interstate Stalking, 18 USC, Section 2261A; Interstate Travel to Commit Domestic Violence, 18 USC, Section 2261; Interstate Violation of a Protection Order, 18 USC, Section 2262.

11. Full Faith and Credit, 18 USC, Section 2265, 2266; Full Faith and Credit for Child Support Orders Act, 28 USC, Section 1738B; Civil Rights, 42 USC, Section 13981, 2000.

12. During the O.J. Simpson media frenzy in 1994-1996, more stories and feature stories on domestic violence issues appeared in print and electronic media venues than perhaps at any time in the last 40 years explaining the apparent reality that Americans understood the importance of family violence issues during this period of time. This apparent awareness level faded in the consciousness of most Americans as media focus dissipated.

13. The battered women's movement had finally succeeded. The groundwork of the 1980s was not reaping dividends. Susan Schecter said it well over 20 years ago, referring to the brief time between the mid-1970s and the early 1980s: "To start 500 shelters, win legal and social service reforms in hundreds of localities, form almost 50 state coalitions and capture the imagination of a nation in approximately eight years are extraordinary achievements. We owe a tremendous amount of gratitude to the founding leaders of the battered women's movement for their significant contributions."

14. Perhaps the best on-line compilation of research on domestic violence related to the positive impacts of the expenditure of resources is found at www.mincava.umn.edu. The Minnesota Center Against Violence and Abuse, led by Dr. Jeffrey Edleson, maintains a massive database with a host of resources analyzing the progress of the domestic violence movement over the last 20 years. The California Attorney General's Office also maintains on excellent site at www.safestate.org with recent research on effective domestic violence initiatives. See also *50 Strategies to Prevent Domestic Violence,* National Crime Prevention Council, 2002.

15. Malcolm Gladwell, *The Tipping Point: How Little Things Make a Big Difference*, Little, Brown & Co., Boston, 2000.

16. Fernando Mederos, "Batterer Intervention Programs: the Past and Future Prospects, Community Responses to Domestic Violence," In *Coordinated Community Responses to Domestic Violence: Lesson From Duluth and Beyond,* Sage Publications, Thousand Oaks, CA, 1999.

17. L. Mills, *Insult to Injury: Rethinking our Response to Intimate Abuse*, Princeton University Press, Princeton, NJ, 2003.

3

After Thirty Years, We Have a Big Problem

Yvette moved in with Mitch six months after they met in a karate class. She worked in a photography store. He was a former teacher, now a law student. He had teenage children and was a single father after his wife had died from cancer. He was winsome and physically fit, and quickly fell madly in love with Yvette as soon as they met. His constant attention, notes, phone calls, flowers, and compliments overwhelmed her within weeks of their decision to get involved with each other. But she did, in her heart of hearts, enjoy all the attention. They bonded quickly and when he asked her to move in, it seemed to make sense.

Within weeks of giving up her apartment, she saw his rage for the first time. It was over something stupid. But his rage was consuming and terrifying. Within days, the rage turned physical. Yvette called the police the first time Mitch hit her. She soon realized she must leave him. He was a dangerous man. Though some personal contact continued as she slowly extricated her life from his, she knew that it would never be a healthy relationship. By then, however, she had developed a close relationship with both his daughters. They still worked out at the same karate studio. And they had quickly developed mutual friends.

Police took a report of Mitch's first physical abuse, but he successfully convinced Yvette that he would leave her alone if she would not press charges. She feared his legal training and did not want to have to face him in court. She never recanted her statement, but she did not return the domestic violence detective's phone calls.

Within days of promising to leave her alone, though, Mitch started calling her, writing her notes, and begging to get back together. Yvette did everything she was supposed to do. She called the Volunteer Lawyer Program and soon obtained a restraining order. Each time Mitch contacted her, she called the police. She kept a journal and contacted a private lawyer. In a four-month period, Yvonne ended up dealing with more than 10 agencies and individuals in the criminal and civil justice systems as she tried to get help. She was forced to tell her story over and over again. She was referred from one agency to another.

Incidents happened in multiple jurisdictions, and different agencies referred her to other agencies. As she sank into depression from the constant harassment, the bewildering system she was supposed to seek help from became a confusing blur of jurisdictional lines, differing policies and procedures, and multiple locations. She met with the District Attorney's stalking team but was later referred to the City Attorney's Office. She almost lost her job and finally had to contact a private therapist for help.

I met Yvette after the case was forwarded as a simple restraining order violation to the San Diego City Attorney's Office. Though I was serving as the elected City Attorney, I had taken six weeks out of my regular job that summer to handle a caseload in our specialized Domestic Violence Unit. Sitting in a little office in the middle of the 35-member prosecution unit, I read the police report, which described an incident in which Mitch had been found lying on the front seat of his car around the corner from Yvette's job. She called the police, believing she had seen him watching her. As officers approached the car, Mitch pretended to be asleep. After they asked him to step out of the car, he told them he dropped off his daughter at her school nearby and then got sleepy while driving home and parked the car. The officers informed him he was less than 1,000 yards from Yvette's employment location, and though not technically within 300 yards of her person, his behavior was harassing and menacing. Mitch told the officers Yvette should not be afraid of him. He said if he really wanted to kill her, he would use one of his high-powered rifles and shoot her from a long distance. He said if he was really stalking her, she would never know he was there.

After two interviews with Yvette, we pieced together the long history of stalking in the relationship. We identified over 60 illegal contacts Mitch had made, contacted the 10 agencies that had been involved, and identified a host of witnesses who had valuable information about Mitch's harassing behavior. We arrested Mitch on the day of his last final in his last year of law school on a $500,000 bench warrant. Later that day, we seized 11 of Mitch's firearms from his father's house, including automatic handguns and a number of rifles with high-powered scopes. Finally, we pulled all the pieces together and started connecting all the agencies that had been involved with this couple in order to hold an abuser accountable and provide safety and support to an extremely traumatized victim of violence and stalking.

Mitch and Yvette's case played itself out two years before the opening of the San Diego Family Justice Center. It became powerful encouragement for collaboration between agencies, even in a case with a happy ending. Although more than 10 agencies had been involved, none knew what the other agencies were doing. Agency personnel never met together to work on the case. The agencies never sent staff to one place for Yvette's benefit. Yvette had to go from place to place in the middle of shock, trauma, and fear to try to get help. Her effort to get agencies to pay attention to her took nearly a year. Thankfully, she did not give up or die during that terrifying 12-month period! But still today when she e-mails me or calls to say hi and touch base, I am reminded how courageous she was in persevering through San Diego's domestic violence intervention system.

Yvette's story frames the problem. It is a long-standing problem from a historical perspective. Violence in the home has been around for thousands of years. Only in the last 30 years have significant resources been allocated to address the issue. Only in recent decades has the battered women's movement evolved and produced major changes in the culture and the substantial increases in resources. But committing significant resources has spawned another major problem.

We keep adding agencies and programs across the country and in local communities to help victims of domestic violence and their children.[1] As attention focused on the issue of family violence and laws and policies started changing, programs began to multiply and not just in traditional intervention agencies that had participated in domestic violence task forces or coordinating councils. The business community, the medical community, the law enforcement community, and the court system all started new initiatives, including agencies that traditionally did not work with domestic violence victims.

Employment programs, colleges, law schools, medical schools, churches, the military, schools, animal shelters, service clubs, and other agencies began developing programs to help victims and their children. Though many communities initially focused on law enforcement intervention, expanded opportunities to support victims of domestic violence were soon evident throughout society. As more and more local, state, and federal entities began funding services in the late 1980s and the 1990s, it became clear that the list of services was growing very long, particularly in suburban and urban communities.

The challenges created by the proliferation of programs were identified and regularly addressed in the domestic violence movement through the concept of coordinated community response.[2] The sexual assault movement and the child advocacy movement also promoted the concept of coordinated community response as the solution to coordinating agencies.[3] Task forces and coordinating councils were promoted by many in the domestic violence movement as the solution to the coordination problems.[4]

Though the problem was identified, most of our problem-solving efforts were system-centered, not victim-centered.[5] Though much was studied and written about the developing system challenges, no one stopped to figure out how many places victims would need to go for help as we continued to expand the number of new programs offering services to those in need.

Too Many Places to Go for Help

In 1998, using principles developed by Ellen Pence and her team in Duluth, we created a type of "community safety audit" in San Diego to analyze the system we had created to help domestic violence victims and their children. We spent a number of months talking to victims and survivors and reviewed the list of agencies then being provided by the San Diego Police Department to victims at the scene of each reported domestic violence incident. The question was posed: How many places does a victim have to go to get all the help she/he needs in San Diego?

Within a few months, we were able to identify 32 different agencies that had services for victims of domestic violence. And few of those agencies were in the same place! Creating a coordinated community response, developing a task force, creating a host of specialized units to provide services to victims had not solved the problem; we had made it worse.

Any reader might say, "Wow! San Diego really created a mess by having so many programs run by so many different agencies." Sorry, no community gets off the hook so easily. San Diego's reality had also become America's reality. Perhaps San Diego had a few more places that offered help than some smaller communities, but the problem was the same across the country.

A number of communities are now studying how many places their victims need to go to get help. Rural communities are reporting that their victims need to go to five to seven places, suburban communities are reporting 15 to 20 agencies where victims need to travel, and metropolitan communities are finding an even larger number of places where their victims need to go to get help, including medical services, counseling services for themselves, counseling services for their children, safety planning, legal services, law enforcement assistance, spiritual support, job training, financial/credit counseling, shelter services, criminal prosecution assistance, home security advice, transportation assistance, court involvement—and the list goes on. Indeed, Brooklyn, New York, recently identified 64 partner agencies that needed to collaborate in their new Center![6]

Many looking at this issue for the first time, who do not work in the domestic violence field, would think: "Surely there must be one agency that already provides all this help." Battered women's shelters, after all, have been moving down this road toward multidisciplinary services for their clients for years. But the reality is clear. Even the most well-funded shelters only have a few of the services their clients really need. Shelter victims wanting help may get short-term housing and support groups or counseling at the shelter, but generally must go elsewhere for other services. Rarely is a full-service employment training operation available in a shelter. Victims need legal assistance including restraining orders, divorce assistance, and immigration law advice. But even if the shelter has a legal advisor on-site for these diverse needs, a victim still must go to court to get a restraining order, not to mention the myriad other legal assistance she needs.

And what if the victim needs law enforcement assistance? Only a handful of shelters in the country have police officers and prosecutors available at the shelter. It gets even more complicated when a community has five to 10 law enforcement agencies in one county or parish and perhaps both a county prosecutor's office and a city prosecutor's office. No existing agency in the country provided access to all such service providers from a single location in 1998.

To be sure, some communities went down the road toward co-located services.[7] A few communities had police officers and prosecutors housed together. Some shelters had five to six disciplines represented in a single location. But in most places, victims traveled from place to place to place to tell their story over and over in an attempt to get the help they needed.

If a victim needed medical help, she would go to a hospital emergency room. If she needed follow-up assistance, she would go to her primary care doctor (if she had one). If she wanted to go to a battered women's shelter but needed to have her pets cared for, she had to find someone to take her pets. If her children were actually physically abused, they would end up in the child protective system, and a whole new set of agencies would be necessary. If the victim had been sexually assaulted, sexual assault protocols would kick in, and a long list of agencies and services would be added to the referral sheet handed to her by well-meaning professionals.

Are you tired yet? Getting dizzy? If you are a survivor reading this, you know how difficult it was in San Diego—and still is in most communities—to find everything you needed on a map, let alone actually going to those locations.

By 1998, we could not deny the reality. We had created a gauntlet for victims of domestic violence and their children. At one end of their journey was the violence and abuse; at the other end was supposed to be safety and healing. But in between, we made them run through a nightmarish, confusing obstacle course of agencies. To fit our policies, protocols, and procedures, we were sending victims careening back and forth across the community for help. To make it convenient for our bureaucratic systems to provide services, we were demanding almost superhuman tenacity and endurance from victims. The more I think about it, the more dumbfounded I get. We created a system for the convenience of system professionals, not for the convenience of victims and their children.

Victims of violent crime, including sexual assault victims, victims violated by their most intimate partners, often in shock and suffering severe physical, mental, emotional, and spiritual trauma, were being sent on a scavenger hunt to end all scavenger hunts if they wanted to get help. Scavenger hunts are fun in church youth groups. Easter egg hunts are hilarious when you are five years old and in the safety of a backyard. But when put in the light of stalking, sexual assault, and domestic violence, the hunt was at best "cruel and unusual punishment" for a victim.

However, the irony surpassed even the obvious abusiveness of the process. This is the victim we are talking about, not the perpetrator. We have laws and even a constitutional amendment against cruel and unusual punishment for criminal defendants. Criminal defendants have rights! We provide "one-stop shop" court systems in one courthouse for them. They can get a lawyer, see the judge, talk to their probation officer, and often even sign up for counseling or other rehabilitation programs there. But what did we have for victims? We had no such co-located services in San Diego in 1998, and no such place of safety when our victims sought help.

So what happened to our victims in San Diego when we put them through the gauntlet? It was no different than much of the rest of the country is today. They did not make it through the system. They might get to a police department, but they would never make it to the prosecutor's office. They might spend a few days in a shelter, but they would never make it to the restraining order clinic. It should have been no surprise. Most of our victims were returning to their abusers without comprehensive intervention ever occurring.

Conclusion

Here we were, 30 years into the battered women's movement, and we had a big problem. We were not providing the necessary services to those in need. We had, through a very well-intentioned series of actions, created a nightmare for victims and their children. We understood the importance of coordinated community response. We worked hard to facilitate it. But simply trying to get everyone on the same sheet of music through a task force or coordinating council was not good enough. We had to do better. We had to move beyond protocols and policies. We needed to provide a closer connection between community-based organizations and government agencies. We needed to engage the San Diego community, in large numbers, to support a better approach to meeting the needs of victims and their children.

By 1998, we had little doubt what we needed to do in San Diego. We needed to lead the way for so many other communities in showing what needs to come after coordinated community response. We needed to resist the urge to rest on our laurels and be thankful for the tremendous progress of the last 20 years. We needed to build on the relationships we had cultivated between so many different agencies. We needed the Family Justice Center vision! Yvette's courageous journey through the system while trying to stay alive taught us that very clearly.

Endnotes

1. Joan Kuriansky, *Promising Practices: Improving the Criminal Justice System's Response to Violence Against Women,* prepared by the STOP Violence Against Women Grants Technical Assistance Project, 1998, NCJ 172217. [By 1998, the STOP TA Project had identified 19 national organizations with major roles related to domestic violence initiatives in America.]

2. *Building an Effective Coordinated Community Response: Grants to Encourage Arrest Policies,* conference manual of the Battered Women's Justice Project, Washington, D.C., July 28-30, 1997.

See *Family Violence – Building a Coordinated Community Response: A Guide to Communities,* Chicago, IL, 1996.

See Barbara Hart, *Coordinated Community Approaches to Domestic Violence,* paper presented at the Violence Against Women Research Strategic Planning Workshop, National Institute of Justice, Washington, D.C., March 31, 1995.

3.   K. Barnes et al., *Developing a Coordinated Community Response to Sexual Assault and Domestic Violence,* Ending Violence Against Women Project, Colorado, 1996.

4.   *Model Protocol for Local Coordinating Councils on Domestic Violence,* Kentucky Governor's Council on Domestic Violence, 1997.

5.   *Coordinating Community Responses to Domestic Violence,*. Melanie Shepard and Ellen Pence (eds.), Sage Publications. Thousand Oaks, CA, 1999. [Ellen Pence has done an excellent job throughout her career of identifying the way system responses are generally developed to assist system professionals. Such protocols and policies are not generally designed with the victim's comfort and ease in accessing services as the primary goal.]

6.   See http://www.nyc.gov/html/ocdv/html/home/home.html, accessed December 10, 2005. The New York City Family Justice Center (Brooklyn) is one of the 15 federally funded Family Justice Centers under the President's Family Justice Center Initiative funded by the U.S. Department of Justice, Office on Violence Against Women.

7.   See www.dvert.org. The Domestic Violence Enhanced Response Team (DVERT) in Colorado Springs, CO, has been operating since 1997. DVERT is operated by the Colorado Springs Police Department and has been nationally recognized for its successful collaborative approach—developing partnerships with 38 different public and private agencies. DVERT was one of the first co-located, multidisciplinary service approaches to domestic violence in the country. Intensive case management, crisis response, and a coordinated community response have been cited as the reason for successful outcomes in cases handled by DVERT.

4

The Next Step: the Family Justice Center

Eden walked into the San Diego Family Justice Center the day we were moving in.[1] We were not open. We had no sign; we had no agencies set up to offer services. Boxes were everywhere as Sgt. Robert Keetch assisted advocates and prosecutors from seven different local agencies who were moving staff into the new Center. Within months, staff from over 25 agencies would work out of the newly created one-stop shop, but that day only a handful of people were there helping to get everyone situated in the new office. The Center was not slated to open for nearly two weeks, but Eden had already heard about it. She was being abused chronically and severely by her boyfriend. After getting off the elevator on the new community agency floor, Eden spotted Sgt. Keetch. Though a 15-year police officer, he was not in uniform that day. It didn't matter to Eden. As soon as he identified himself as an officer, she threw her arms around his neck, weeping and begged for help. She did not understand the complex system that our community had created. But she had heard that she could now go one place to get all the help she needed. She did not really know what she needed, but she knew that she wanted the violence to stop and she wanted to be safe.

When Eden threw her arms around Sgt. Keetch's neck, she knew only that he was her best hope. Sgt. Keetch is one of the good guys. He is a cop who understands that services for domestic violence victims involve far more than cops. He is a person of color who understands that people of color experiencing intimate partner violence need to be welcomed into a place of safety where those providing services look like them and respect their cultural and ethnic heritage. Even today, three years later, as Operational Manager of the Center, Robert Keetch realizes the diversity and complexity of the needs of terrorized, traumatized, confused victims who simply want to come to one place and say they need help. With little or no understanding of the system, they want to bring all their difficult issues somewhere and simply be welcomed as someone in need of help by a community that cares. Eden walked into the Center as a victim of domestic violence. She walked out a survivor.

I first proposed the concept of a one-stop shop in August 1989 after four years as a domestic violence prosecutor. It was not a new concept, but it was already becoming clear to me and many others that the system was too hard for victims to navigate. Services were expanding. Agencies with programs were multiplying rapidly. It was good news that proved we were beginning to realize the importance of dealing with violence. But the length of our referral list was already beyond a single page!

Communities around the country were beginning to co-locate prosecutors and police officers to deal with domestic violence.[2] Some were bringing together staff from nonprofit, community-based organizations and law enforcement officials. The child advocacy movement had already proved that co-located services worked well. Battered women's shelters were expanding their services to meet needs beyond emergency shelter and food. But there were already far too many places for a victim to go if she needed help with many different needs. So I wrote a proposal for our community.

An Idea Whose Time Had Not Come

The original proposal for a Center was about 10 pages long and was directed at the local District Attorney and City Attorney in San Diego. The proposal was simple: Bring together in one place, representatives from the District Attorney, City Attorney, Police Department, Sheriff's Department, the local battered women's shelter, and other social service providers. Then invite victims to come get help in one place. It was logical and just sheer common sense.

I was a young, new city prosecutor asking the elected County District Attorney to listen to me. Because my boss, the elected City Attorney, agreed to support my vision, the District Attorney gave me an audience with nearly 20 of his management staff. I passed out my proposal, made a 10-minute presentation, and sat down. Questions were few and discussion was limited. The next day I received a phone call from the Assistant District Attorney. The call was short, the message simple and direct. The DA did not support my proposal. My 1989 idea for a one-stop shop was an idea whose time had not come! Many of us were discouraged, but not deterred.

Starting Small With the Vision for Co-Located Services

Working with advocates from two local battered women's shelters, San Diego Police Department management, and other domestic violence prosecutors in the City Attorney's Office, we went forward with a portion of the concept anyway. With the blessing of then-San Diego City Attorney John Witt, we carved out three empty offices in the city prosecutor's office on the same floor as our specialized Domestic Violence Unit. We offered this space to the Police Department (to help us coordinate on the investigation and prosecution of cases), the YWCA Battered Women's Services (to offer support and advocacy to victims in our criminal cases), and the

Center for Community Solutions (to operate a restraining order clinic). Their staff would do their own work with current caseloads in their current assignments while using the free office space. We offered this in return for only one promise: If we had victims on pending criminal cases who came to the City Attorney's Office, staff of the three invited agencies would sit down and talk to them and offer services as appropriate. It was a humble beginning.

As noted earlier, San Diego was not alone. Similar efforts were underway in Hennepin County, Minnesota; Mesa, Arizona; San Jose, California; Colorado Springs, Colorado; Albuquerque, New Mexico; and Indianapolis, Indiana. Some multidisciplinary centers were based in hospitals, others in law enforcement agencies, others in battered women's shelters, courthouses, prosecutor's offices, and family advocacy programs on military bases. Depending on the strengths of a particular community, the approach might vary.

In communities with strong child advocacy centers, child advocacy programs began expanding their services to meet the needs of the adult victims of domestic violence while meeting the needs of abused children. The overarching goal of all similar programs was the same: Provide more services to victims and their children from one location instead of expecting victims and their children to travel to many disparate agencies. The research supports our early vision, particularly with criminal justice system services included. A victim is more likely to use a system in the future knowing that the criminal justice system acted in a coordinated way in the past to support her.[3]

San Diego's journey continued during the 1990s without the support of the elected District Attorney. First, we co-located a few advocates with our prosecutors. Then we started rotating cops and prosecutors into each other's agencies a few days a week. Soon, we added a partnership with Children's Hospital by supporting a new initiative developed by the Center for Child Protection, known as the Family Violence Project.[4] Slowly, we experienced firsthand the benefits of co-location, a multidisciplinary approach, and stronger day-to-day working relationships. Living together was so much more powerful than a community task force, a coordinating council, a phone list of resource agencies, or an e-mail distribution list. Living together as professionals was complicated, but it was evident early in our experience that it was providing the most efficient and effective services to victims we had ever delivered.

Finally, in 1998, we conducted our own version of a community safety audit (Chapter 3).[5] The idea was to evaluate how well we were doing in keeping battered women safe in our community. There were many aspects to the safety audit, but only one was necessary to prove the need for a Center. It was early in the audit that the following question arose: How many places does a victim of family violence have to go to get all the help she needs in our community? No one knew the answer. Some of us guessed five places—some estimated 10 places. We have touched on this in the previous chapter, but the answer deserves repeating again as we flesh out the Center vision. The answer would motivate us to begin the long journey toward changing the world.

After a day of brainstorming, charting, and evaluating, we were finally able to answer the question—*In our community, in order for a victim to receive all necessary help she would have to go 32 different places!*

32 Places to Go . . . What Now?

Results of the safety audit gave us our challenge. We knew our old idea's time had come; we resurrected that 1989 proposal. San Diego's Police Chief at the time, David Bejarano, was a community-oriented policing disciple. Dave Bejarano was part of San Diego's growing national reputation, built by former Chief Jerry Sanders, as a department focused on problem-oriented policing. Indeed, by 1999, San Diego had officers doing tremendously innovative work with community organizations, using problem-oriented policing approaches to address chronic and entrenched problems.

By then, I had become the elected City Attorney. The City Attorney's Office developed a Neighborhood Prosecution Unit, which was supported by Chief Bejarano. The concept was simple. If it was effective to have police officers working in neighborhoods to address crime issues with community members, it would be even more helpful to have prosecutors assisting in the problem-solving process where the problems were actually occurring—in the neighborhoods.

Once the Neighborhood Prosecution Unit was created, the Chief and I sat down to talk about the community safety audit related to our domestic violence services. My proposal was straightforward: We needed to bring service providers together instead of requiring victims to go so many places for help. Though we did not know how many agencies might be willing to move portions of their staffs to such a location, we could certainly start with cops and prosecutors. By late 1999, the Police Department had a specialized Domestic Violence Unit with 24 detectives handling misdemeanor and felony domestic violence cases, supervised by four sergeants and a lieutenant. The City Attorney had a specialized misdemeanor prosecution unit with a staff of 32, including 13 prosecutors, two investigators, three advocates, and support staff. After all our work together, we could lead the way. We would move in together, and we would invite social service providers and other public agencies to join us in rent-free office space.

The Logical Extension of Community Policing

It took only one meeting for Chief Bejarano to figure it out. After I presented my proposal, he reflected on it briefly and then said these words: "This Center is the logical extension of our community policing and neighborhood prosecution work." Under the leadership of former Police Chief (now Mayor) Jerry Sanders, the San

Diego Police Department had, as noted, become a national model for community-oriented policing. Chief Bejarano clearly saw the Family Justice Center as the next step in the Department's community policing work. And the hard work began!

The Chief's support was conditional upon a comprehensive study of the feasibility of such a Center with a law enforcement presence. He chose former Sgt. (now Lt.) Monica Kaiser in the Domestic Violence Unit to oversee the study. The study took approximately 18 months, as Sgt. Kaiser pulled together a team that included prosecutors, police officers, system advocates, and community-based advocates. They traveled the country looking at other types of one-stop shops, including child advocacy centers, sexual assault response teams, shelters, and other small domestic violence programs with multidisciplinary services. They met with police officers, detectives, prosecutors, and local community agency staff. They analyzed the potential case flow issues. They evaluated the protocols necessary to protect chain-of-command issues with the different agencies. The study's conclusion was clear: The Family Justice Center idea could work with enough buy-in from policy makers, elected officials, and community agencies.

> It was an honor for me to be part of the original team that developed a model that was right for San Diego. Each community will need to figure it out for themselves and custom fit the Family Justice Center model to meet their needs, their strengths and weaknesses. But our journey has been worth the effort.
>
> —Lt. Monica Kaiser, SDPD

Name Based on Survivor Input

During the evaluation process, the concept began to emerge under the working title of "San Diego Domestic Violence Service Center." With more discussion, the name evolved into "San Diego Domestic Violence Justice Center." However, after Sgt. Kaiser's study gave the green light to the vision for the Center, our growing coalition agreed it was time to float the idea with funding sources and, most importantly, with our potential clients—current victims and survivors of domestic violence in San Diego. So focus groups were developed and meetings were organized, as we reached out to talk to potential funders and clients.

Within a matter of weeks, the message came through loud and clear. Victims did not want to go to a *service center*. They did not want to go to a Center with the name *domestic violence*. Funding sources did not want to fund *domestic violence*. We considered and evaluated other names, and a clear consensus emerged: the San Diego Family Justice Center. Everyone supported *families*, and *justice* was critical in the process of stopping family violence. Input from victims and survivors was also vital in concluding that offenders could not receive services at our Center. If we were going to create a safe environment for victims and their children, we must have a facility akin to a battered women's shelter, one where offenders were not welcome. The San Diego Family Justice Center would be solely a victim-centered facility, and victims would give support to one another.

By October 2001, the concept was crystallized. The Center was viable. We had built a strong coalition. Nearly 20 years of raising awareness, collaboration, and specialization had produced a foundation for a Center with co-located services. But now how would we pay for it? The City of San Diego faced significant financial challenges. Social service programs already scrambled annually for scarce money. Where could we turn for support? Would the Mayor and Council appropriate general fund revenue for a new initiative like this? With so many competing priorities in local government, how could this one rise to the top of the list? We discuss resource issues and funding for the Center vision in Chapter 6, but long before we figured out the larger business case, we had to fund our San Diego vision.

There's such a sense of security here. After experiencing what we go through you can become desensitized to the whole thing. Coming here provided me with a backbone. Here I was seeing other people who were here, all kinds of people, professional, from the street, people you would walk by everyday from all walks of life and have no idea they were going through the same thing that you were going through, too. It made me feel like I was not alone; other people have experienced what I went through, too. The people here who I talked with understood my situation and validated my experience. That made me stronger.

—*Anonymous Family Justice Center Client, 2005*

Finding the Money

Our first funding application went to the United States Department of Justice, Office on Violence Against Women (OVW) in 2001. We reasoned that this national idea should be endorsed at the federal level and San Diego should help lead the way. It made good sense, with so much federal money now focused on addressing family violence issues, that the Justice Department should support our exciting vision. But only months after applying for money, our application was rejected!

Though there were many reasons for our rejection, we received feedback from OVW that included two comments. First, we had asked for money to rent office space to create the Center, but at that time OVW provided funds only for program services. Second, our proposal had not fared well during the peer review process. OVW's peer review brought in domestic violence experts from across the country to evaluate all funding requests before staff made a final decision. Clearly, we failed in articulating our vision and/or the peer reviewers did not understand the concept of co-located services for victims of domestic violence and their children.

Though OVW rejected our first application, we had simultaneously submitted our application for rent and infrastructure costs to the California Endowment, a large private foundation focused on funding health-related initiatives in California. The Endowment carefully considered our proposal for many months. While our proposal was pending, we scheduled a public hearing in October 2001 before the City of San Diego's Public Safety and Neighborhood Services Committee. Made up of five members of the San Diego City Council, the committee was our first public presentation of the vision. We invited our Program Manager at the Endowment, Greg Hall, and other potential funders to the hearing.

We filled the committee hearing room with community supporters from a host of potential partner agencies. Momentum was building! Front and center were the Police Chief and the Fire Chief, in uniform, standing side by side with domestic violence advocates in support of a new public safety initiative in San Diego focused on helping victims of domestic violence. The committee heard the pitch, and they too saw the vision. They were moved as survivors shared their stories and the need for more accessible services. The hearing was not, however, about *those women* or *those victims*. We focused on the responsibility of our entire community to stop family violence. The committee voted to support the vision, though money still needed to be identified. Poignantly, two of the five members of the committee shared their own experiences with family violence, and both of them wrote a personal check to support the Center on the spot.

Though new to the California Endowment, Greg Hall too saw the vision that day. Greg's insight and wisdom was the key turning point for the Center. Under the leadership of Dr. Robert Ross, the California Endowment became our gateway to success. Experienced in public health prevention and intervention models, Dr. Ross understood the concept of trying to bring all services together and developing a community of caring professionals who could focus on healing for victims.

In March 2002, the California Endowment offered the City of San Diego a $500,000 challenge grant. If the City would match it, the Endowment would provide $500,000 over a three-year period to help make the Center a reality. Within 30 days, the Mayor and City Council pledged city community development block grant funds, and we had enough money to get started.

Though the Endowment was critical, we had pursued a series of strategies in the event their funding did not materialize. City Attorney's Office press secretary Maria Velasquez played a crucial role in developing a promotional video in partnership with the City's television station (City 24) that helped explain the vision of the Center. She assisted in developing letters of support from key community leaders and recruited the local ABC affiliate (KGTV, Channel 10) to become a media sponsor for the Center.

At every turn, we remembered the words of David Starr Jordan, the first President of Stanford University: "The world steps aside to let anyone pass who knows where they are going." We simply kept articulating where we were going until everyone around us came to believe it was true.

On April 9, 2002, then-Mayor Dick Murphy and a unanimous San Diego City Council authorized a five-year lease on privately owned downtown office space for the new Center. A local businessman, who had been touched by family violence in his own life, offered us three floors in a downtown high-rise at a reduced rent. And the space planning and detail work began in earnest.

> I felt at home when I walked into the lobby. As I entered into the kitchen/family room I was already impressed with all the services being provided to people.
>
> —*Marie, Family Justice Center Client, 2005*

Over the next six months, an implementing team of police officers, prosecutors, and community-based advocates led by Assistant Chief Rulette Armstead, Lt. Jim Barker, and Assistant City Attorney Gael Strack began figuring out what it would look like to have a few staff members from many different agencies move in together. There were myriad questions to be answered in planning for the actual operation of the Center:

- How much space would each agency get?
- Would the agency staff members be interspersed or segregated?
- Would all client services be provided on one floor or on multiple floors?
- How could the police officers be protected from supervision by prosecutors?
- How could the community agencies be assured that cops would not try to control them?
- What would the on-site governance structure look like?
- Who would be in charge?
- Who would be the final decision maker?
- Could a collaborative decision making model be used?
- How would non-governmental agencies have a say in day-to-day operations?
- How would clients enter the Center?
- Who would they see first?
- Who would decide the order of services to be provided?
- What records would be kept on clients?
- How would information on clients be shared between agencies?

The *Family Justice Center Manual,* to be printed and published separately from this book, will address the detailed steps necessary to open a Center.[6] The manual is based on the learning process we engaged in as we moved from concept to reality between October 2001 and October 2002, and is then supplemented with the

---

Family Justice Center On-Site Partners

Adult Protective Services

Cal Western Law School—Legal Internship Program

Camp Hope

Center for Community Solutions—Temporary Restraining Order Clinic

Chaplain's Program (Modeled after San Diego Fire & Police Departments)

Children's Hospital—Chadwick Center, Family Violence Project

Home Start

Military (Navy & Marine Corps)

San Diego City Attorney's Office—Domestic Violence and Special Victims Unit

San Diego Deaf Mental Health Services

San Diego District Attorney's Office—Family Protection Unit

San Diego District Attorney's Office—Victim Assistance Program

San Diego Domestic Violence Council

San Diego Family Justice Center

San Diego Family Justice Center Foundation

San Diego Family Justice Center—Volunteer Program

San Diego Police Department—Domestic Violence Unit

San Diego Police Department—Elder Abuse Investigations

San Diego Probation Department

San Diego Volunteer Lawyer Program

Sharp Grossmont Healthcare—Forensic Medical Unit

Teen Court

Travelers Aid

UCSD—Paralegal Program/Residency Program

UPAC—Union Pan Asian Communities

lessons learned in the Center during the past three years of operation. But the reality was crystal clear: Courageous public officials and a generous, forward-thinking community foundation had taken the critical step toward making the San Diego Family Justice Center a reality.

The Family Justice Center Today—Renee's Story

What is the Center today? Gael Strack's Christmas surprise perhaps best describes what a victim in need finds there today. It was the holiday season, and Gael had just been named the Director of the new city department, the Office of the Family Justice Center. She left City Hall intent on enjoying a two-hour shopping spree at Horton Plaza, the city's downtown shopping mall. But her attention was drawn to a young woman with a suitcase at her side sitting in the lobby of City Hall. Her head was buried in her hands; a small child tugged at her side. Gael could not walk by. She stopped and asked the young woman if she was okay. The woman looked up and began crying.

The young woman had just been beaten. Her injuries were obvious. Fleeing her boyfriend, she had ridden the city's mass transit trolley system to downtown San Diego. She did not know where to go or what to do. She had so many concerns and needed help with so many different things. Gael never got to the shopping mall that day. Within 30 minutes, she escorted Renee to the nearby San Diego Family Justice Center. Kimberly Pearce, the Director of Client Services, welcomed her. A dedicated volunteer took the traumatized child, changed her diaper, provided a snack, and engaged the child with toys on the floor of the children's room. Kimberly informed Renee of the options available to her and developed a plan of action. A forensic nurse conducted a medical exam and documented Renee's injuries.

Next, Renee took a hot shower in the Forensic Medical Unit and received a clean set of clothes. A San Diego police officer took a courtesy report, though Renee lived outside of the city limits. She was afraid to call her dad. Instead, she chose to meet with Chaplain George Barnes and receive some spiritual support. At Renee's request, Chaplain George called her dad for her and talked him through the unfolding drama. A social worker from Traveler's Aid assisted in making arrangements for Renee to travel to the Midwest the next morning to stay with her parents.

Shortly thereafter, Renee met with a shelter representative and received authorization for emergency shelter. We ultimately purchased her bus ticket and provided her $20 in spending money. Chaplain George transported her to the nearby shelter that night. The next morning, Chaplain George, who Renee had connected with on a very meaningful level, brought her to the Center for follow-up services.

Renee asked to meet with Gael before she left. She said she had no idea that such a place existed. Gael told her of the Center's recent beginning and reflected with Renee that if they had met just two years earlier in that City Hall lobby, Gael's only recourse would have been to refer her to the series of places she needed to go for help. Gael and Renee had both experienced the power of the Family Justice Center, and Renee and her little girl's life would never be the same. Later in the morning, George Barnes drove her and her daughter to the bus station and waited until the bus departed for home, where her parents were waiting for her.

Family Justice Center Off-Site Partners

Access Center

Adams and Adams Consulting & Training, Inc.

Casa Cornelia

Center for Community Solutions—Project Safe House & Hidden Valley House

Child and Adolescent Services Research Center

Child Welfare Services

Citizens Diplomacy Council

Crisis Response Team

Crime Victims Fund

El Nido, Interfaith Shelter Network

Episcopal Community Services—Sanctuary

Gavin De Becker, Inc.

Gay and Lesbian Center

Indian Health Council

License to Freedom

Libre—Community Resource Center

PERT—Psychiatric Emergency Response Team

Rancho Coastal Humane Society

SANDAG

San Diego Superior Court

San Diego Workforce Partnership

San Diego Youth & Community Services—Human Trafficking Project

Sexual Assault Response Team (SART)

SDSU—Disability Awareness Program

South Bay Community Services

UCSD—Medical Center

Verizon Wireless

Women, Infants and Children (WIC)

Women's Resource Center

YWCA—Emergency Shelter

Over 600 clients per month come to the Center, including 200 children. Each day 120 professionals from 25 agencies are there to provide services. The clients, through a client intake process, decide which agencies they want to see. Nearly half the clients never interact with criminal justice system professionals, choosing rather to receive services from community-based organizations only.

During the breakfast hour, they are served breakfast. During the lunch hour, they are served lunch. If they need a cell phone, they can get one with 3,000 minutes of airtime for free from Verizon Wireless.

They can get a restraining order without having to go to court (electronic filing); they can receive medical services, attend a support group, obtain counseling for their children, and receive a host of other services.

Current Family Justice Center services include:

- Food
- Clothing
- Restraining orders without going to court
- Free cell phones with free minutes
- Free Internet access
- Spiritual support
- Transportation assistance
- Free medical and dental assistance
- DA Victim-Witness Assistance services
- Counseling
- Support groups
- Safety planning
- Child care
- Support services for children
- Law enforcement assistance
- Free locksmith services
- Pregnancy counseling

Providing services all in one place made my visit easier, with all the information in one place instead of searching for all my options.

—*Gardenia, Family Justice Center Client, 2005*

And all the services are in one place! They are real and tangible. But the current services are only a beginning.

The Center's strategic plan, developed with input from our clients in focus groups, is now aiming toward adding even more services, including:

- Economic/financial assessments
- Financial/literacy/credit counseling
- Credit repair
- Asset development
- Educational classes
- Personal coaching
- Mentoring opportunities for all clients (adults and children)
- Job training
- On-site housing—emergency, transitional, and affordable
- On-site job availability for victims and children through corporate partnerships with responsible retailers
- Thrift store/retail store called "All Things Purple"
- Coffee shop for clients

Client complaints, though a very small percentage of feedback received, focus on services they still want us to add and on the waiting time when we have many clients going through the intake process at the same time.

> The dining room is freezing. Way too cold.
>
> *—John-Michael, Family Justice Center Client, 2005*

We accept the complaints and try to respond to them if at all possible. But even beyond the amazing array of services now being provided from a single location, the Center has also developed an ever-growing vision statement that points the way into the future and can point the way for communities across America. The vision statement guides the available services today and points the way to greater goals for the years to come.

The vision is big and sometimes hard to make tangible. The motto we have adopted to keep us moving forward keeps it simple: DREAM BIG! Daily, the dedicated professionals of the Center challenge each other to dream big and keep listening to clients as they tell us what is working and what is not. Our clients each dream of lives free from violence and abuse. The least we can do is dream with them as we continue to build partnerships with more and more agencies that can wrap their arms around our clients whenever necessary.

San Diego Family Justice Center Vision Statement

A future where ALL the needs of victims are met, where children are protected, where violence fades, where economic justice increases, where families heal and thrive, where hope is realized, and where we ALL work together…

The bigger you dream, the more you can do to give hope to those in need. In the beginning, for example, I never would have imagined that we would make spiritual support a priority in a domestic violence center with cops and prosecutors present, but we listened to our clients, looked at the research, and dreamed big! Today, chaplains participate in a nonsectarian, interfaith program that helps meet needs throughout the Center and provides powerful encouragement to clients suffering from trauma and in shock.

Everyone was friendly, attentive, and comforting. No one judges you or makes you feel dumb or worthless. A lot of agencies have a talk-down mentality, but that attitude isn't here at the Family Justice Center. This is a great place and much needed. It would be nice to be given an envelope for legal papers so no one can see what I am carrying when I leave. When I go home, if he's there, I don't want him to see what I have."

—*Lillian, Family Justice Center Client, 2005*

The power of dreaming big produced tremendous encouragement to staff and clients through the dedicated service of a host of volunteer chaplains!

Is there more to be done? Yes. We don't have enough services to help victims get job training and jobs. We don't have enough legal services. We need to do more to provide affordable, long-term housing for clients. We have a long way to go, but the Center vision is moving us forward one step at a time!

Conclusion

Communities now have a model. They can use the San Diego Family Justice Center example to see how we went from vision to reality. It was a long journey. It was years and years of relationship building. It was strong, decisive decision making at a moment in time that said, "We must do this though the unknowns far outnumber the knowns." With a tremendous team of supporters, the Center became a reality—now 120 professionals from 25 agencies work together every day in 40,000 square feet of office space in downtown San Diego.

In the chapters to come, the concepts of the Center will evolve, but it was evident at a certain point that we could not continue to talk about and plan for it. We had to do it! We talked often of building and flying the plane at the same time. While no one would want to fly on an airline with that motto, in the world of co-located services, you can talk about it forever or you can do it and figure it out while you fly!

> More often than not, attending to a client's emotional and physical needs is a spiritual endeavor. At the Family Justice Center, the chaplains are available to serve the professionals and the clients. We can provide victims with spiritual support outside the courtroom and emotional support inside the courtroom. We serve breakfast and lunch, help care for children, and even assist them in getting free dental assistance and locksmith services!
>
> *—Family Justice Center Chaplain George Barnes*

There is now a model. San Diego's journey was an example for other communities. This new service delivery model can be done and is a promising approach to dealing with the current services for victims and their children in many communities that requires victims to go from place to place, agency to agency, telling their story over and over again. Many victims like Renee and Eden need you to dive into the hard work of making this vision a reality.

Endnotes

1. Eden is pictured with Robert Keetch in the photo section of this book.

2. A host of communities developed some version of co-located domestic violence services during the 1990s that included a number of law enforcement professionals, including Santa Clara County, CA; Seattle, WA; Colorado Springs, CO; Newport News, VA; Nashville, TN; Memphis, TN; Chattanooga, TN; San Jose, CA; Quincy, MA; Hennepin County, MN; Phoenix, AZ; Mesa, AZ; and Indianapolis, IN.

3. E. Gondolf and E. Fisher, *Battered Women as Survivors: an Alternative to Treating Learned Helplessness,* D.C. Heath and Co., Lexington, KY, 1988.

4. The Family Violence Program was developed by Sandy Miller, M.S., after she was hired by the Center for Child Protection at Children's Hospital in 1989 to assist in reducing foster care placements within the child protective system. Sandy was a domestic violence-trained advocate who developed a specialized advocacy unit with trained domestic violence advocates assigned to work with battered women where there was a co-occurrence of child abuse and domestic violence.

5. Ellen Pence and her team in Duluth, MN, have developed the concept of a community safety audit, a process by which a community evaluates its systems and intervention responses. Though Ellen has had a strong partnership with San Diego, she did not participate personally in our 1998 assessment process. We did, however, use the assistance of a number of consultants who had received training in Duluth on the community safety audit process.

6. The *Family Justice Center Manual* will be published by Volcano Press, Volcano, CA, in early 2007.

5

Caution: Not All Communities are Ready

"It is easy for you to come and talk about collaboration and co-located services in our community because you don't know anything about our community! You don't know what our struggles are, you don't know what our problems are, and you don't know that collaboration has become the vehicle for government mandates that are endangering battered women!"

It was November 2005 and excitement was growing in Calgary, Edmonton, Saskatoon, and the greater Toronto communities of Waterloo, Durham, and Scarborough about the Family Justice Center vision. I had just finished describing the vision on a panel with the president of the National Network to End Domestic Violence, Lynn Rosenthal, and a key Center advocate, Felicia Collins-Correia from Tulsa, Oklahoma. We had each offered some practical ideas for how to start moving down the road to a Center. Then a woman stepped to the microphone and delivered her impassioned rebuke, commanding the immediate respect of the audience.

Though excitement was high about the vision, the anger and frustration in her voice was palpable. At first, I was perturbed. The presentation and the questions were being webcast live on the Internet across Canada and around the world. I wanted excitement from the crowd. I wanted to recruit change agents to help move the vision forward in more U.S. and Canadian communities. But here was a very angry survivor and advocate who I immediately knew was not interested in the vision.

This woman, I later learned, had spent over 30 years advocating for battered women in Canada. She was a victim and ultimately a survivor of domestic violence. Her experiences with the system left her with little room for optimism. The hurt and pain were visible on her face. She continued to talk about her frustration with Canadian government mandates related to collaborating with the child protection movement, representing the fear and resentment of many shelters. She said that in her interaction with portions of the Canadian government, her agency had been threatened with loss of funding if they did not share information with child protection agencies.

When she finished speaking, there was dead silence in the room. Then the advocates in the room became obvious. They stood in unison and clapped for this powerful, articulate, seasoned survivor and advocate who spoke truth in the face of growing momentum towards co-located services in Canada. My response was careful and deferential. She was right, of course. We knew nothing of her experience or the challenges that she and her agency faced. I knew nothing of how the Center vision would or should interface with her community. She had reminded us of a reality that needs to be acknowledged as the Family Justice Center movement evolves: The vision is not necessarily right for every community in every country in every part of the world.

While some communities may find that a Center is not suited for their particular circumstances, more commonly others find they are simply not yet ready to pursue the Family Justice Center vision. Once the idea, the vision, and the possibilities of a Center are understood, each community must consider how its agencies get along, what the relationships between leaders of those agencies are, and how well they are doing currently in working together to help victims.

I really enjoyed my visit; the staff was so friendly and helpful. They answered all my questions. At the end of my visit, I felt like I had many friends. I wasn't alone anymore.

—*Carolyn, Family Justice Center Client, 2005*

The Center vision can be articulated, but it can and should only become a reality through an organic process in a community. The vision cannot and should not be imposed from the outside or from the top down. It must grow from the bottom up. It is based on relationships between individuals and agencies. Those relationships must evolve over time and develop to a point where moving in together is a healthy idea.

Bad intimate relationships rarely get better when partners get married or decide to live together. Just like people, agencies that don't trust each other and don't know how to work together should not live together. Let's look more closely at both concepts being developed here: 1) The Center vision must grow out of a long, organic process of collaboration and specialization within a local community; and 2) communities should assess whether they have the building blocks for development of an effective Center. *If communities are not ready, they should not pursue this vision.*

I was so impressed with the Family Justice Center. I was not aware of this facility. I came to support my friend and was treated so well. I will share with everyone about this wonderful, comfortable place. The staff and volunteers were awesome and worked so well together. Thank you all for what you do.

Patricia, Friend of Family Justice Center Client, 2004

Respecting and Understanding the Relationship—Building Journey

No community can wake up one day and decide to build a Center. It has to grow into the idea over time. The cops and prosecutors need to have learned how to investigate and prosecute batterers successfully. The shelter advocates need to have developed close working relationships with those cops and prosecutors. Bringing everyone to a meeting, putting name tags on them, and then telling them they are now going to live together 16 hours a day in a Family Justice Center is not a good idea.

San Diego's relationship-building journey toward a Center began over 20 years ago. It had its roots in the decision of feminist advocates to build relationships with criminal and civil justice professionals. It grew because of the decision of feminists in San Diego to include men. Former YWCA Battered Women's Services Director Ashley Walker recently recounted the intentional choice to reach out to men in the early and mid-1980s, seeking alliances instead of engendering conflict.[1]

San Diego never had a class action lawsuit against law enforcement agencies for failing to protect battered women. Little animosity ever developed there between battered women's shelters and criminal justice professionals. The cooperative spirit was aided by a core group of key system professionals who allied themselves with feminist advocates from 1986 to 1988.[2] As a result, there was a relationship of collegiality and camaraderie from our earliest task force planning meetings.

Indeed, I remember vividly the laughter and jokes surrounding our first major decision together: Should we create our own stationary in an effort to attract the attention of policy makers? The answer was a resounding *yes*. We gleefully decided to put all of our names on the letterhead so each of us would seem important. It was the first time any of us had ever seen our names on letterhead. We were all trench workers. We were not policy makers. For the most part, we were not agency heads. We were *grassroots*. We had no power so our early challenge was creating the illusion of power. Our challenge was pooling our resources and sharing strategic ideas to impact systems we did not control. Stationary became our first tool in the struggle to change the world!

In many communities, the nature of the relationship between shelter advocates and criminal and civil justice professionals will be the key dynamic that determines whether a Center can evolve and flourish. Communities where, for a variety of reasons, conflict and mistrust exist between shelter advocates and law enforcement professionals are likely to find it difficult to build a collaborative approach that can lead to co-location of services.

Key Steps in the San Diego Journey

Key steps were evident in San Diego's journey, actions we took before even beginning to plan for a Center that may help other communities trying to pursue this vision, including the following:

- Established and operated domestic violence task force.

- Created specialized Domestic Violence Units in the DA's Office, City Attorney's Office, Probation Department, and Police Department.

- Created permanent Domestic Violence Council (after our two-year Domestic Violence Task Force).

- Developed small pilot project initiatives experimenting with co-location.

- Established public support from the all police chiefs in the county and other elected officials.

- Successfully completed an 18-month community safety audit.

- Successfully completed an 18-month feasibility study.

- Held community forums and victim focus groups confirming the need for a Center.

- Obtained unanimous approval from the Mayor and City Council, including a funding commitment for the Center.

- Maintained a close working relationship with the statewide domestic violence coalition.

At every turn, San Diego's journey progressed, sometimes slowly, toward the ultimate vision of a Center. Key steps that have been identified in the development of a strong coordinated community response were all present in San Diego.[3] Many authors have also identified the importance of community leaders dedicated to advancing social reforms in the domestic violence field.[4] San Diego had strong leadership from key policy makers, including agency heads and elected officials.

Key Elements of a Community Ready for a Family Justice Center

In the last three years diverse communities—tribal, rural, suburban, and urban—considering the Center vision have found over and over that key elements must be in place for successful development of a Center. Anyone in a community advocating for creation of such a Center needs to know what pieces must be in place for those agencies and people who can make it a reality.

- Critical partners necessary to a Center, including law enforcement, prosecution, probation, military (if applicable), community-based advocates, civil legal services, medical, and diverse community-based organizations, must be willing to first study the practical implications of moving in together.

- Criminal justice agencies should have a history of developing aggressive arrest, investigation, and prosecution policies that keep victims safe while the system prosecutes the batterer. *Criminal justice agencies with dangerous or irresponsible policies, such as condoning high mutual arrest rates or revictimization of victims by officers or system professionals, are not ideal candidates for co-located services with community-based shelter organizations.*

- Potential Center partnering agencies must be willing to accept the victim-centered service delivery model of the vision and reject on-site services for batterers. The vision is to provide on-site services to victims and their children only in order to avoid the increased danger and intimidation that comes from batterers being allowed access to them when victims come forward for help.

- The core community partners—police, prosecutors, and community-based advocates—should have a history of specialization in their domestic violence intervention work—specially trained advocates, police officers, prosecutors, judges, court support personnel, and medical professionals who focus most, if not all, of their time and energy on handling domestic violence cases.

- Local elected officials engaged early in discussions about the development of a Center and pledging their public support, is crucial to success, along with active participation from other government policy makers.

Quite a list, isn't it? Just when this book started to get you excited about the Center vision, you see a checklist that makes creating the right foundation a very tall order indeed. But the basics should be clear. This list was not made up out of the blue. It was forged in the experience of "pouring the footings" for the San Diego Family Justice Center and confirmed over and over again as we began to work with other potential Center sites in the United States, Canada, Great Britain, Mexico, and Australia. Creating a Family Justice Center is not so easy. No great idea, no matter how simple, is easy.

Assessment Questions for any Community

In some cases, asking questions may be a better way to get at the issues discussed previously. We have identified a series of 10 questions to be applied by potential funders of a Center proposal.

Any community that is considering developing a Center should answer the following questions itself in an honest, open, objective community conversation. Community members advocating for creation of a Center can ask their elected officials to hold public meetings and discuss these questions. They are an excellent starting point for discussing whether your community has the right background, history, and committed partners to make a Center work.

1. Do you have protocols for every agency in your community on how it responds to domestic violence? When were the protocols last updated?

2. Does the state domestic violence coalition work closely with your community or strongly support your existing protocols and procedures?

3. Do you have a history of agencies that provide domestic violence services working together? Do you like each other?

4. Do you have domestic violence specialists in your law enforcement agencies and in your prosecutor's office?

5. Do you have a domestic violence task force or coordinating council?

6. What is the greatest accomplishment of that task force in the last year?

7. Who will be your strongest partner in pursuing the Center vision?

8. Who will be your weakest partner in pursuing the vision?

9. How much local money is already being spent in your community to help victims of domestic violence? Has the amount of money gone up or down over the last 10 years?

10. What will you do to pursue the Center vision if you cannot initially find funding?[5]

Recognizing the Truth—Even if It Hurts

No community wants to conclude it is not ready for the exciting vision of a Center model. Sharon Denaro from Dade County, Florida, agrees that the readiness issue is huge for any community:

> *When the President's Family Justice Center solicitation came out, we wanted to apply. We had a core group of individuals who wanted to see it happen and we had a wonderful history of working together especially in developing a domestic violence court. However, we also discovered we were*

not ready. The idea of a Family Justice Center was new and it had not been discussed with everyone. We needed to get buy-in from key government officials, our advocacy community and a Champion needed to emerge. The good news is the solicitation gave us an opportunity to begin the discussion. We now have some great discussions going on and the pieces are falling into place. We've been energized by the Family Justice Center concept. We have hope that we can make a difference in Dade County with this vision but we are not ready yet.[6]

As this book continues, the powerful success of the San Diego Family Justice Center will be evident. Any community leader or agent for change will catch the excitement and want to be part of it. But it does a great disservice to the complexity of this vision and to the unique nature of different communities if we pretend the vision is right for every community everywhere.

Okay To Not Be Ready

The message here is to relax—slow down! Don't try to force-feed this vision to anyone. Every community needs visionaries and advocates for creation of a Center. But it takes time for everyone to see the vision and be ready to pursue it. We need to continually acknowledge the following:

+ Not all communities can do this.

+ Not all communities are ready.

+ A history of collaboration between diverse agencies is critical.

+ A history of interdisciplinary relationships is important.

+ Many communities may need to step back and work on the building blocks first.

+ Many need to dream big but start very small.

Why will communities want to ignore these realities and move forward anyway? First, if money is available, every community will want to think they are ready. Second, it is hard to admit that your community is not doing good work with families in need. We want to be proud of our community. We want to celebrate all we do well and only want passing reference to our weaknesses as a city, a county, or a community. But we cannot talk about making Centers work until we step back a few steps and remember that no matter how exciting the concept, how powerful the potential result, and how positive the potential relationships between agencies, if our foundation is rotten, the house will not stand strong.

As embarrassing as the incidents were, I was made to feel comfortable and was not judged. Greatly appreciate assistance. I was utterly flabbergasted. The entire process was family friendly, organized and professional, yet nurturing and caring. Everyone treated me with dignity and respect. They even fed me and thought about my children who weren't even here at the Center. Why hasn't this Center been available for us before?! I praise God for each of you. And I thank you fore your patience and kindness. God be with you.

—*Amber, Family Justice Center Client, 2005*

Over the last three years, as the Center movement has developed, it has become clear that not all communities are ready to have use such a model. Some communities may never be ready. Centers must be organic; they must grow out of the soil of each individual community. They must have the foundation prepared before the house is built.[7]

What will happen if a community ignores this challenging list and just forges ahead? Will they be able to create a Center without this foundation? Will they be able to develop relationships quickly that have never existed? Doubtful! Can they still make a Center work even if their collaboration history is bad, their interagency relationships are ugly, and agencies have not previously prioritized work to stop family violence? Unlikely!

The experience in San Diego and elsewhere indicates that any community that cannot survive the assessment elements and the assessment questions should think long and hard before moving forward with plans for a Center. What can a community do to keep moving toward the vision even in incremental steps? Certain actions helped San Diego move forward toward the ultimate plan of co-located services with many diverse agencies. These actions can be considered and applied in other communities—whether rural, tribal, suburban, or urban—to lay the groundwork for a future Center.

Actions to Prepare Communities for Center Vision

Many of the actions listed below must be pursued in a community for years to prepare everyone. Others simply need to be instituted during the planning process, but they clearly support the process of developing consensus around the creation of a Center. If you conclude you are not ready to pursue immediate development, a slower, longer, evolutionary process will be the right course for your community. Consider these ideas for slowly moving your community closer to pursuing a Center:

- Get police and prosecutors talking to each other in weekly/monthly round tables about their handling of cases.

- Get police and prosecutors in the same room with advocates to talk about the good and the bad of their work together on behalf of victims.

- Stop the finger pointing! Blaming each other for problems solves nothing!

- Create an open dialogue on each agency's views of system problems.

- Build one-on-one relationships and alliances, one friend at a time, with like-minded policy makers, elected officials, and community leaders. (Do lunch!)

- Look for opportunities for agencies to work together on individual cases.

- Ask victims and survivors what will serve them best—ask them what they need. Use focus groups. Use victim surveys—let them be anonymous!

- Identify how much money is being spent right now by all agencies and any other special domestic violence initiatives. Brainstorm how working together could make resources go further

- Challenge everyone to think of the Center as a public safety initiative.

- Seek consensus on this principle: We cannot protect children if we do not protect their mothers[8] If your child protection system will not agree with this principle, it should not be part of your Center.

- From the beginning, bring in those with a fresh perspective of concept evaluation—yes, the outside consultant who has experience with the Center model!

- Consider using the services of a trained facilitator/strategic planner in evaluating your community's readiness.[9]

- Consider a pilot project involving co-located services if a small number of local agencies do have a strong history together and could form the nucleus for an initial experiment in living together.

- Consider building the Volkswagen before you try to build the Cadillac.

- Dream big, and start small if key partners are not willing to pursue the vision but other agencies are strongly supportive.

- Remember: Test all ideas and proposed pilot projects by asking victims and survivors to reflect with you on the viability and helpfulness of the proposed idea.

Conclusion

The message to remember here is simple: Not all communities can or should pursue the Family Justice Center vision. Communities with a history of mistrust, bad interagency relationships, or a lack of specialized intervention initiatives in domestic violence should not co-locate their existing services. Nothing could be worse for victims than incompetent, uninformed, and victim-endangering policies being enhanced by joining forces with other poorly trained and uninformed agencies. Local battered women's shelters and state domestic violence coalitions are often the best judges of the nature of interdisciplinary working relationships in a community. Such entities should play key roles in evaluating the appropriateness of the Center model for a community.

If an assessment shows that the community is not ready, it can still take steps to move toward development of a Center in the future. Often, even if key partners are not ready to pursue the vision, other public and private agencies may pursue a pilot project or small co-located services initiative to advance the vision. The *dream big—start small* motto may be the best approach in communities where collaboration is an untested concept and potential unanticipated consequences have not been identified.

Endnotes

1. Ashley Walker, *Battered Women and the Law,* presentation for Cal Western School of Law course facilitated by Professor Gael Strack, January 2005.

2. The San Diego County Task Force on Domestic Violence Planning Committee played a powerful role in laying the groundwork for later collaboration. The 1988 members included: Murray Bloom, Director, San Diego Superior Court, Family Court Services; Lt. Commander Chuck Ertl, Ret., NAS Miramar; Joyce Faidley, Center for Women's Studies and Services (now known as Center for Community Solutions); Gene Fischer, Deputy Director, Family Service Center, Marine Corps Recruit Depot; Dee Fuller, Director, District Attorney Victim Assistance Program; Betty White, Center for Community Solutions; Casey Gwinn, San Diego City Attorney's Office; Kate Yavenditti, San Diego Volunteer Lawyer's Program; Katy Lancaster, San Diego County Probation Department; Lee Lawless, family law attorney; Lt. Leslie Lord, San Diego Police Department; Elly Newman, Legal Advocate, YWCA Battered Women's Services; Ashley Walker, Director, YWCA Battered Women's Services; Ruth Hansen, San Diego County Probation Department; and Marilyn Cornell, San Diego County Probation Department.

3. Casey G. Gwinn and Anne O'Dell, "Stopping the Violence: the Role of the Police Officer and the Prosecutor," *20 Western State University Law Review,* 1993, 298, pp. 300-03.

4. Meredith Hofford and Adele V. Harrell, "Family Violence: Interventions for the Justice System," cited in *Battered Women and the Law,* Clare Dalton and Elizabeth M. Schneider, Foundation Press, New York, 2001, pp. 576-78.

5. Each of these questions can illuminate certain strengths and weaknesses in a community that will inform the discussion about a community's readiness to move forward with the Family Justice Center vision.

6. Interview with Sharon Denaro, December 8, 2005.

7. Systems and even states should be conducting similar assessments of their laws, policies, and procedures. In California, Attorney General Bill Lockyer convened the Attorney General's Task Force on Local Criminal Justice Response to Domestic Violence. Our report, entitled *Domestic Violence—Keeping the Promise: Victim Safety and Batterer Accountability,* was a critical analysis of California's compliance with nearly 20 years of legislation and related policies and procedures now in place. The report hails the Family Justice Center as a model for addressing poorly coordinated system responses in local communities. For an on-line copy of the report, go to www.safestate. org/domesticviolence.

8. This principle will inform a community's ability to bring together child advocacy and domestic violence professionals. In the absence of this commitment, domestic violence advocates will find a child protective system far more likely to revictimize battered women, prosecute victims of domestic violence for failure to protect, and fail to create a juvenile dependency system where batterers are held accountable for their violence against intimate partners in the context of identified child abuse allegations.

9. While many strategic planners will argue that subject matter knowledge is irrelevant to a planner or facilitator, I would argue that an experienced Family Justice Center planner from San Diego or from one of the other operating Centers around the country will be far more helpful than a facilitator with no knowledge of the vision you are considering. For more information on the role of a strategic planner, see www.adams2. org. Judi Adams serves as the San Diego Family Justice Center strategic planner and has overseen the strategic planning efforts for all sites in The President's Family Justice Center Initiative.

6

Don't Buy the Lie That You Can't Afford It

By Casey Gwinn and Gael Strack

> San Diego Union Tribune, March 27, 2004 – "Police arrested an 18-year old man yesterday in connection with the fatal shooting of his 15-year-old girlfriend. ...The medical Examiner's Office identified the girl as Daniela Lopez ..."

Daniela was the first domestic homicide victim of 2004. It was a sobering event for staff at the San Diego Family Justice Center because we had adopted a goal that no one would die in a domestic violence homicide in the City of San Diego in the calendar year.[1] Later, Daniela's boyfriend was arrested for her murder, and her family and friends planned her funeral. Many of us from the Center attended her funeral and watched from the back of the church. We were there to give our condolences and show our support to the family. As Daniela's casket was being carried out of the church, everyone wept.

Later that month, the Center held a vigil for Daniela at her favorite place, a local park. We wanted to let her family, her friends, her school, and the community know that help was available. We talked to her mother, teachers, best friends, even her little sister. They were in pain, trying to make sense of this madness and trying to find a way not to let Daniela die in vain. This beautiful young woman with a strong sense of humor and a love for life was robbed of her dreams and her laughter so young. She was a victim of teen relationship violence and then she became a homicide victim. They took every brochure and bookmark we had on teen relationship violence, pledging to pass them out at school and to friends who were experiencing violence with their boyfriends.

Assistant Police Chief Rulette Armstead from the San Diego Police Department pledged her renewed support to help Daniela's school and her community. She extended Juvenile Police Officer Ben Jolly's assignment at the Center and asked him specifically to address the issue of teen relationship violence. Officer Jolly turned out to be a gift. He immediately reached out to the students and teachers at Daniela's high school and made presentation after presentation about teen relationship violence. More awareness initiatives were launched that year in an effort not to forget her short life. This chapter is dedicated to the memory of Daniela Lopez.

The San Diego criminal justice system went on to prosecute Daniela's killer. The approximate cost? About $2.4 million. A killer was held accountable, but the system failed. We spent our money far too late in our effort to help Daniela and hold her abuser accountable.

The Family Justice Center is Worth The Money

Any community considering development of a Center must invariably address the financial issues that come with pursuing such a vision. Is the cost of a Center worth it? Will it save money in the long run? In a world of scarce resources, is a Center a wise investment of money? Sadly, most communities have never done the evaluation necessary to determine whether co-located services are cost-effective and therefore financially viable. But in San Diego we have and the news is good. The Center is worth the money. If it saved one life, it would be worth it morally and financially. But it can save far more than one life.

We will spend some time in this chapter on the general cost estimates of domestic violence for society and for the criminal justice system. Then we will look at the minimal costs of running a Center. But before we do that, let's be frank. As soon as supporters start talking about a Center, they are going to hear it all:

- We need a federal grant.
- We don't have enough money in our community to support even our existing programs.
- We cannot do this without more financial support from the state.
- We are cutting programs right now—we cannot add another one.
- If we had strong leaders in this community, we could do it, but our Police Chief does not support our work to stop domestic violence.
- I am just a PTA President; I have no power to make something like this happen here.
- I'm a pastor, not a politician.
- No one will listen to me if I start pushing for this in our town because I am a homemaker.
- I'm a judge—this is not my job.
- Our District Attorney isn't even prosecuting these cases; everything gets plea bargained or dismissed.
- Maybe we will have our act together some day and can do this kind of Center, but we just are not ready right now.

We will touch on some of these lies, excuses, and half-truths in the pages that follow. But what is the number one answer to why leaders will say there cannot be a Center? *We cannot afford it.*

And the main message of this chapter? *Don't buy the lie!*

The Truth About Priorities, Values, and Resources

If you have stayed with the book this long, it is probably time to be brutally honest. It is probably time to speak the cold hard truth about priorities, values, and resources in our communities, our country, and our world. We are all responsible for family violence. Batterers get away with their violence because our communities let them. Battered women don't get the help they need because we don't provide it. We clamor for better schools, newer roads, nicer parks, and lower taxes. We clamor for an end to hostilities in the Middle East when a soldier loses his life. But we don't clamor for Family Justice Centers.

Everyone was very kind to me. I expected to be herded through like a number, but I have been treated with compassion and understanding by everyone.

—*Beth, Family Justice Center Client, 2005*

We don't picket politicians who fail to make family violence a priority. We settle for a few dollars here and there in our community-based social service organizations from local government. We watch our local, state, and federal government spend millions and even billions on water and sewer systems, airports, mass transit systems, public employee pensions, public safety services, redevelopment projects, the military, subsidized airline travel, financial aid to other countries, and a host of other priorities. We call for more resources to build prisons and put more police officers on the street to protect us from gangs, street violence, and even consumer fraud. But we don't demand the same level of support from our governments and social institutions to stop family violence. We tolerate it. We become silent co-conspirators with those who continue to visit violence on their families.

Martin Luther King, Jr. said it many years ago. His context and topic were different, but his point was well-taken: "We in this generation must repent, not only for the words and deeds of the bad people but for the appalling silence of the good people." His indictment still rings true today in a country saturated with family violence. When was the last time you engaged in civil disobedience to protest a judge's mistreatment of domestic violence victims in court? When was the last time you wrote a letter to the editor demanding the elected officials step up and do something to stop family violence? When was the last time you called a local elected official to urge proactive effort to reduce violence in the home? When was the last time you heard a politician say, "We cannot afford these new programs for domestic violence victims and their children," and you stood up and replied, "Liar, liar, pants on fire!"

We address these issues in Chapter 8, as well, because the vast majority of criminals in this country grew up in violent and abusive homes. But instead of dealing with it and preventing the criminal conduct to begin with, we wait and spend our money later. The National Institute of Justice estimates the cost of crime in the United States, including medical costs, lost earnings and public program costs related to victim assistance, at $105 billion.[2]

So we are spending the money. We just spend it way too late. We have learned to send ambulances to the bottom of the cliff instead of building fences at the top of the cliff. We wait until the children of domestic violence grow up and move on to populate our juvenile halls and adult prisons. We spend the money then! We don't spend it stopping the violence before lives are deeply scarred.

Why Not Build Fences at the Top of the Cliff?

Why do we wait so long to deal with the consequences of violence and abuse? First, we don't think it is about us. As we have emphasized throughout this book, we think it is about *that* socio-economic group or *that* ethnic group." Second, we think it is somebody else's job to deal with it. Leave it to the professionals—let the government take care of it. Third, we think it does not impact our day-to-day lives personally or financially—our families, our jobs, our businesses, our churches and synagogues, our schools. We really don't think it costs us anything. Setting aside the moral and social irresponsibility of such an argument, we will devote much of the remainder of the chapter to the cost issues in helping many conclude the cost of a Center is minimal. But let's look briefly at the first two responses above before we spend the rest of the chapter on the costs you are paying for family violence one way or another.

Not About 'Us' and 'Them'

Is it about us or is it only about *those* people? Is it only about *those* women? We touched on this earlier in the book. All the research refutes the myth that it is not about all of us in our society. Women, men, and children from all socioeconomic groups, all ethnic groups, and all faith groups experience family violence.

The day the Oprah Winfrey Show came to film the story of the San Diego Family Justice Center, nine new clients showed up at the same time, and the reception area was chaos. We all pitched in to help with the intake process. I (Casey) introduced myself to a middle-aged woman in dark glasses and designer clothes. She asked why there was a film crew there. I told her it was the Oprah Winfrey Show but that no one would be filmed without their permission. The look on her face was priceless. She was excited and embarrassed all at the same time.

Sgt. Robert Keetch with the first client of the Center approximately 30 days before we even officially opened. She walked in a victim. She walked out a survivor.

The staff of the Center at the official Grand Opening on October 10, 2002.

The ribbon cutting ceremony with elected officials on October 10, 2002.

The first Volunteer Academy graduating class of the Center.

Strategic planner Judi Adams leading one of the many strategic planning meetings held regularly as the Center moves forward.

The client kitchen, available to clients and their children, while they are receiving services from all on-site agencies.

One of the "living rooms" designed for interviews of clients.

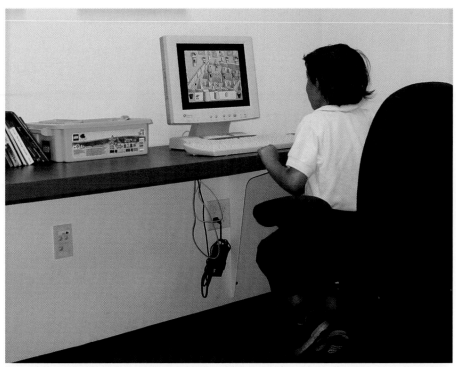

One of the special children's areas in the children's wing of the Center.

An examination room in the Forensic Medical Unit.

Rachel and her children. Rachel delivered the first "FJC" baby after coming to the Center for services during her pregnancy. Rachel tells part of her story in Chapter 7.

Volunteer Photographer Lawrence Lima and the Portraits of Courage photos, stories of courageous Center clients that hang in the lobby of the Center.

The FJC staff softball tournament—enjoying shared experiences that build community among the many agencies with on-site staff at the Center.

Gael and Casey celebrating the expansion of the Center from 20,000 to 40,000 square feet.

Claudia Fernety's depiction of the Center created through a partnership with the arts and culture community in San Diego.

Campers and staff during the summer camping season at Camp Hope, the special camping initiative of the Family Justice Center. The Camp Hope story is told in Chapter 9.

The boys of Camp Hope enjoying tubing at the lake. Boys growing up in an abusive home now given the opportunity to break the cycle by making new choices.

Frog catching became a special memory from Camp Hope for Jasmine. Jasmine's story is told in Chapter 9.

Celebrating the 3rd Anniversary of the Center in October 2005.

FJC Foundation Board member Kimberly Weisz and Casey Gwinn announcing the Center's new public awareness campaign with San Diego Padre pitcher Trevor Hoffman as the spokesperson.

She was an Oprah watcher. Her reaction was more amazement than frustration. As she described her long journey and the beautiful home she was leaving in the high-end Rancho Santa Fe of San Diego County, she said, "I can't believe it. It has taken me 18 years to come forward for help after knowing that what I was experiencing was not right. And after I finally get up the courage to come forward, I show up on the day Oprah Winfrey is here!" The point of the story, however, is not Oprah's involvement. This was one of the first times we had seen an upper-income victim of domestic violence in our system.

Since awareness about the Center has risen, we see upper-income victims regularly. Ten years ago they would have rarely darkened the door of the Police Department or the prosecutor's office, but today they are willing to come to a professional office building in downtown San Diego. They are willing to come to a place where they are treated with respect and dignity. And the myth has been shattered. It *is* about upper-income women.

Not About My Faith Community

Another myth is that married women of faith do not experience family violence. It is about women who shack up with their boyfriends and party on weekends. Happily married women from the local Baptist church don't deal with family violence...or so we are told. Jewish women, Muslim women, Catholic women don't deal with this issue...or so some say. It, too, is a lie.

> The chaplain was a great inspiration. I have future goals to accomplish with God! Thank you. One day I will offer my assistance to help others who are victims.
>
> —*Carolyn, Family Justice Center Client, 2005*

A number of years ago, a dear pastor friend of mine took me out to lunch to talk about my work in family violence. He pastors one of the largest churches in San Diego County and enjoys a national radio ministry. We talked about the tragedy of family violence. He asked me a host of questions about domestic violence in the church. He was extremely thoughtful in his comments and questions.

After nearly an hour, I finally had to ask whether he had ever preached on the topic of family violence. His answer was *no*. I had to ask why. His next answer was extremely honest and revealing: "Based on everything I am learning, if I spoke on it, we would not be able to meet the needs of all those that would come forward." Well, there it was. Perhaps in the early years of his ministry he did not think it was an issue in his faith tradition. But eventually he knew it was; he just did not know how to deal with it. If you are a person of faith reading this book, don't buy the lie that it is not about your friends.[3]

It Is Not My Job!

Too often, we try to convince ourselves and others that even if family violence is a scourge on society, it is not our scourge to deal with. We lament politicians that don't do something about it. *They* really messed that up. *They* did not protect her. *They* really need to get their act together. *They* never should have lifted that restraining order. *They* should have arrested him when they had the chance. *They* never should have let him out of jail.

> My priest told me to go home and be a better wife. The Family Justice Center chaplain told me it was not my fault.
>
> —*Sonya, Family Justice Center Client, 2004*

We can sit at Starbucks and sip our latte and condemn those who didn't do their job. But it is our job, as we will see in the last chapter. And you cannot sit at Starbucks in San Diego anymore without realizing you are part of the solution. Every Starbucks in downtown San Diego is supporting a public awareness campaign of the Center using the well-known face of San Diego Padre baseball player Trevor Hoffman[4]. Starbucks *gets it!* Other businesses, churches, and elected officials are *getting it.* They are realizing it *is* their job.

I remember hearing the Chief Executive Officer of Liz Claiborne, Inc., Jerome Chazen, say a few years ago: "We in corporate America cannot afford to stand on the sidelines if we hope to protect the well-being of our employees and the health of our company." Of course Liz Claiborne gets it. We have also enjoyed strong support from Mary Kay, Inc., Verizon Wireless, Cox Communications, Sharp HealthCare, Jeromes Furniture, EDCO Disposal Corporation, SBC, Gateway Computers, and a host of small local companies in our development of the San Diego Center. Indeed, many companies across the country are stepping up as responsible corporate citizens to help address issues of family violence. Hopefully, many more will follow them in the years to come.

> I felt better speaking to this staff versus the officers who came to take my report. It was so much more informative and assuring here. Everyone seemed to be on my side.
>
> —*Anonymous Family Justice Center Client, 2004*

The Truth About Resources

Not only do the resources exist in our culture to help victims and proactively implement programs to stop family violence, but we are presently paying millions to deal with what we are not stopping. Consider this: In 2004, the San Diego County Health and Human Services Department engaged in an evaluation to determine how much money the criminal justice system spent on each domestic violence homicide in our county. The result: Each one costs the system approximately $2.5 million, including the cost of lifetime incarceration for the killer.[5] So we are spending the money. We are spending it on other things, and we are spending it at the wrong time. We wait until the victim is dead, the family is destroyed, and the children are scarred for life before we spend the money to address the issue.

A similar study was recently performed in Great Britain by a professor at the University of Lancaster. It was prepared to evaluate the appropriateness of the cost associated with opening the first Center in the United Kingdom. The study found enormous cost to the taxpayers from domestic violence.[6]

The Business Community and Taxpayers Foot the Bill

The business community often thinks domestic violence has nothing to do with them. They are simply out there fueling the American economy with services and products. But the research is compelling. Let's look at what we know about the cost of family violence to the business community and the tax paying public. Research has confirmed over and over the impact on employees experiencing family violence, including:

- Loss of productivity
- Higher stress
- Increased absenteeism
- Increased employee turnover
- Higher health care costs
- Reduced staff morale

The cost of a violence epidemic that most CEOs and corporate executives don't think really impacts them is enormous to American businesses. The Bureau of National Affairs has estimated the cost at $3 to 6 billion. These costs are not simply due to lost productivity or increased medical costs. The violence does come to work. Over 60,000 violent incidents where the worker knows the attacker occur in the workplace each year.[7] In California, assaults and violent acts have been the leading cause of death in the workplace—31.2%.[8]

Thirty-seven percent of women who experience domestic violence report the abuse had an impact on their work performance in the form of lateness, absenteeism, keeping a job, or career promotions.[9] Domestic violence in the workplace may manifest itself as harassment via threatening phone calls or stalking. A significant number of workplace homicides are related to family violence. It is estimated that women lose nearly $18 million in earnings each year as a result of partner violence, and organizational costs associated with partner violence are estimated to be up to $5 billion annually in terms of absenteeism, tardiness, lowered productivity, turnover, and increased security and medical costs.[10] Battered women incur an estimated $24 million a year in medical expenses, much of which is paid by employer-sponsored health care plans.[11]

In fact, for over a decade we have known that murder is the leading cause of on-the-job deaths of women in the U.S.[12] More than 13,000 reported acts of violence against women in the workplace occur every year by husbands and boyfriends.[13] Seventy-four percent of employed battered women are harassed by abusive husbands and partners at work.[14]

Unaddressed domestic violence in the workplace poses a safety risk to other employees as well. It is not always the victim who is shot or killed. We even have a phrase for it based on the number of postal workers with domestic violence histories who have killed a mate or coworker. We call it "going postal." We should not pick on the U.S. Postal Service, though. It is everywhere. According to the National Safe Working Place Institute, in 1994 over 40% of workplace homicides were perpetrated by men with a history of violence against women. In another study, one-third of workplace homicides were family violence-related.[15]

Diving Deeper Into the Costs

The first step to measuring cost is to determine the true prevalence of domestic violence in society. The 2003 report published by the Centers for Disease Control and Prevention, *Costs of Intimate Partner Violence Against Women in the United States*, pointed out the struggles with gathering the statistics and determining the prevalence of domestic violence.[16] It cited lack of consensus about terminology, variations in survey methodology, gaps in data collection, different time frames, reluctance to report victimization, the repetitive nature of domestic violence, limited populations, and survey limitations. The Bureau of Justice Statistics reported in June 2005 that 41% of all family violence assaults go unreported.[17] Other studies suggest the number of unreported cases could be as high as 98%.[18]

What Is the Prevalence?

Recognizing these challenges, we must start somewhere and accept that, by any measure, estimated costs will be conservative. It is estimated that from 960,000 to

3 million women are abused by their husbands or boyfriends each year.[19] Around the world, at least one in every three women has been beaten, sexually abused, or otherwise abused during her lifetime.[20] A California study estimated that approximately 700,000 women in California are victims of domestic violence over a 12-month period, which represents only one-third of the criminal cases reported to the California Department of Justice by law enforcement agencies in a year.[21]

When it comes to homicides, an average of more than three women are murdered every day as a result of domestic violence in this country. In 1999, 1,642 murders were attributed to domestic violence, and 1,218 of the victims were women.[22] In 2000, 147 murders were attributed to domestic violence in California,[23] and 16 were from San Diego County.[24]

What should be calculated?

After determining the prevalence, it's a good idea to examine the actual costs of investigation, prosecution and incarceration for both arrests and homicides. The criminal justice system represents another major cost of domestic violence. Joan Zorza identified the issue in her article, "Women Battering: High Costs and the State of the Law,"[25] when she pointed out that domestic violence incidents are the largest category of calls to police each year. One-third of all police time is spent responding to domestic violence calls.[26]

The New York City Police Department made 12,724 domestic violence arrests in 1989 at an average cost of $3,241 per arrest. Although the cost of indigent defense attorneys was not included, the city paid at least $41 million in police services, court costs, and detention time arising from domestic violence arrests. The National Institute of Justice estimates that 15% of all law enforcement costs are due to domestic violence, totaling $67 billion per year.[27] Of course, not all reported intimate partner incidents result in arrest. In San Diego, only 33% of such cases do so.[28]

Intrafamilial homicide was estimated to cost this country $1.7 billion annually, according to research by Murray Straus in 1986.[29] The National Institute of Justice estimates the average cost at $2.4 million per domestic violence homicide. An analysis conducted by Miami-Dade County[30] determined the cost of 62 local domestic violence homicides per year averaged $500,000 per homicide. That estimate, however, did not include services to survivors and families, dependency proceedings regarding termination of parental rights, and long-term costs of incarceration. And in a study conducted by the San Diego County Fatality Review Committee, the cost of a single domestic violence homicide was estimated at $2,555,793.[31] Below is the analysis.

Table 6-1. Cost Per Domestic Violence Homicide in San Diego County	
	Cost
Four police responses	$ 582
Two temporary restraining orders	400
180-day jail term	19,292
Two years' probation	4,104
One emergency room visit	855
Two weeks in a domestic violence shelter	2,094
One week at Polinsky Center for three children	4,200
One year of foster care for three children	18,756
Two coroner's autopsies	5,510
Homicide investigation/court system prosecution	1,500,000
State prison sentence	1,000,000
TOTAL	$2,555,793

Clearly, these numbers do not take into account the human costs of pain and suffering. When you think of the brutal (and preventable) murder of Daniela Lopez, the hard costs described above barely register. We can't help but think about the pain and suffering of Daniela's family, friends, fellow students, and teachers—all who knew and loved her. In one study conducted in England by Professor Sylvia Walby, the costs of pain and human suffering were estimated at 17 billion pounds (approximately $30 billion, U.S.).[32]

What About Health Care Costs?

Domestic violence also inflicts major costs on the health care system. About half of all female victims report an injury of some kind, and about 20% of them seek medical assistance.[33] It is estimated that one million women seek medical care for abuse-related injuries in the United States each year.[34] The American Medical Association estimates that 28% of women seen in ambulatory clinics have been battered at some time during their lives.[35] Approximately 20 to 25% of pregnant women seeking prenatal care are experiencing intimate partner violence.[36] It has been reported that as high as 37.6% of the women in a sample of pregnant adolescents were experiencing domestic violence.[37] Battered women account for 25% of women who attempt suicide and 25% of women using a psychiatric emergency service.[38] One study determined that approximately 63% of female psychiatric inpatients had a history of physical abuse, the majority of which was inflicted by adults sharing their homs.[39]

In *Guidelines for the Health Care of Intimate Partner Violence for California Health Care Professionals*, Dr. Connie Mitchell looked at the health care financial impact of this large amount of domestic violence. She cited the costs of both medical care and lost days of productivity related to domestic violence between *$3 and $10 billion annually*.[40] She reported on a study that compared health care costs for victims of partner violence with non-victims in a large Midwest health plan and found victims incurred $1,775 more in health care costs in a single year of study than non-victims did.

> I so appreciate the patience and empathy everyone has shown me. The doctor and nurse were so detailed and understanding.
>
> —*Anonymous Family Justice Center Client, 2005*

The Pennsylvania Blue Shield Initiative recently estimated that domestic violence health care costs to the state are $326.6 million per year, which, if extrapolated nationwide, would amount to over $6.5 billion annually.[41] This figure does not include mental health costs related to the abuse of women nor the fact that many women's injuries are never connected to prior abuse. Nor does it take into account that battered women are 15.3 times more likely than non-battered women to seriously consider suicide and battering is the single greatest context identified for—and possibly associated with—half of female alcoholism.[42]

Are you getting tired yet? We are not done. There are more costs being passed on by businesses to consumers and passed on by government to the taxpayers.

What about Shelter costs?

California alone has approximately 112 shelters, 98 of which receive state and federal funding through the state Office of Criminal Justice Planning and the federal Department of Health Services (DHS).[43] Emergency domestic violence shelters in California work within tight funding restrictions, which limits the length of stay to 30 to 45 days. According to data gathered by DHS, in the year 2000, 80,000 women received services at shelters while 23,388 individuals were turned away because the shelter was full. [44] Between 2000 and 2003, DHS funded 91 shelters, awarding each of them between $150,000 and $190,000 annually. The average total annual shelter budget was determined to be $1,231,910. These shelters received a total of approximately 266,000 calls to their hotlines in a one-year period. The annual budget for one California shelter completely supported by private funds was $2,686,658.[45]

In addition to emergency shelters, many communities may have their own facility for transitional housing for domestic violence victims and their children. In San Diego alone, there are 12 such facilities.[46] Many receive public funding, a cost borne by the taxpayers. If there was truly a way to stop the violence and stop the next generation of victims, it would indeed change the world and save money!

What about animal abuse?

There is a growing recognition that domestic violence, child abuse, and animal abuse often occur in the same households.[47] Frank Ascione found that nearly two-thirds of battered women seeking shelter in safe houses report that their abuser threatened to harm or actually harmed or killed their pet[48]. Witnessing this type of abuse can be devastating to anyone, especially children. Battered women and their children have a tendency to worry about the safety of their pets and sometimes are reluctant to leave an abusive situation because of them.[49] Needless to say, there are significant costs associated with the investigation and prosecution of animal abuse cases, the sheltering of pets, animal shelters, and vet bills. Though no studies have been conducted on these costs, we should at least note them.

What About Litigating Divorces and Child Custody Proceedings?

In 1998, the National Center for Health Statistics reported 1,135,000 divorces occurred in the United States, representing a rate of 4.2 divorces per 1,000. Many involved children; millions of children across America have experienced the pain, confusion, and grief that result from divorce,[50] in addition to an ugly, costly custody battle. The consequences for children depend on the degree of parental conflict prior to divorce.[51] In domestic violence cases, the conflict may likely continue after separation, causing even more pain to children. "Fatality reviews and inquests around the world point dramatically to the increased risk when abused women and children attempt to leave their batterer. In 1996, the rate of spousal homicide for separated women was 79 per one million, compared with 3 per one million for married women. This statistic clearly suggests that separation can be a particularly dangerous time for women, which is consistent with the definition of domestic violence as abuse of power and control.[52]

Batterers are also twice as likely as non-batterers to apply for custody of children.[53] Their fight for custody and visitation rights, as a way to further control victims, increases the costs of litigation and drains the financial resources of abused victims. Often the family courts rely on custody evaluators and mediators to help them make these determinations, and access to children after separation may require specialized supervision facilities to protect both the children and victimized parents from ongoing abuse. Court costs and the costs for supervised visitation centers must be added to the overall cost of domestic violence, along with the costs of child abduction and child homicides. Again, the costs of the family court system in processing the enormous number of family violence cases has not been calculated, but the numbers are clearly substantial.

So how do these costs compare with running a Center that reduces homicides and reduces repeat offenses against women and children? Simply, the cost of one homicide is more than $1 million in any community in America. In many communities, the cost is much higher when you factor in long-term incarceration for the killer. So what is the cost of running a Center?

Todo estubo exelente. Me sentoi protegida, bespetada y pode enterarme de mis derechos como madre que ignoraba la Senoirita Angela fue muy amabil y me hablo con Onestidad y respecto Gracias Angela. Everything was excellent. I felt protected and respected. I learned about my rights as a mother. Miss Angela was very kind, she spoke to me with honesty and respect. Thank you, Angela."

—Guadalupe, Family Justice Center Client, 2005

The Cost of Running a Family Justice Center

In contrast to the already existing costs of domestic violence described above, Center costs are minimal. When compared to the financial impacts of domestic violence on the business community and the health care system, a Center, with all costs included, becomes an overwhelmingly cost-efficient service delivery model.

For purposes of making a financial case for a Center, let's use the National Institute of Justice estimate of $2.4 million per domestic violence homicide as we frame the costs of operating a Center. The operating cost of the San Diego Family Justice Center is $1.5 million a year for four floors of office space, approximately 40,000 square feet, parking, utilities and a staff of six. In the first three years of operation, the City of San Diego has seen a nearly 50% drop in domestic violence homicides (from nine in 2002 to five in 2005). While we readily acknowledge the complexity of shifting costs in the criminal justice system from the back end to the front end, there can be little argument that preventing homicides is right morally and financially.

Based on the big picture, launching a Center is relatively inexpensive. It is not creating a bureaucracy. It is efficiently bringing together those who already work in the field of family violence prevention and intervention. However, every community partner must contribute existing resources to the project, such as dedicated staff, equipment, and supplies.

The budget for a Center has three major categories: 1) start-up costs, 2) operations; and 3) expansion/long-term needs.

What Were San Diego's Start-up Costs?

Table 6-2. Start-up Costs For San Diego Family Justice Center		
Item	Amount	Total
Move-in costs	$8,620	
Data	240,000	
Furniture	86,798	
Systems furniture	158,668	
Audiovisual needs	15,220	
Shelving	14,759	
Subtotal		524,065
Space/rent for 10 months	444,832	
Utilities	43,200	
Parking	85,895	
Subtotal		573,927
Grand total		$1,097,992

What Is the Annual Department Budget?

Table 6-3. Fiscal Year 2005 Budget	
Item	Amount
Salaries and benefits	$447,525
Non-personnel expense	16,245
IT budget	56,260
Total	$520,030

Operation costs may also include new staff (if any); parking for clients, staff, and site visitors; phones and computers for community partners and volunteers; Internet connections; supplies; brochures and written materials; Web site development and maintenance; volunteer training; supervision and recognition; staff appreciation; food for victims; meetings; and training and hiring consultants.

What Are the Expected Expansion and Long-Term Needs?

Within three short years, the Center has already experienced tremendous growth, given the 600 clients, 3,000 phone calls, and 400 site visitors we interact with every month. This growth led us to lease an additional floor to provide services and to

> You all made an extremely uncomfortable and embarrassing experience bearable. I found this setting to be very comfortable and the staff very professional including the volunteers.
>
> —*Sally, Family Justice Center Client, 2005*

become a city department in order to ensure the long-term sustainability of the Center.

The Center initially started out with the following staff: a director to run the Center; an executive secretary to support the director and the department; a manager of client services to assist with the day-to-day-service delivery and coordination of community partners; an analyst to oversee the department's budget and grants administration; and a receptionist for incoming clients and visitors. Additionally, the San Diego Police Department assigned Sgt. Robert Keetch to operate as the manager of operations to oversee the logistics of all partners, security issues, and the volunteer program. On our wish list for the next fiscal year is a volunteer coordinator to manage the 100 active volunteers who have been recruited to date; an information systems analyst to oversee the information and technology needs of the Center, community partners, and volunteers; and an administrative assistant to assist with responding to numerous requests for information, special events, various meetings, and site visitors.

Within five years, the Center envisions moving into a permanent site. Our sights are already set on San Diego's old library building located across the street from the current Center. The existing library is a city-owned facility with approximately 140,000 square feet, more than enough space to accommodate all the partners responding to family violence, such as domestic violence, elder abuse, child abuse, sexual assault, and teen relationship violence. We anticipate this permanent site will need approximately $10 million in renovations along with additional staff to oversee the day-to-day operations.

Conclusion

The money is there to develop Centers across America. Local, state, and federal governments spend it now—but they spend it too late. Businesses spend billions now to deal with family violence – but they spend it too late. So many not only spend it, but they spend it over and over as the cycle of violence repeats itself from generation to generation.

To begin to change the spending priorities of government and the private sector, we must reject the lie that there are not enough resources to deal with the issue of family violence. Once we refuse to buy the lie, we can start talking about the reallocation of scarce resources. We can start talking about promoting peace at home in order to have peace abroad. We can start talking about ways to export our Center vision for healing families in the United States and around the world by stopping violence in the home.

Daniela Lopez needed our help long before her murderer was prosecuted. We failed her. Perhaps, in her memory, the next time you hear someone say we cannot afford to develop Centers, you can say "Liar, liar, pants on fire!" We are convinced it would make Daniela smile.

Endnotes

1. Casey Gwinn, "Aiming for Zero," *San Diego Union Tribune,* opinion/editorial section, October 10, 2002.

2. Ted Miller et al, *Victim Costs and Consequences: A New Look*, National Institute of Justice research report, June 1996.

3. Reverend Al Miles, *Domestic Violence: What Every Pastor Needs to Know*, Augsburg Fortress Press, MN, 2000, p. 25.

4. Sponsored by the San Diego Family Justice Center, October 2005.

5. Amelia Barile Simon, *San Diego County Fatality Review Committee Report*, Department of Human Health and Human Services, 2004.

6. Professor Sylvia Walby, "The Cost of Domestic Violence, University of Leeds/Lancaster, http://www.womenandequalityunit.gov.uk/research/cost_of_dv_Report_sept04.pdf.

7. *National Crime Victimization Survey,* U.S. Dept. of Justice, 1999.

8. *Guidelines for Workplace Security,* Cal/OSHA, 1999.

9. *The Cost of Domestic Violence,* EDK Associates, New York, September 1997.

10. A. Moe and M. Bell, "Abject economics, the Effects of Battering and Violence on Women's Work and Employability," *Violence Against Women,* January 2004, 10(1).

11. L. Greenfeld et al., *Violence by Intimates: Analysis of Data on Crimes by Current or Former Spouses, Boyfriends and Girlfriends,* U. S. Department of Justice, March 1998.

12. Jim Kouri, "Murder and Violence in the Workplace," Michnews.com, November 2004, http://www.ojp.usdoj.gov/ovc/assist/nvaa2002/chapter22_5.html.

13. Ibid.

14. L. Friedman and S. Cooper, *The Cost of Domestic Violence,* New York, Victim Services Research Department, 1987.

15. *Workplace Violence: A Report to the Nation,* University of Iowa Injury Prevention Research Center, Iowa City, IA, 2001.

16. *Costs of Intimate Partner Violence Against Women in the United States,* report by Department of Health and Human Services, Centers for Disease Control and Prevention, Atlanta, GA, 2003.

17. *Family Violence Statistics,* report by Bureau of Justice Statistics, June 2005, NCJ 207846.

18. R. Emerson Dobash and Russell Dobash, *Violence Against Wives,* Free Press, New York, 1979.

19. Greenfeld. See also *Health Concerns Across a Woman's Lifespan: 1998 Survey on Health,* The Commonwealth Fund, May 1999.

20. L. Heise et al., *Ending Violence Against Women,* December 1999.

21. Alicia Bugarin, *The Prevalence of Domestic Violence in California,* California Research Bureau, November 2002.

22. *Intimate Partner Violence and Age of Victim,* Bureau of Justice Statistics Special Report, October 2001.

23. Bugarin, *Prevalence.*

24. Interview by Gael Strack with Linda Wong-Kerberg, Chair, San Diego Domestic Violence Fatality Review Committee, December 2005.

25. Joan Zorza, "Women Battering: High Costs and the State of the Law," *Clearinghouse Review,* 1994 Special Issue, pp. 383-88.

26. Ibid.

27. Bugarin.

28. Kate Sproul, *California's Response to Domestic Violence: A History of Policy Issues and Legislative Actions to Combat Domestic Violence in California,* California Senate Office of Research, June 2003.

29. Dr. Connie Mitchell, *Guidelines for the Health Care of Intimate Partner Violence for California Health Professionals,* California Medical Training Center, 2004, p. 17.

30. Jennifer Glazer Moon, unpublished research memo prepared in 2005 for Miami, Dade County, FL, conducting a feasibility study for the creation of a Family Justice Center.

31. Simon.

32. Walby.

33. *National Crime Victimization Survey, 1992-96,* study of injured victims of violence, 1994.

34. *1998 Survey of Women's Health,* Commonwealth Fund.

35. P. Salber and E. Taliaferro, *The Physician's Guide to Domestic Violence: How to Ask the Right Questions and Recognize Abuse,* Volcano Press, Volcano, CA, 1995, p. 9.

36. Ibid., p. 10.

37. M. Curry et al., "Effects of Abuse on Maternal Complications and Birth Weight in Adult and Adolescent Women," *Obstetrics & Gynecology,* 1998, 92(4), pp. 530-34.

38. Salber, p. 9.

39. Ibid..

40. P. Tjaden et al., *Comparing Violence Over the Life Span in Samples of Same-Sex and Opposite Sex Cohabitants.*

41. Zorza.

42. Ibid.

43. Bugarin.

44. Ibid.

45. Ibid.

46. Presentation by the Shelter Committee of the San Diego Domestic Violence Council, November 2005.

47. B. Boat, "The Relationship Between Violence to Children and Violence to Animals," *Journal of Interpersonal Violence,* 1995, Vol. 10, pp. 229-35.

48. Frank Ascione, "Battered Women's Report of Their Partners' and Their Children's Cruelty to Animals," *Journal of Emotional Abuse,* 1998, Vol. 1, pp. 119-33.

49. L. Kogan et al., "Crosstrails: a Unique Foster Program to Provide Safety for Pets of Women in Safe Houses," *Violence Against Women,* April 2004, 10(4), p. 418.

50. P. Jaffe et al., *Child Custody & Domestic Violence—a Call for Safety and Accountability,* Sage Publications, Thousand Oaks, CA, 2003.

51. Ibid.

52. Ibid.

53. Janet Bowermaster, "Relocation Custody Disputes Involving Domestic Violence," *University of Kansas Law Review,* 1998, 46 (3), pp. 433-63.

7

Cops and Prosecutors Matter

Maria had been married for four years in 1989. She married Philip for many reasons. He was kind, thoughtful, even doting. He was a successful businessman and well-connected in the community. She was "marrying up." She was from a working class family. He was from a wealthy Japanese family. He owned a beautiful home in La Jolla, California, and he made it clear that everything he had would be hers as well. They met at a community social event and were together constantly after that first moment. He wanted to be with her every day. He said he was so passionate about her that he could hardly bear to be away from her. He thought about her constantly, and he did not want to miss a minute in life that he could be with her. She had never had a man so focused on her. It was dangerous and exciting and flattering. They went on dates and outings constantly. Soon they started enjoying weekend trips. Their sexual attraction to one another was powerful. She had never experienced such intensity in a relationship. She had never been loved like this.

The first time she saw his temper was understandable. He had planned a special evening together, and she was late. She was taking classes at a local community college, and the professor ran over the allotted time. By the time she got to Philip's house, he was angry. Where had she been? Why hadn't she called? He was so hurt. The beautiful dinner he had fixed was dried out. His timing for each course was totally thrown off. While his anger took her aback, it really was her fault. He loved her so much. He had worked so hard, and now it was ruined because of her thoughtlessness. She quickly took the emotional blame without a word from him. Eventually he calmed down and they had a special evening together. They made love late into the night, and she made sure he knew how desperately sorry she was for hurting him by being late.

Two months later, Philip asked her to move into his home. He wanted to get married, but he felt neither of them was ready yet. He just could not stand to be away from her. His house was large, and he lived there all alone. She had been spending most weekends and many weeknights there anyway. She was thrilled. Though he was eight years older than she, it was very clear that they were falling deeply and hopelessly in love. Moving in together was the right thing to do. She had no doubt about it.

In the months to come, they spent every moment together except when he was away on business or she was taking classes. He was becoming more possessive and jealous of any contact she had with men in her life, but she thought nothing of it. He loved her. He could not live without her. She became far more determined to meet his needs and respond to him with the same passion he had for her. She worked hard to come home on time or to call if she was going to be late, and she always left notes to describe her schedule.

Slowly, she lost contact with her friends from school and her previous job as a library assistant. There was little free time available, and Philip wanted to be with her night and day. He was more moody as the months went, by but he was having trouble with his business investments and was under a great deal of stress.

Finally, 14 months after meeting, Philip proposed to Maria and she accepted without hesitation. They were married in a small, private ceremony weeks later. The whirlwind romance had become marriage. It was passionate. It was all-consuming.

The first time Philip pushed her, it was completely unexpected. They were arguing about the amount of time she was spending at school. He asked her to drop out of school and she refused. She was determined to graduate from college, and since they were not planning to have kids for a few years, she had the time now to finish her education. He said she did not need a college degree. He did not have one and he did not need one. They were financially taken care of with his father's money, and they lived in a beautiful home. He towered over her as they argued; she decided to end the argument by leaving the room. As she tried to walk past him, he pushed her backwards. She was stunned, but the push was not terribly forceful. He told her they needed to talk it out. An hour later, they agreed she would drop two of her three classes. They would spend the extra time together.

For the next three months, things went smoothly, though Philip was often frustrated or angry about silly things. He found ways to blame her for his moods. She was not sensitive enough. She was not focused on his needs. She was not respectful enough. She was not willing to surrender her schedule when he needed her support. He told her of his mother's willingness to give up her priorities to help his father become successful. Now he needed her as he was trying to take his inheritance and invest it in real estate for their future. He was also starting to sell real estate with Century 21, and he needed her help organizing his appointments and marketing meetings with clients.

Maria dropped out of college two years into their relationship to help Philip with his real estate business. He was so happy when she told him. He said it would bring them closer together. But within months, his now regular tantrums and outbursts actually increased. He said she did not listen to him and would lightly tap her on the side of the head when she was not paying close enough attention. He would often joke with her that her inability to focus on his directions must be a result of low intelligence. She gained 20 pounds as she spent more and more time sitting at a desk in their home, helping with the real estate business. He told her she was getting too fat to fit into her clothes. But there was a blessing for him, he said; no other man would find her attractive.

In their third year of marriage, Philip started making rules for Maria about when meals should be ready, rules about her time away from the house, and rules about the way she talked to him. When she didn't follow the rules, his anger sometimes exploded into a barrage of verbal abuse. Unlike the typical abuser, he was rarely sorry for his outbursts and usually blamed them on her insensitivity to his needs.

Four years into the marriage, the taps to the side of her head turned harder and harder. He called it "cuffing her." His blows, though now common, never left a mark. He said it was a little "love thing" between them. She told him not to hit her and told him how much it hurt. His only response was that if she listened with more respect, he would not hit her.

One night, they had their first truly violent altercation. He had been drinking before dinner and was not pleased with her dinner menu. After dinner, she asked him to help her do the dishes and he refused. As she walked toward the kitchen, he pushed her from behind; Maria pushed him back. As he began to come toward her and berate her, she ran. Philip chased her and caught her around the waist in the kitchen. He threw her to the floor. Her left arm was caught under her body. She knew almost immediately that it was broken. She screamed out in pain as Philip helped her up and over to a kitchen chair. He was so sorry but reminded her it was her fault; she should not have pushed him. He was only defending himself. She should not have run. They needed to work out their problems face to face.

Her first thought was to call the police, but Philip convinced her that if she did, both of them would go to jail. They were both to blame—the police officers would take them both to jail. She continued to tell him that she wanted the police to come. Philip, however, made clear that if they were both arrested, he would not bail her out. And all the neighbors would see police cars in front of their house. It would bring shame on both of them. Within an hour, they had crafted a plan to take her to the hospital emergency room to treat her broken arm.

When Philip and Maria arrived at the emergency room, he filled out the paperwork while she told her admitting clerk that she had slipped and fallen on the stairs in their home. It was stupid. She was not paying attention and she landed on her arm. It was 1986 and no one asked any further questions. Philip was by her side throughout her time in the ER. Two hours later, with a cast in place, Philip and Maria returned home.

Co-conspirators now in deceiving others about their violent relationship, Philip and Maria felt a bond in the weeks after the emergency room visit. Philip went out of his way to care for her and help her as her arm healed. He hired a housecleaner and often cooked for her. It was a special time in their relationship. Though he was still verbally abusive on a regular basis, he used no violence of any kind toward her for months.

By their next physical altercation, they had been together nearly five years. It started with an argument over laundry she had failed to get done for him and ended in the kitchen when she threatened to defend herself if he hit her again. Philip flew into a rage and grabbed a knife from the butcher block. Maria ran and he chased her into the living room. Her head start allowed her to get upstairs and into their bedroom ahead of him. She locked the door and grabbed the phone. As she called 911, Philip pounded on the door, demanding to be let into the room. He did not hear her call 911, and after she described what was happening, she hung up. Minutes passed; he calmed down and told her to open the door. She refused but told him how much he had scared her. Philip explained how much it hurt him to have her think he was going to hit her. He had not hit her in months and was shocked that she would threaten him simply because they were arguing. Moments passed, but Maria did not open the door.

Less than five minutes after she had called 911, San Diego police officers rang the doorbell. When the doorbell rang, he went downstairs and opened the front door. Officers asked to come into the house and told him they had received a 911 call from a female in the house saying her husband was chasing her with a knife. Philip had left the knife outside the bedroom door, but the officers demanded entrance to the home and informed him they had a right to search the home in order to check on the welfare of his wife. He protested but had little choice.

One officer stayed with Philip while the other went to check on Maria. Officer Johnson identified himself to Maria and she opened the door. She gave Officer Johnson a complete statement. Twenty minutes later, Philip was placed under arrest and taken to jail for brandishing a weapon. It was a misdemeanor offense, but by 1987 in San Diego this was a mandatory arrest situation with a mandatory booking into county jail. The officers gave Maria a sheet of resource information, completed the scene investigation, made the arrest, and left the scene.

Within days, Maria was calling to drop the charges. She contacted the detective assigned to the case, San Diego Detective Jim Tomsovic, and pleaded with him. She said she was responsible for the violence, she had provoked her husband, and she would recant her original statement. If Maria's case had happened before 1986, the case would have been dismissed upon her request with nothing forwarded to the prosecutor's office. But by 1989, San Diego had become one of a handful of jurisdictions to implement an evidence-based investigation and prosecution approach. We had learned that if the victim was in charge in deciding the outcome of the investigation, we were in fact drawing a target on her chest. We were telling the batterer that all he had to do was threaten and manipulate her into dropping the charges and nothing would happen to him. Maria was told the case was out of her hands; her husband had committed a crime and he would be held accountable.

Phillip was ultimately convicted. The judge sentenced him to serve six months in custody in a work-furlough program. He was placed on three years probation and ordered to complete a 32-week batterer's intervention counseling program and an alcohol treatment program, and to pay a fine, which went to the local battered women's shelter that ended up providing services to Maria. It was not an easy journey from arrest to conviction. Maria tried repeatedly to get the case dismissed. The judge had a hard time caring about the case when Maria did not appear to care, and the detective and I worked long hours trying to figure out how to win at trial. But what amazed me the most was Phillip's attempt to manipulate me, the prosecutor. It even happened in my own office in the Child Abuse/Domestic Violence Unit!

He is Really a Very Nice Guy

Two weeks before Phillip's case was set for trial, I got a call from his defense attorney. He said this case should not be going to trial. Phillip was a good man who was married to a very troubled woman. Phillip's reputation and career were being destroyed for nothing. He said, "If you could only meet him, you would see what a nice guy he really is." Though I had not done it before and such a move was fraught with peril for a prosecutor, I told the defense attorney I would be happy to meet with him and Phillip in my office before I decided whether to dismiss the case or give him a better deal than I had previously offered.

Four days later, Phillip and his attorney arrived at my office. Phillip carried a large cardboard box in his arms. We agreed that nothing said in the meeting would be admissible in court if the case went to trial. A few additional ground rules were agreed upon, and then the defense attorney asked Phillip to tell me his life story. He started with his birth in Japan and continued through his growing-up years. He described coming to the United States over 20 years earlier and becoming a successful business owner and then real estate broker. He opened the cardboard box and lifted out trophy after trophy and plaque after plaque from his professional career. He talked about his Japanese culture and all that mattered to him as a Japanese man.

Finally, after 30 minutes, I interrupted. "Phillip, why are you here in my office today?" I asked. His response was immediate. "Because my wife and I cannot get along." I said, "I don't prosecute people for not getting along. Why are you here in my office today?" He tried another approach. "Because my wife and I are very unhappy together." I said, "I don't prosecute people for being unhappy together. Why are you here today?"

And so the conversation went for another five minutes. I tried again. "Phillip, I prosecute people who commit crimes against their partners, and I am prosecuting you. So why are you here today?" And a sliver of truth emerged as Phillip said, "Because I cuff her from time to time." His defense attorney turned white. "What do you mean you cuff her?" I asked. His answer had no hesitation, "It's just a little love thing between her and me. She does not always pay attention when I am talking, so I tap her on the side of the head sometime to get her attention, and she really hates it."

Phillip never admitted to anything besides cuffing, but it didn't matter. He eventually pled guilty, Maria broke free of him, and the San Diego criminal justice system worked to hold a batterer accountable. We required Philip to plead guilty rather than *no contest* and then put Maria in contact with a young San Diego personal injury lawyer named Chris Johnson. Maria sued Phillip and won a trial verdict of $800,000 against him for his violence and abuse during their marriage—the largest trial verdict in a domestic violence case in the history of San Diego. Even with an uncooperative victim, an offender was held accountable, and the violence stopped because the criminal and civil justice systems had worked well.

We are devoting this chapter to fleshing out the issues around the criminal justice system's response to domestic violence. Understanding the role of the criminal justice system is crucial to understanding how a Center should operate. This truth about the vision must not be missed: *No community can create an effective Family Justice Center without a basic, solid, specialized law enforcement response to domestic violence.* Cops and prosecutors matter to the Center vision!

> At first I did not want to be here but the more I talked to the detectives and the counselors here the more I realized they were helping me, not against me. Thank you.
>
> —*Michelle, Family Justice Center Client, 2005*

The entire vision depends on effective, responsible, informed criminal justice system responses to domestic violence. If the cops and prosecutors in your community don't *get it*, if they are doing bad things to battered women, don't race forward to open a Center! If you want to co-locate certain services without the involvement of police and prosecutors, you may consider that—but it will not be consistent with the vision articulated in this book if it does not include specially trained police officers and prosecutors.

Communities that go forward with Centers but fail to understand the importance and centrality of well-trained cops and prosecutors do a great disservice to battered women and their children. Batterers must be arrested and then prosecuted if we are going to stop family violence. You can put 50 social service agencies in the same place to help victims, and you will never stop the batterer. People with badges and guns stop batterers. Arresting and prosecuting batterers is one crucial piece in an overall plan to protect victims from further violence. Prosecutors who advocate passionately in court *for* victims and *against* abusers help stop domestic violence.

Surely, you think, there is some way to get around bad police work and poor prosecution policies in the handling of domestic violence. *There is not!* You might

> I have never in my life been through a more wonderful experience trying to get help with anything. I can't believe there is a great system like this. I felt safe. I was treated with respect and was made to feel comfortable. Thank you so much for all the help from so many different people.
>
> —*Brandy, Family Justice Center Client, 2005*

think, if we have other agencies that understand this vision, let's just pull them together in one location. As noted in our cautions in Chapter 6, this might be possible, but beware. It will not be as effective in helping victims as including good cops and good prosecutors. And it may put staff and victims in more danger!

If you create a public facility with co-located services but you don't have a powerful and substantial law enforcement presence, you better have good private security! Such a facility could end up with a target on its front door, and offenders will come to threaten, intimidate, and hunt for their victims with impunity. The facility will *not* send out a loud zero-tolerance message to offenders and victims, and no one will think of domestic violence as a serious crime that you are committed to stopping.

Some May Misunderstand the Anti-Arrest Research

Today, some critics of the criminal justice system attempt to argue that arrest and prosecution cannot and will not stop domestic violence. The logical conclusion would therefore be that the criminal justice system should not be central to the Center vision. Books have been written, papers published, and debates organized around the country as critics argue that there are negative impacts from pro-arrest and pro-prosecution policies.[1] The critics are not without some evidence to support them. Increased focus on the criminal justice system has, in some places, led to adverse consequences for battered women.[2] Victims have been arrested, offenders have gone free, and prosecution has not stopped batterers from reoffending. The criminal justice system also arrests and incarcerates more people of color than it should. It is without question a blunt instrument in dealing with a very complex set of interpersonal issues.

For over 20 years, debate has raged about the effectiveness of arrest in stopping family violence.[3] Millions of dollars have been spent to conduct arrest studies to determine whether a 12-hour or 24-hour arrest deters future violence by a batterer. Some argue in favor of mandatory arrest laws, others argue against them based on this research.[4] The entire debate is a waste of money. *News flash!* Twenty-four hours in a cell with "Bubba" will probably not solve the complex issues that have been developing since a batterer's childhood. Arrest alone is not the magic cure for domestic violence. Uninformed, poorly trained police officers will arrest a lot of

> The longer I worked at the Family Justice Center, the more convinced I became that victims acted very differently with us when they realized we were part of a team and not just the big, bad criminal justice system trying to make their lives more difficult.
>
> —*Detective Tyrone Crosby, San Diego Police Department*

battered women if they don't know how to determine the "primary aggressor" at the scene of the crime.[5]

The same debate is now raging about pro-prosecution and evidence-based prosecution approaches advocated by prosecution leaders in Duluth, San Diego, Baltimore, Milwaukee, Quincy, Oakland, Riverside, Brooklyn, Dallas, Austin, and other leading prosecution agencies around the country over the last two decades. *Message to funders: save your money!* Don't do a lot of research on whether prosecution alone will stop batterers and end violence and abuse. The result will be the same.

Prosecution alone is not the answer. Though some research does show encouraging results from pro-prosecution initiatives,[6] criminal prosecution is not the magic potion to stop violence. No one can dispute that when the batterer is in jail, the victim is not being beaten, but when he gets out of jail the victim may well be in more danger than before prosecution if the system does not provide comprehensive services. Research has also confirmed that even if the physical violence does stop because of criminal justice system intervention, verbal and emotional abuse often continues in the relationship.[7] Prosecution is only one piece of the social control mechanisms that must be arrayed to stop battering in America.

> I need this help to find out what to do to not be afraid. I am glad I asked the police to help me get a restraining order.
>
> —*Anonymous Family Justice Center Client, 2004*

Criminal Justice System is Central to the Center Vision

Four points are critical to remembering the centrality of the criminal justice system as the Center vision moves forward. First, domestic violence must continue to be treated as a serious crime. Second, powerful evidence already exists that the criminal justice system is a positive force for change in stopping family violence. Third, if the criminal justice system is broken in some communities, and it is, we need to fix it, not abolish it. Fourth, the Center is actually a force for positive change in shaping the criminal justice system response into what it should be.

Domestic Violence Must Continue to Be Treated as a Serious Crime

If we say domestic violence is a serious crime in our culture, we must treat it as a serious crime. If we want to stop violence in intimate relationships, there must be consequences for those who choose to use violence. We could decriminalize bank robbery, but no one is arguing to do so, even though treating bank robbery as a serious crime tends to put more people of color than other ethnic groups in jail. There is no effort to reduce bank robbery prosecutions, because bank robbery is universally accepted as a serious crime.

> Probation plays an important role in breaking the cycle of violence. When batterers reoffend, we need to hold them immediately accountable. Through the partnerships at the Family Justice Center, we can work with law enforcement to make immediate arrests and provide long-term support to victims. I look forward to developing a program at the Family Justice Center that targets repeat and high-risk offenders.
>
> —*Vince Iaria, Chief Probation Officer, San Diego County*

Domestic violence too should continue to be treated as a serious crime. The criminal justice system is the ultimate statement about what we will and won't accept in our culture. As former Nashville Police Sergeant Mark Wynn says, "The criminal justice system is where the law keeps its promise." If the system is not keeping its promise to battered women, we should not reject the system. We should work harder to ensure that it does keep its promise to provide *equal protection under law* and *due process* for all victims of sexual assault, domestic violence, and stalking.

Some writers have called for the decriminalization of domestic violence in America.[8] Some have advocated for solid walls of separation between advocates and law enforcement authorities. Some are calling for more victim control over whether the criminal justice system gets involved in family violence cases at all. But 20 years into efforts to increase arrest and prosecution of offenders, we cannot turn back from attempting to hold criminal abusers accountable.

For decades, even centuries, abusers avoided accountability and exercised domination and control over their partners with impunity. We are finally beginning to see abusers arrested and prosecuted. Is the criminal justice system a blunt instrument? Yes. Does it sometimes arrest and prosecute the victim instead of the perpetrator? Yes. Have some communities failed to properly implement appropriate investigation, documentation, and prosecution protocols to determine the true primary aggressor in the relationship? Yes. But that should not lead us to reject the importance of criminal justice in making domestic violence a serious crime.

> I had a marvelous detective (Greg Olsen) and a counselor from Center for Community Solutions. They got me through the devastation and the physical injuries. They were a godsend for communicating with the DA and everyone, especially after my phone was shut off. With my father with Alzheimer's and a lot of deaths in the family, I was able to come here to get assistance, take a breath, have tea, and get help. Almost daily I commuted from Oceanside, used the phone here, and met with anyone who could help and see me. I'd been here so often it was my second home.
>
> —*Anonymous Family Justice Center Client, 2004*

Many domestic violence victims seek help through the criminal justice system. A recent study showed that "more than 70% of the domestic violence victims who sought help at some point had sought assistance through the criminal justice system. Women's rights activists have advocated that batterers be arrested, prosecuted and sentenced in the same manner as other violent offenders."[9] Police officers and prosecutors have always been central in dealing with criminal conduct, and we should not turn away from their central role now. The Center vision embraces the ongoing centrality of their role in reducing family violence. Cops and prosecutors matter to victims of domestic violence. And when they do their job well, they offer life-saving help and hope to victims.

The Criminal Justice System Has Already Produced Tremendous Results

Aggressive pro-arrest and pro-prosecution policies have led to increased criminal prosecution of offenders and a strong societal statement against violence in intimate relationships. Though we talk in this chapter about the failures of the criminal justice system, the successes have had a powerful and positive impact in reducing homicides and violence in intimate relationships.[10] Over the last 20 years, intimate partner homicides are down, violent crime by gender is down, violent crime by gender and race is down, firearm-related domestic violence incidents are down, and sexual assault is down.

We Must Fix the System, Not Destroy It

Imagine if during the civil rights movement, civil rights advocates bemoaned the atrocious conduct of police and prosecutors in enforcing the civil rights laws? But instead of calling for stronger enforcement, they called for overturning the civil rights laws? What if activists argued that the laws were being ignored or abused in order to revictimize victims of discrimination and racial hatred? What a travesty would have occurred! Thankfully, civil rights activists did not demand the repeal of those laws. They did not call for a different strategy that excluded criminalizing racial crimes. They called for additional strategies. They called for new approaches.

But they did not reject the fundamental notion that the criminal and civil justice systems had a powerful social change role to play in stopping discrimination, violence, and abuse based on hate and intolerance.

Similarly, the civil rights movement condemned poor practice but still pursued new efforts to support victims of violence and abuse. They asked how it could be done better, how systems could improve, and how critical mass could continue to build in social change theory. They looked for other allies to recruit in the growing social reform movement. Martin Luther King, Jr., did not call for abolishing the role of police and prosecutors. Instead, he hailed those who were courageous enough to enforce the law and hold racists accountable for criminal conduct. And he called for mass mobilization of all elements of society to stop the violence and discrimination.

Today we must continue to understand the importance of the criminal justice system in stopping violence against women, men, and children while looking for new initiatives to move us forward. We must look for ways to improve the system and change it for the better. We must hold government leaders accountable for irresponsible behavior in dealing with family violence.

It's great to have the police here at the Family Justice Center. Many victims are afraid to call the police because they don't know what will happen next. You can tell they're on the fence. But when they find out who's here, what services are available and how the system works, you can immediately see it reduces their anxiety level. Knowledge gives them the courage to take the next step. If not today… maybe tomorrow.

—*Kimberly Pearce, Family Justice Center Director of Client Services*

The Center as Positive Force for Change

Even given our obvious mission to improve the system rather than destroying it, no one to date has looked at the potential solutions to problems of revictimization by the criminal justice system through the developing national Center vision.

This book is perhaps the first effort to say that a Center, if developed properly, can help improve and develop an effective criminal justice system response over time. The Center *community* that evolves can assist in shaping the views of law enforcement officers toward victims and the complex emotional issues they struggle with during the intervention process. The solution to dysfunctional local criminal justice systems is to educate, train, create accountability systems, and build closer collaboration among survivors, advocates, and law enforcement professionals. Judges need education, training, and accountability.[11] Prosecutors need the same and so do police officers.

We need to build closer working relationships with those who don't *get it*. We cannot turn away from the challenge of changing systems simply because systems are difficult to change. Change did not happen because shelter advocates and feminist leaders hid in a secret place and avoided the criminal justice system. Change happened because they engaged the system, pushed legislation, and called for accountability.

It was the San Diego Police Department that has really helped me. At that point, that I got help and support, my life was changed a lot. I was very surprised because I went to different places and nobody helped me. But, they helped me here. I was really lucky to be here. My life is much better now than it was before. I feel more able to care of myself and stronger. Before I cam here I was scared of everything. It has changed me a lot. I can stand up for myself more. I'm not as afraid.

—Anonymous Family Justice Center Client, 2005

One of the great ironies of the feminist movement is that some feminists are still arguing that we should kick the criminal justice system out of the movement! Now that many police and prosecution leaders have joined the effort, some "founding mothers" and others in the battered women's movement are not so sure they want them involved. Founding mother Ellen Pence regularly makes the point that the movement got what it asked for—the system just did not become what they hoped for.[12] The criminal justice system is now "in the house" though, and we have to figure out how to get along, find common ground, and develop informed law enforcement responses

So what does the Center concept offer to help us get police, prosecutors, and judges on board with effective intervention strategies? Perhaps the best starting point to answer this question, given the topic of the chapter, is to focus on the benefits of the Center model for police officers and prosecutors.

Center Benefits for Cops and Prosecutors

We can identify four major benefits for law enforcement officers and prosecutors. First, the Center model produces closer relationships, greater collaboration, and therefore less finger pointing and blaming of other agencies. Second, it produces better police investigations. Third, prosecutors try fewer cases because the evidence is stronger, and fewer victims recant because of the support and services they receive. Finally, the Center vision offers the opportunity to recognize, reward, and therefore reinforce good police work.

Relationships and Collaboration

Without question, the greatest mechanism in social change theory is relationships. By developing strong personal relationships in local communities, domestic violence advocates play powerful roles in bringing about change. Advocates successfully recruited elected officials and policy makers, police officers, clergy, prosecutors, judges, doctors, private attorneys, business leaders, and a host of other change agents to move their vision forward. While it is rare to find a successful community without individual charismatic, determined change agents, it is equally rare to find a community that has made great progress in victim safety and offender accountability that has not worked hard at personal relationships with key community members. No intimate relationship or marriage can succeed without the hard work of developing a strong relationship, and no local coordinated community response can thrive without strong personal ties among key leaders.

The Center vision brings both peril and possibility to the fundamental importance of relationships. If there is power in healthy relationships, there is even greater professional intimacy, communication, and support where those professionals work together every day—where they work side by side and deal with challenges, problems, and the needs of victims together. There is, however, also peril. Two people with a bad relationship usually don't find it gets better if they move in together. If a relationship is fraught with mistrust, dishonesty, and hostility, getting married or moving in together will not create a healthy relationship! But the basic idea that good relationships can become closer and more effective with daily interaction cannot be disputed. The structured environment of a Center provides the opportunity to move from sporadic interactions among well-meaning agencies to dynamic, powerful, effective relationships in a centralized facility.

> Finally, we were on the same page with community agencies that might have just criticized us five years ago. Now they saw our volume and our struggles. We all saw ways we could help victims to navigate our complicated criminal justice system.
>
> *—Detective Deborah Berger, San Diego Police Department*

In Brooklyn, New York, the first federally funded Center to open in the President's Family Justice Center Initiative brought together individuals from 34 agencies providing services to battered women and their children. The Center opened on July 20, 2005. Prior to the Center process, most of the professionals working in those 34 agencies did not even know each other. Day in and day out they toiled in their own organizations to meet the needs of victims, but they rarely shared information, sat together to strategize intervention plans, or even spent time understanding each other's role. Soon after the Center opened, staff members realized they now had the opportunity to personally know each other, socialize together during lunch hours, share information, and develop a closer working relationship. In San Antonio, Texas, the same dynamic evolved soon after their Center grand opening in August, 2005.

The power of relationships is enhanced dramatically when people spend time together, get to know each other, develop protocols for supporting each other, and slowly develop shared experiences together. The Center vision offers all of this. So we understand the importance of relationships in general, but what about police and prosecutors?

Law enforcement has its own culture and its own view of the world. Anyone who knows a cop knows this is true. Officers tend to socialize together, share challenges with each other, and develop a close bond. This bond is reinforced through their stressful work environment, life-and-death situations, long hours, and the powerful opportunity to support each other. Prosecutors likewise have their own culture, which bonds professional trial attorneys who have devoted their career to prosecuting criminals. These two cultures, however, have only recently begun building structural opportunities to interact with the community as a whole and with each other.

Community-oriented policing initiatives have built bridges between police officers and local communities. Neighborhood prosecution initiatives have taken community policy to a new level by adding prosecutors to the partnerships. These two arenas have already demonstrated for us the positive power that can develop as close working relationships evolve among police, prosecutors, and community members.

The Center vision, however, takes these concepts even further. In San Diego in 1998, when I first asked then-Police Chief David Bejarano to support our Center vision, he immediately realized the connection. Chief Bejarano did not have a specialized background in domestic violence work. He was, however, as was his predecessor, Chief Jerry Sanders, nationally and internationally recognized for San Diego's problem-oriented policing initiatives and his commitment to the philosophy of community policing. After hearing our vision, the first words out of Chief Bejarano's mouth indicated his insight into the importance of relationships to the vision: "I will support this vision because it is the logical extension of community policing." David Bejarano knew that community policing was all about making law enforcement more effective by building closer working relationships with community organizations and community leaders. If those relationships had the opportunity to increase community safety and reduce crime, then it made sense that actually co-locating community and social service organizations with law enforcement officials would make the relationships even stronger.

With over 10 Centers now operating across the United States, England, and Canada, the evidence is already clear. David Bejarano was right. The Center vision can offer a closer working relationship among law enforcement officials, domestic violence advocates, and other system professionals, such as therapists, doctors, and nurses, than we have ever seen anywhere else.

Supervising sergeants at Centers are already seeing the benefits. In San Diego, the number of *uncooperative* or *nonparticipating* victims has already dropped dramatically. Victims who come to the Center wanting to drop charges often leave realizing that abuser accountability is an important component of their safety and healing. Detectives dealing with hysterical victims find that once the victims have received all available community services, it is much easier to develop the case, get a clear history of the violence, and help the victim identify exactly what the abuser did in the incident that brought her to the Center. Throughout this chapter, you will see the testimonies of those who have made the Center a reality, but look at a few interview comments focused on the benefits to police officers:

I remember the old system where victims would have to tell their stories over and over again—each time falling apart in the process. The new system is much more compassionate. We're also able to provide a safe and comfortable place for victims to be interviewed and for children to play. It makes for a better investigation. Our detectives are even beginning to like the purple sofas. (Captain Kathy Healey)

I was not there long before I wondered why we had not done this a long time ago. It was the best thing that has ever happened to our Police Department's Domestic Violence Unit. (Sgt. Jim Arthur)

The world can be a lonely place for victims of violence. The Family Justice Center provides a safe environment where the abused can heal and find hope for the future. Without the Center, many victims and their children would have nowhere else to turn for help. The Center provided more resources for detectives to immediately offer to victims than we had ever imagined before. (Sgt. Brian Ahearn)

Being at the Center was like being at a domestic violence conference every day! Every day we came together with people who cared about victims and could offer so much of the help that I as a detective could not provide myself. (Detective Tony Johnson)

Victims acted very differently when they realized how many people were there at the Family Justice Center to help them. It was not just about cops and prosecutors going after an offender. It was now about a busload of people all trying to help her at the same time. (Detective Simon Ty)

A detective with a close working relationship with advocates at the Center now finds that he or she can call the advocate and work as an ally in supporting the victim. Once the Center opened, *uncooperative* or *hostile victims* began to decline immediately. The need for comprehensive advocacy and the benefit of such a wrap-around service delivery approach has been well documented.[13] And at the core of all the endorsements listed above? Relationships! Relationships, in turn, produce closer collaboration.

If relationships are the first major by-product of pursuing a Center vision, collaboration is a related by-product. It is a benefit for police officers, prosecutors, and every other partnering agency. Through task forces, coordinating councils, protocols, and policies, we have tried to identify ways to get everyone in our communities on the same sheet of music. The call to collaboration has been a call to share information, coordinate services, and ensure that agency policies are not working at counter-purposes.

The National Council of Juvenile and Family Court Judges was one of the first national organizations to focus on the importance of collaboration in the early 1990s. Books have been published, articles have been authored, and conferences have been held to develop the concept. Mimi Carter at the Center for Effective Public Policy has distinguished collaboration from networking, cooperating, and coordinating. She defines networking as the exchange of information for mutual benefit.[14] She defines coordinating as the exchange of information and the altering of activities for mutual benefit. She adds to these two processes the sharing of resources to come up with a definition of coordination. But she defines collaboration as working together to achieve a common goal that is difficult or impossible to reach without the assistance of another.[15]

Thus, collaboration is networking, cooperating, and coordinating combined. Yet, there is an even deeper significance to true collaboration. Mimi Carter argues that collaboration shifts organizational and individual focus in multiple ways:

- From competition to consensus

- From working alone to working together

- From thinking about activities to thinking about results

It is this insightful analysis that indicts most current efforts that we call *collaboration*. In most communities, we may do some networking around family violence issues. We may even attempt some cooperation and coordination. But we are not truly collaborating. Most organizations still struggle to give up their egos and turf long enough to build meaningful collaborations. In a world of scarce dollars, most nonprofit community organizations see themselves as competitors for funding, and they jealously guard their client statistics as their primary vehicle to prove their relevance and obtain future funding for their operation.

The result of such approaches is only partial coordination among local community organizations and very little collaboration. Victims get lost in the white water of organizations churning feverishly to survive. And they end up, as we have established throughout this book, going from agency to agency to obtain needed services—telling their story over and over again.

Collaboration now happens naturally at the Center. Within a few months of being opened, we noticed many more victims seeking temporary protective orders through the services being provided by the Center for Community Solutions (CCS), our on-site legal clinic. Victims preferred coming to the Center where they didn't have to worry about parking, their safety, their children, or where to find food to eat while they were getting legal help.

I think it is wonderful that food and beverages are provided for clients and everyone I spoke with today was encouraging.

—*Tiffany, Family Justice Center Client, 2005*

The problem, however, was that victims still had to go to civil court to file their orders. That didn't make sense to anyone. After hearing our clients identify this problem, Steve Allen, the Legal Director for CCS, and others initiated a meeting with Family Court Judge Timothy Tower and court staff to find a solution. Prosecutors, civil attorneys, detectives, and advocates from the Center also attended the meeting.

Within a very short period of time, Judge Tower agreed to begin a new procedure called *fax filings* and authorized the Center to prepare fax petitions for temporary protective orders for approval without requiring the victim to be in court. The court in turn would fax back the signed order while the victim continued to receive services at the Center. That first meeting between professional from Family Court and the Center brought results. The group has been meeting monthly ever since, finding solutions to similar problems within the civil justice system.

The Center vision offers the domestic violence movement the greatest opportunity for true collaboration ever attempted in the effort to stop family violence. What will happen in a community if the focus becomes not activities but results? What will happen if we start actually asking victims if they want to come to one place for their services? What will happen to a victim's interaction with the criminal

---

The synergy of community partners, law enforcement and prosecutors working together, creates a novel and formidable force to be reckoned with.

—*Steve Allen, Center for Community Solutions, Legal Services*

> The Family Justice Center finally put services for victims we were dealing with right down the hall instead of across town.
>
> —*Sgt. Dan Plein, San Diego Police Department*

and civil justice systems if she is actually safe, cared for, and wrapped in services? What will happen if our entire focus shifts to providing the best possible services to victims and the greatest possible accountability for offenders?

The answer is clear: True collaboration will begin to emerge. Community organizations will come to see they are often helping the same families. Law enforcement agencies will come to realize that having social services easily accessible makes their victims so much more open to law enforcement intervention. Social service agencies will realize that abuser accountability is directly tied to effective law enforcement investigations and prosecution techniques. Prosecutors will realize that far fewer victims recant their original statements to police when they are wrapped in services, safety, and support.

When a client comes in and all agencies are in the same place, if the focus stays on meeting the needs of the client, all agencies begin looking at their roles differently. They are no longer competitors; they are now collaborators. They are true partners in a grand vision: keeping victims and their children safe. The primary focus and responsibility for intervention usually placed on law enforcement begins to shift toward a far more holistic community intervention model. Not surprisingly, police officers and prosecutors, as the quotes earlier in the chapter demonstrate, begin to feel the power of working alongside others. They begin to see themselves as only one piece of the complex puzzle of support and assistance for victims.

Better Investigations

The Center produces better investigations by officers, a tremendous benefit to officers and victims for a variety of reasons. First, victims are in a better state of mind to provide meaningful details when their immediate needs are being met by staff at the Center. They are far less stressed as well when they are not worried about their children. They are not hungry because food is available. They are not worried about having enough money in the meter because parking is free. They are not distracted by their environment because the Center is such a pleasant, special, safe environment for them. The Center intake process seeks to eliminate the distractions and reduce the anxiety level of victims, thereby allowing them to be more focused when an investigator starts to ask about the facts of their criminal case.

Second, victims feel a much greater level of support by Center personnel that they first work with. By the time they interact with detectives, a level of trust in the entire system has developed, which reduces a victim's anxiety and distrust and increases her willingness to work cooperatively with the detective. When victims

> Our youngest victim thus far has been 17, and the oldest victim 67. Obviously domestic violence is not selective. As an ER physician, I became weary of what I would see everyday in the Emergency room… dozens of women who come very close to a homicide—the stabbings, broken arms—the sad and horrific cases. The Family Justice Center is a place where hospitals can refer their patients for follow-up medical documentation, legal and social services. The Forensic Medical Unit is a place where victims can seek help early without shame. And if victims don't seek help early on—then I will undoubtedly see them in the ER or at the coroner. Domestic Violence is like cancer . . . if caught early—it can be treated. If ignored, it will kill you."
>
> —*Dr. George McClane, Director of the Forensic Medical Unit*

are supported throughout the process, they are much more likely to see the detective as another ally on the team seeking to support and protect them. Third, with the victim's consent, investigations are being corroborated by additional information being provided by other community partners. It is like putting the pieces of the puzzle together. The investigation becomes substantially stronger with a forensic medical examination, a copy of the victim's declaration in her protective order, and prior unreported domestic violence incidents that have been documented by advocates within the Center intake system.

> I have a new appreciation for strategic planning. It can be extremely painful but absolutely necessary. It's the key to our success. We are going to trial less. We went from 80 jury trials in 2002 down to 32 in 2004. When detectives work together with the Forensic Medical Unit to put together a well-investigated case, those cases don't go to trial.
>
> —*Former Head Deputy City Attorney Tim Campen*

Less Recanting of Victims and Fewer Trials

Prosecutors in the City Attorney's and District Attorney's Domestic Violence units have all concurred with the powerful endorsements of the police officers who have worked at the Center. Former Head Deputy City Attorney Tim Campen reports that trials in 2004 declined from 80 to 30. He credits the decline to the benefits of the Center: Better police investigations led to better cases, which led to far fewer trials.[16] He estimates that within the three years the Center has been operating, the City Attorney's Domestic Violence Unit went from seeing 70% of their clients not wanting to participate in the prosecution process to seeing nearly 70% willing to participate.[17]

Rewards and Recognition

Beyond relationship benefits and collaboration, the Center concept also offers a tremendous opportunity for affirmation and encouragement for good police officers and prosecutors. We all need a healthy balance of affirmation and accountability.

The Center vision has created a mechanism for the accountability side of the equation with its focus group system (discussed in Chapter 11). We all need support, praise, and encouragement for what we do well or try to do well, and we need consequences and accountability when we mess up, make bad choices, or otherwise compromise what is right. Those principles have applied since we were small children. It should be no surprise that police and prosecutors need the same in their work to respond to family violence incidents well. After 20 years of passing laws related to domestic violence, we have finally developed programs for rewarding the good behavior of intervention professionals and established feedback systems for the clients we serve to help hold police officers and prosecutors accountable in a supportive, collaborative way instead of an adversarial way.

The Center concept provides a ready-made environment for affirmation and accountability. Within a short time of opening the San Diego Family Justice Center, we had 500 to 600 clients per month coming to one place and 25 agencies with staff on-site. What better opportunity for encouraging those who do good work and addressing problems with those doing poor work with our clients? Within months, we were able to create focus groups to seek feedback from the clients. We also created special awards and recognitions for high-performing employees and volunteers.

Everyone was helpful. Detective Goodman brought me here and walked me through everything. He was wonderful—he was really nice, called me at home and he greeted me at the door. I came back the next day for paper work. Socorro (legal clinic) was so nice to me. At the time, I was fueled by fear and anger. I ran in here dirty and tired. I was on the verge of tears. In all this, the detective and Socorro were great. Everyone was helpful and reassuring even though I was pretty nervous. The judge (Judge Jessup) helped me. So did the sheriff's deputy in the courthouse.

—Anonymous Family Justice Center Client, 2005

Beyond receiving input from clients and altering services based on such input, the San Diego Family Justice Center also created systems for rewarding staff members who did their job well. Too often, domestic violence intervention systems do not spend enough time rewarding those who provide excellent services to victims in need. Rewards and recognition are part of accountability. Accountability cannot simply be about disciplining or punishing those who make mistakes. It must also be about appreciating and acknowledging those who pursue excellence.

The Center has created a host of awards and other simple inexpensive strategies for recognizing and rewarding excellent work. One of the most popular and significant awards for police officers is the Wambaugh Award, named after best selling author Joseph Wambaugh. We created it to recognize detectives who write the best police reports in domestic violence cases. Joe Wambaugh himself presents the award to the officer receiving it in the presence of the Police Chief. We also created awards for Employee of the Month, Volunteer of the Month, Employee of the Quarter, Volunteer of the Quarter, Employee of the Year, and Volunteer of the Year. By elevating such awards to highly esteemed honors, we have encouraged accountability through affirmation. Without a doubt, police officers and prosecutors have benefited from these kinds of awards.

> I was not there long before I wondered why we had not done this a long time ago. It was the best thing that has ever happened to our Police Department's Domestic Violence Unit.
>
> —*Sgt. Jim Arthur, San Diego Police Department*

Another annual award is the Fearless Pilot Award. This is given out to an individual at the Center who shows tremendous leadership and perseverance. It is acknowledgement for willingness to try new things, build new things, and make good things happen. Much like a trained pilot who must pay attention to every detail and work with an entire crew to ensure safe travel for his or her passengers, a leader at the Center must pay attention to the details, bring people together, and as a team ensure the safety of victims and their children throughout the process.

During my time as the elected City Attorney, I also made efforts to have special perks for domestic violence prosecutors assigned to the Center, including providing special law enforcement badges, regular raises, compensatory time off, and special notes of appreciation. We also looked for opportunities to profile the heroic acts of police officers who did their jobs well.

On one occasion, we sought and obtained special commendations for police officers from a neighboring city for saving a domestic violence victim's life. The officers had responded to the 911 call of a victim who told the operator that her boyfriend had just called and said he was on his way over to "make her pay." Officers arrived at her apartment, escorted her to a neighbor's unit and then waited in her dark for 45 minutes. After almost an hour, the ex-boyfriend kicked the front door open and met two armed and well-trained police officers. After a struggle of several minutes in the dark, officers turned on the lights and pulled a 14-inch butcher knife out of the suspect's belt! Those officers deserved praise and honor, and the domestic violence community rallied to give it to them. We put them on television. We advocated for special awards from their police chief. We jumped in to praise them publicly as true heroes.

On the other side, communities must also pursue accountability for police officers and prosecutors who fail to protect domestic violence victims and their children. By creating protocols and then enforcing them, a Center can raise the bar for services from police officers and prosecutors. In 1998, we revised the domestic violence law enforcement protocol to include a clear position statement that failure to comply with the protocol was dereliction of duty for officers. Such a statement encourages compliance. Today, however, these protocols and policies are more important than ever in a Center where we can rally all agencies together in support of the protocol. Because of close, day-to-day working relationships, we all become better able to hold each other accountable for protocols we have all agreed to follow.

Accountability at the Center happens frequently, quietly and respectfully. We have discovered that when prosecutors reject a case for prosecution, our domestic violence detectives are not happy about it. In years past, they would have simply been annoyed and ruthlessly criticized the City Attorney's Office for not prosecuting cases. Today, detectives simply walk upstairs to the City Attorney's Office, sit down, and talk to the prosecutor to find out why the case was rejected. If more work needs to be done, they can do it. However, once the prosecutor actually talks to the detectives and understands the significance of certain facts and the time investment of the detective, he is are more willing to reconsider the decision and file the case.

The Family Justice Center as an Antidote

Two final issues must be addressed before we move beyond the discussion about the centrality of police officers and prosecutors in the Center vision. Both issue relate to recent decisions of the United States Supreme Court that have sent shock waves through much of the domestic violence movement. But the Center becomes an antidote for the potentially poisonous and disastrous impact of each court decision.

Crawford v. Washington

On March 8, 2004, the United States Supreme Court decided an important case that has had and will have dramatic impact on domestic violence prosecutors and police officers across the United States. Crawford v. Washington dealt a blow to our 20-year effort to prosecute domestic violence cases without calling the victim to the witness stand.[18] As discussed earlier in this book, *evidence-based prosecution* evolved over many years in an effort to help police officers and prosecutors use circumstantial and hearsay evidence to prove a batterer's guilt even if the victim was not able or not willing to testify against her abuser.[19] The Crawford case involved a criminal defendant who was convicted of attempted murder for stabbing a man he believed had raped his wife. The wife refused to testify at trial, but statements she had made to police during the investigation were used against her husband. On appeal, the United States Supreme Court overturned decades of precedent (prior court rulings) by deciding that out-of-court statements should not be used in most cases unless the defendant had a chance to cross-examine the person who made the original statement.[2]

> Being at the Family Justice Center has been a very humbling experience. I now realize how many victims are depending on us to get this right and that the case doesn't end with a conviction. The healing process is much bigger than just one system's response. Victims need all of us—medical, legal and social agencies—to work together. And when we do, you can literally see the difference. They reclaim their inner strength and beauty much faster.
>
> —*Gael Strack, Director, San Diego Family Justice Center*

The legal issues in the case are complex, and the implications are far reaching, but the impact on criminal justice system efforts to hold abusers accountable is straight-forward. If prosecutors can no longer use the crime scene investigation statements (e.g., my boyfriend hit me in the face) without putting the domestic violence victim on the witness stand at trial, it will be tougher to convict offenders. Many victims recant after the initial investigation or refuse to testify against their partner when the case goes to trial six months after the incident. As noted earlier, before opening the San Diego Family Justice Center, the vast majority of victims was unwilling to participate in the criminal prosecution of a partner. Understandably then, if prosecutors across America can no longer use hearsay statements in court to prove what the batterer did without the testimony of the victim at trial, fewer offenders will be successfully prosecuted.

One exciting benefit of the Center model, however, is the reality that once victims receive services and are safe, they are far more willing to participate in the criminal justice process. They do not recant their stories as often. And if the prosecutor needs to put them on the stand in order to prove the crime, they are far more likely to testify. As Gael Strack has put it, "We didn't know Crawford was coming, but we opened the Family Justice Center just in the nick of time. Because of the Family Justice Center, we have felt the impact of Crawford to a far lesser degree than prosecutors who don't have a Family Justice Center."[21]

Rachel's Story

With the Crawford case in mind, Rachel is a perfect example of the benefit of the Center. Previously, the City Attorney's office had prosecuted Rachel's husband for domestic violence. By the time the case went to trial, Rachel had recanted. She did not return the prosecutor's phone calls and refused to testify for the prosecution. At trial, she testified for the defendant and told a new story of what happened that night and how the officer got it all wrong. Her recantation was effective in helping the batterer avoid accountability.

Within a year, we had another case involving Rachel's husband, but this time the Center was open. Rachel met with the detective, the prosecutor, the advocate, the forensic nurse, and a chaplain during her first visit. Feeling supported, she did not recant. During a medical examination in the Forensic Medical Unit, she discovered she was pregnant. Rachel came back to the Center many times after that to meet with her advocate and to seek spiritual counseling. One day, she walked into Gael Strack's office to say hello and to let her know she had moved. She knew the trial was coming up and wanted to make sure everyone had her information. Gael practically stopped breathing.

In Gael's 17 years as a prosecutor, a victim had never called her up or stopped by to say hello, let alone remind her about an upcoming trial. Gael called the prosecutor, the investigator and the advocate on the case. They all walked upstairs to Gael's office on the community floor and met with Rachel. Rachel advised them of her new contact information. The prosecutor talked with her about the trial and what to expect. The advocate went over safety planning, and the investigator respectfully served Rachel with a subpoena. Rachel testified during the prosecutor's case. She was supported in the courtroom by one of the Center chaplains. She told the truth. The jury ultimately convicted her husband, and the judge sentenced him to the maximum in county jail.

My daughter became the first Family Justice Center baby. The Family Justice Center gave me many resources so we could be safe from my abuser. My life has had many changes but, through the Family Justice Center and the great people that work there I can stand on my own two feet again. I'm a proud mother and have learned how not to be a victim.

—*Rachel Goodman*

Rachel chose to keep her baby. One year later, the Center hosted their first baby shower for a client. Surrounded by a caring community that wrapped her in support, Rachel wept as she celebrated the birth of her son, who had been fathered by her abuser. Two years later, Rachel is remarried and involved in a healthy relationship. She is working full-time as a real estate agent and regularly speaks for the Center. She is a survivor and we honor her courage every day. In October 2005, the Center launched "Portraits of Courage," which includes six portraits of clients seeking services at the Center who have reclaimed their lives and dignity. They beautifully portray the inner beauty and strength of men and women who have survived domestic violence and are willing to share their inspirational stories with others. All six portraits hang at the Center for others to see, read, and be touched by their stories of courage and hope.

Town of Castle Rock v. Gonzales

In 2005, the United States Supreme Court declined to recognize a constitutional duty for police officers to comply with the law in enforcing court-issued domestic violence restraining orders. In the case of *Town of Castle Rock v. Gonzales*,[22] officers failed to enforce a restraining order when a father did not return his children from a visitation appointment in a timely manner. The mother feared her children were in danger, but officers refused to attempt contact with him or even look for him, even though the mother frantically begged for help. The suspect eventually killed all three children and opened fire on the Castle Rock Police Department before being killed by officers. The Supreme Court's refusal to allow the grieving mother to bring litigation against Castle Rock reminds us all that we must pursue alternate approaches to holding police officers responsible for protecting battered women and their children. The American Bar Association Commission on Domestic Violence has sponsored a resolution calling on communities to create statutes, protocols, and policies to increase accountability for police officers in the face of the Castle Rock court decision.[23]

The Center vision, however, can play a powerful role in recognizing the importance of law enforcement in dealing with domestic violence and can assist in creating accountability and affirmation approaches with police officers and prosecutors. A closer look at the Castle Rock situation points out the many other resources that were not readily available to the victim. She had to rely on a small, poorly trained police department for protection and assistance. Without question, Castle Rock needs a collaborative community response, which, hopefully, will one day include a Center. The Center offers the kind of wraparound service delivery model that can increase protection for victims and provide greater accountability for police officers working with them.

Conclusion

The criminal justice system will never solve the complex social problem of family violence. But it is an important partner in holding criminal domestic violence offenders accountable for their conduct. The Center vision does not make law enforcement the central focus of intervention and prevention efforts, but because of the criminal nature of most violence and abuse, we must continue to see the importance of police officers and prosecutors in the overall approach of these Centers.

Batterers rarely stop without intervention, and experienced abusers will not stop abusing until there are serious consequences for their behavior that often include incarceration, long-term accountability, and monitoring. If the criminal justice system is not working in certain communities, we need to fix it. If the unintended consequences of certain law enforcement policies are revictimizing victims and their children, we need to adjust our policies. But we must see treating domestic violence as a serious crime as crucial to the ongoing social change movement toward stopping family violence. While some communities are not ready to pursue the Center vision, particularly if they don't have a strong criminal justice system response, the vision can still challenge them to improve their law enforcement responses by enhancing relationships among advocates, community-based agencies, prosecutors, and police officers. Philip and Maria remind us that the hard work of improving the response of cops and prosecutors is worth it. When the criminal justice system works well, justice is done, offenders are held accountable, and victims get the help they need.

Endnotes

1. David A. Ford and Mary Jean Regoli, "The Criminal Prosecution of Wife Assaulters: Process, Problems, and Effects," in *Legal Responses to Wife Assault: Current Trends and Evaluation,* N. Zoe Hilton (ed.), Sage Publications, Thousand Oaks, CA, 1993, , pp. 127-64.

2. Leigh Goodmark, "Law Is the Answer? Do We Know That for Sure?: Questioning the Efficacy of Legal Interventions for Battered Women," *St. Louis U. Pub. L. Rev,* 2004, 1(7), p. 23.

3. E. Buzawa and C. Buzawa, *Do Arrests and Restraining Orders Work?,* Sage Publications, Thousand Oaks, CA, 1996, pp. 34-37. .

4. Evan Stark, "Mandatory Arrest of Batterers: A Reply to Its Critics," in , Chapter 8 in Buzawa, p.115. See also JoAnn Miller, "An Arresting Experiment: Domestic Violence Victim Experiences and Perceptions," *Journal of Interpersonal Violence,* 2003, 18 (7), pp. 695-716.

5. In 2005, the Connecticut Legislature debated a new primary aggressor law. During the debate, advocates from the Connecticut Coalition on Domestic Violence reported that in one community the dual arrest rate was 75%!

6. Robert C. Davis et al., "Effects of No-Drop Prosecution of Domestic Violence Upon Conviction Rates,". *Justice Research and Policy,* 2002, 3 (2), pp. 1-13. See also *The Effects of Domestic Violence Prosecution,* study of five no-drop jurisdictions funded by American Bar Association, 2000. Available upon request at www.familyjusticecenter.org.

7. Ibid. [The American Bar Association Study found that 37% of victims interviewed after successful prosecution reported ongoing verbal and emotional abuse.]

8. Linda G. Mills, *Insult to Injury: Rethinking Our Responses to Intimate Abuse.* Princeton University Press, Princeton,,NJ, 2003.

9. L. Ventura and U. G. Davis, "Domestic Violence: Court Case Conviction and Recidivism, *Violence Against Women,* February 2005, 11 (2).

10. *Family Violence Statistics Including Statistics on Strangers and Acquaintances,* report by Bureau of Justice Statistics, June 2005, NCJ 207846. See www.ojp.usdoj.gov/bjs.

11. The National Council of Juvenile and Family Court Judges has led the nation for over 10 years in providing domestic violence training and resources for judges. See www.ncjfcj.org for further resources.

12. Presentation by Ellen Pence, Ouachita Parish, Louisiana, October 12, 2005. Conference sponsored in conjunction with the grand opening of the Ouachita Family Justice Center.

13. Nicole E. Allen et al., "Battered Women's Multitude of Needs: Evidence Supporting the Need for Comprehensive Advocacy," *Violence Against Women Journal,* September 2004, 10(9), pp. 1015-35.

    Barbara Hart, *Coordinated Community Approaches to Domestic Violence,* speech delivered at the Strategic Planning Workshop on Violence Against Women, National Institute of Justice, Washington, D.C., retrieved December 7, 2005, from www.minicava.umn.edu/hart/nij.html.

    Ellen Pence, "Some Thoughts on Philosophy," in *Coordinating Community Responses to Domestic Violence: Lessons learned from Duluth and Beyond,* M.F. Shephard and Ellen Pence (eds.), Sage Publications, Thousand Oaks, CA., pp. 25-40.

14. Madeleine Carter, *Principles and Models of Collaboration,* presentation at the U.S. Department of Justice Conference on Missing and Exploited Children, April 2005, Philadelphia, Pennsylvania. Available upon request from the Center for Effective Public Policy, Washington, DC., www.cepp.com or Center for Effective Public Policy, 8403 Colesville Road, Suite 720, Silver Spring, MD, 20910, phone (301) 589-9383, fax (301) 589-3505.

15. Ibid.

16. Interview by Gael Strack with former Head Deputy City Attorney Tim Campen, December2005.

17. Ibid.

18. Crawford v. Washington (2004) 541 U.S. [124 S. Ct. 1354, 158 L. Ed. 2d 177, 2004 U.S. LEXIS 1838, 2004 WL 413301].

19. See www.familyjusticecenter.org/library for sample Power Point training presentations by Casey Gwinn on the philosophy and implementation of evidence-based prosecution strategies in felony and misdemeanor domestic violence cases.

20. Major treatises are now being written, and organizations such as the American Prosecutor's Research Institute have prepared tremendous training materials to assist prosecutors in child abuse, domestic violence, sexual assault, and elder abuse cases in blunting the impact of the court ruling.

See Allie Philips, Senior Attorney, *Striking a Balance in the Wake of Crawford v. Washington*, American Prosecutor's Research Institute, available at www.ndaa-apri.org.

21. Much will be examined and written about the implications of <u>Crawford v. Washington</u> in the years to come, but it is important to note early in the fallout of the 2004 decision that communities with Family Justice Centers will likely see far less impact on their prosecution and conviction rates than communities without the Center model.

22. <u>Gonzales v. Town of Castle Rock</u>, 125 S. Ct. 417 (2005).

8

Helping Children Caught in the Crossfire

James didn't pick his family. He never had the chance to say that he did not want to be exposed to violence and alcohol abuse during his growing-up years. He was a victim, a child caught in the crossfire of family violence. By seven years old, he had experienced the pain of open hands, closed fists, and screaming rage. He often went to bed scared for his mother and terrified of his stepfather. By the time he was 14, he was hitting his first girlfriend. By 20, he was a father and was already abusing his girlfriend and her two young children. At 22, he was in the San Diego Municipal Court being prosecuted by the San Diego City Attorney's Office for spousal abuse.

I met James in court. His defense attorney said he was a really nice guy who needed someone to cut him a break. I was advocating locking him up for two years. But before one of the court hearings in the case, I agreed to meet with him and his attorney. We agreed that nothing he said would be used against him in court and nothing I said would be used against the prosecution if the case went to trial.

Within 10 minutes of meeting James, I was almost moved to tears. He was a scared, angry man only three years younger than I was. But he carried baggage that I didn't have. He wept in my presence as he admitted that he did not know how to stop his violence. He told me about his home when he was growing up and how much he loved his step-kids. He knew he was making terrible choices, but didn't know how to stop. It was a powerful education for me as a new domestic violence prosecutor. Putting James in jail for two years was not going to solve anything. He had already spent a week in jail at the outset of the case, and he did not want to go back. He was willing to go to counseling, perform public work service, pay a fine, and do anything else required of him, but he begged not to have to go back to jail.

At first, I was not sympathetic to James. I thought how tough he must have acted when abusing those he claimed to love. And now, here he was, weeping and begging for mercy. I saw him as more pathetic than sympathetic. But as I listened to him and looked into his eyes I was moved by what I heard and saw. There was good in him. There was potential. He did not want to lose his construction job by going to jail. He wanted to provide for his family and he swore that he did not want to keep doing to his kids what he had experienced as a child. I did not demand jail time when the judge sentenced him.

Today, James is the labor relations manager for a large union. He is 15 years past his criminal prosecution, and the generational cycle of family violence in James' family has been broken. James is currently volunteering his time to help develop Camp Hope, the San Diego Family Justice Center's camp for victims of family violence and their children. He has served as a spokesperson for the domestic violence movement and continues to freely share the day-to-day temptations and struggles he faces because of the painful baggage he carries inside him. But he is a messenger of hope and a living testimony to the healing that children of family violence homes can experience. He has overcome powerful forces that could have destroyed him. James' story is the perfect starting point to understanding the issues surrounding domestic violence and children and the role Family Justice Centers can play in healing children before they face the criminal justice system as teens or adults.

> I felt I was safe, not pushed or intimidated. It was a great experience and they even fed me. I was hungry too. I enjoyed seeing my girls be kids again. I was apprehensive coming in and thinking I could do this on my own. Thanks for making me feel at ease and helping me to realize I needed all of you to help.
>
> —*Marie, Family Justice Center Client, 2005*

In America, We Raise our Criminals at Home

The starting point for the call to hope and healing for children through the Center vision must be an honest assessment of the origins of the diabolical nature of family violence. Communities, churches, law enforcement agencies, social service agencies, judges, prosecutors, advocates, medical professionals, employers, and anyone else trying to deal with family violence will make a grave mistake if they do not understand the birthplace of family violence in our society. We cannot create Centers or even begin planning for them in communities across the country and around the world until we understand one fundamental reality: In America, we raise our criminals at home. The birthplace of family violence is the family.

Impacted and shaped by a culture dripping in violence, abuse, guns, and the objectification of women, it is the family that spawns each new generation of offenders. It is in homes touched by domestic violence, child abuse, drug and alcohol abuse, and neglect that we raise those who go on to abuse others in intimate relationships. While good kids from good homes sometimes make bad choices, the vast majority of all domestic violence offenders, child molesters, juvenile criminals, and prison inmates were raised in homes with violence, abuse, and neglect.[1] Research has confirmed this truth for nearly 20 years. The raw reality of this truth deserves a chapter. It deserves our constant acknowledgement and consideration.

It will later inform choices about how to conduct outreach efforts to at-risk families and how to organize services for children within Centers.

Thirty years of only partially successful efforts to reduce domestic violence should convince us that understanding the family genesis of the problem is crucial to ultimate success. Too many communities have ignored the cause in leaping to conclusions about the cure. Too many agencies have implemented protocols and policies and then sunk into despair when those policies and procedures failed to *solve* the problem of domestic violence. We like to talk about new laws and new approaches, but we don't like to admit our part in thousands of years of human history, in a culture that still tolerates and glorifies violence, and in raising children who continue to act violently toward those they try to love.

We don't like complexity in America. We don't like ambiguity. We want good and evil. We want right and wrong. And once we have defined the problem, we like quick fixes. Let's throw some money at the problem. Let's implement a few policies and procedures. Let's pass a couple laws. Homelessness? Let's just build a few affordable housing projects and some homeless shelters. Bad economy? Let's pass a tax relief bill. School shootings? Let's eliminate access to guns, and we will be on the road to success. Violent crime? Let's pass a three-strikes law, or a two-strikes law, or even a one-strike law, and the bad guys will be locked up for good.

We should not pick on politicians who search for the quick fix, the good headline, or the simple solution to social ills. I spent eight years as an elected official. Politicians are a reflection of our culture, our values, and our priorities. The lure of the quick fix is a much more widespread ailment in our world than that practiced by some ambitious elected officials. The minister wants to preach a sermon on this issue or that issue and expect the congregation to *get it* in one sitting. The doctor wants to prescribe the medication and have the problem go away within 10 days. Parents want to give a child a good firm lecture and think they have solved whatever the misbehavior issue might have been. But it is not so simple, is it? Not with personal problems, not with economic problems, not with social issues, not with international problems, not with relationship problems, and not with domestic violence issues.

Human History Makes Our Vision Difficult

In Genesis 2, Cain killed his brother Abel, and family violence became a part of the Hebrew Bible and human history. In 550 B.C., Confucius uttered a value-laden statement that has been ringing down through history: Women are not worth a single testicle. In 584 A.D., the Roman Catholic Church engaged in a contentious and controversial debate on a subject that captivated the scholars of the day. The final vote of the ruling bishops was 34 to 33. Women were declared human by one vote! Without question, much of human history from every part of the globe demonstrates undeniable historical realities of the objectification, dehumanization, and victimization of women. Male privilege and patriarchy have infected virtually every culture in human history. And America cannot ignore its guilt. When the Declaration of Independence declared that "All men are created equal . . ." it did not include women. Indeed, women were not even allowed to vote in this country until the suffrage movement produced the 21st Amendment in 1926. Women have been considered property of the patriarchs since The Ten Commandments and even before. Human history makes our vision for Family Justice Centers difficult indeed.

Beyond, the clear evidence of the subjugation of women in human history, there is also disturbing evidence from the beginning of recorded history of the victimization and control of children.[2] While primarily evidenced in the violence, victimization, and subjugation of female children, male children too have historically lacked both legal rights and legal standing. Over 2,000 years ago, no organized opposition was even recorded when the Roman ruler Herod destroyed every male child in Israel under the age of two in search of a baby boy named Jesus.

While the focus of this chapter is children, the historic discrimination and victimization of disabled children and adults has also drawn our attention at the Center. After hosting a conference focused on victims with disabilities, we all realized how great the need is to reach out to them as well.

The cold hard reality of the lack of equality for women, children, the disabled, and others who lack power in the culture cannot be disputed by any honest, thinking person on the planet. It is equally indisputable that the organized religions of the world have also played a role in the historical conspiracy against women, in particular. Whether by creed or custom, religion has often been used to justify the demeaning and controlling of women. The history of the Jewish faith, the Christian faith, Islam, Buddhism, and Hinduism all have clear connections to the ugly worldwide reality of carnage and genocide that has been justified in the name of God.[3]

To be sure, religion and faith are not the enemies of hope and healing for violent families. Many victims and offenders find help from many different religions and faith traditions. Powerful voices have risen up in recent years calling for people of faith to be a positive force for change including Al Miles, Ann Marie Hunter, and Marie Fortune.[4] I am a follower of Jesus, strive to live my life by the teachings of Jesus, and live my life with great respect for those of other faiths and belief systems. But we cannot ignore where we have been, what we have done, and how those powerful forces have shaped the struggle we now confront in our culture and our world. Many professionals I work with in the domestic violence field do not share my faith or even hold to any faith, but they still struggle with cultural beliefs and biases that lead to discrimination and violence against people of color, women, children, gays and lesbians, and others who lack status or power in the culture.

It should be no surprise then that we find the birth of domestic violence in generation after generation of homes where children grow up witnessing the lives of their parents filled with verbal, emotional, and physical violence. Many years ago in San Diego a child survivor of a domestic violence home was chosen in an art competition to provide the artwork for our Domestic Violence Council's public awareness campaign on family violence. Her poster was a black hole-like image with text that repeated over and over from the outer rim of the hole: Children trapped in domestic violence raise children trapped in domestic violence...who raise children trapped in domestic violence . . . who raise children trapped in domestic violence. . . . The words ultimately faded into the center of the black hole. Her artwork was not only an autobiography; it was a powerful reminder of the reality of family violence.

> Chaplain George does so well. He has an impact on people's lives.
>
> —*Anonymous Family Justice Center Client, 2005*

Nearly 10 years ago, Robin Karr-Morse and Meredith S. Wiley authored *Ghosts From the Nursery: Tracing the Roots of Violence* and looked at the impact on children of prenatal exposure to drugs, adverse experiences in the womb, trauma, head injury, emotional deprivation, and early brain anatomy.[5] Still today, it is an excellent resource in reminding us that child development is the key time in a human being's life where values, beliefs, and world views are formed. It also provides irrefutable proof that the roots of violence are virtually always found in the home.

The research is now undisputed: In America and around the world, we do indeed raise our criminals at home. Most men and women who choose to use violence in intimate relationships learned it in the homes in which they grew up. It is rare that a child raised in a healthy, two-parent family ends up becoming a chronic abuser of intimate partners later in life. No doubt it happens, but it is the exception, not the rule. In the vast majority of situations, children who have grown up in violent and abusive homes come to believe that violence is normative, and they learn to use such power and control techniques as they grow up and become involved in intimate relationships. Some in the feminist movement are willing to acknowledge this reality for boys, but few want to also admit that girls may also grow up to become violent toward their partners due to the "classroom" they grew up in. Or, more commonly, girls simply grow up to believe violence is normative—normal behavior in all families.

The National Crime Victimization Survey for the last few decades has confirmed that women and men can both be violent.[6] Though the crime survey likely provides some misleading information due to its information gathering techniques (telephone surveys), there can be little argument that women use violence at times in intimate relationships. And the children caught in the cross-fire, both boys and girls, are often profoundly impacted by the classroom of the home. While some children are resilient and do overcome the impacts of early victimization and witnessing of violence, most carry the baggage of that violence for the rest of their lives.[7]

So, what are the actual impacts on children who grow up witnessing domestic violence in the home? How many of those children are also physically or sexually abused? It is important to answer those questions in order to understand how we can help children in a Family Justice Center once the dream becomes a reality.

Children's Response to Domestic Violence

After 20 years of research and review, many facts about domestic violence and children are undisputed:

- Between 3.3 million and10 million children in the U.S. witness domestic violence each year.[8]

- Recent exposure to violence in the home is a significant factor in predicting a child's later violent behavior.[9]

- National studies show that being abused or neglected as a child increases the likelihood of arrest as a juvenile by 53 percent and of arrest for a violent crime as an adult by 38 percent.[10]

- Between 45% and 70% of men who abuse their intimate partners also abuse their children.[11]

- As many as 70% of children in battered women's shelters have also been physically or sexually abused.[12]

- Each year 324,000 pregnant women in the U.S. are battered.[13]

- Men who were exposed to their parents' violence are twice as likely to abuse their own wives as sons of nonviolent parents.[14]

Children growing up in domestic violence homes not only carry the baggage of violence and abuse with them, but some of them never make it to adulthood. Children in domestic violence homes are more likely to commit suicide than other children. They are more likely to commit sexual assault as they grow older.[15] And children do in fact act out with their own criminal conduct even early on in life. In fact, one research study found that children growing up in domestic violence homes are 60 times more likely to be involved in delinquent behavior than children from nonviolent homes. They may be as much as 1,000 times more likely to become abusers as adults than children not experiencing violence in their families.[16] Though some children are extremely resilient to the impact of family violence, many suffer profound impacts. Research demonstrates immediate or short-term impacts on many children, including:

- Stuttering

- Eating and sleeping disorders

- Mood swings

- Anxiety

- Fear

- Sadness and depression

- Performance problems in school

- Increased aggression[17]

The long-term impacts of violence on the lives of children, even after concluding their exposure to violence at some point, are also sobering:

- Eating disorders, delinquency, substance abuse, and suicide

- Deficits in social competence, school achievement, and peer relations

- Serious emotional and behavioral problems

- Identification with the abuser by male children by the age of 13 or 14

- Increased likelihood by girls of accepting abuse in their adult relationhips[18]

> Everyone was polite, friendly, professional and understanding. The lounge area was so cheerful and fun and the children's playroom was fantastic.
>
> —*Sherry, Family Justice Center Client, 2005*

Research has also confirmed that children repeat the cycle of violence they learn in the home early in their lives. In 1992, the University of Illinois documented the prevalence of relationship violence among teenagers. Some form of violence in dating relationships was reported by 36% of students. And only 4% talked about it with an authority figure. Children and teenagers too are experiencing violence, and they need our help.

Every year I speak in "Healthy Paths" classes at a local high school about relationship/domestic violence. Recently, during each of my classes I was reminded how easy it is to see the evidence if you look for it. The class started asking questions as I spoke. I engaged them in debate. And slowly, it became clear that at least 1/3 of the class was impacted by verbal, emotional, and physical abuse. I could see it on their faces. I could hear it in their questions: "So, if my mom and dad were to get in an argument and my dad grabbed my mom and wouldn't let her leave the room, is that domestic violence?" There was no doubt what was happening in that home. A man came up to me afterwards and said, "I need to talk to someone but I want to be anonymous." I gave him our DV Info Line at the San Diego Family Justice Center

(866-933-HOPE). I left the school reminded that the next generation of abusers and the hope for the future were all there at the same time in those classes.

Pregnant Teenagers Show Another Side of the Story

In 1997 in San Diego, we looked at the impact on children from a different angle by reviewing our success (actually failure) in dealing with pregnant or parenting teens. The numbers were troubling. Of teen domestic violence cases in the City Attorney's Office, 70% involved pregnant or parenting teens. When we worked cooperatively with the San Diego City Schools to evaluate the relationships of nearly 350 pregnant teens, we found a very significant but disturbing reality:

- 75% of the fathers were in their 20s
- 10% of the fathers were over 30 years old
- Only 15% of the fathers were in their teens[19]

We found the next generation of abusers in the womb. More teenage girls were being victimized by significantly older men with greater social power, greater resources, and a greater ability to emotionally coerce a young girl into a sexual relationship rather than by teenage boys.[20]

With such overwhelming evidence of the impact of domestic violence on children, helping them must absolutely be one of our highest priorities. But isn't that already happening? What about all those child abuse laws? What about all those child advocacy centers that provide services to abused children? Hasn't this work already been done? Let's identify why child advocacy centers and well-meaning child abuse prevention professionals are not enough to help children growing up in domestic violence homes. Let's think through why the current approach is not enough and why the Family Justice Center vision can help.

Are Child Advocacy Centers Enough?

The first and most obvious problem in addressing domestic violence issues through the existing system is that our child advocacy system does not adequately focus on issues involving violence between adults in the home. The child advocacy system in this country was created to protect children. Indeed, the primary focus of the system is not adults but children. Proponents of *child safety* and *family reunification* do not often even address the issue of domestic violence. If they do, the focus is often on the role the mother plays in failing to protect her children from the violence of her partner.[21]

The juvenile and family courts in this country, which most often deal with child abuse and other related violence in the home, are not even equipped or oriented to deal with violence between adults. As a national trainer, I am still amazed at how

little knowledge most child advocacy workers have of the dynamics of domestic violence. The juvenile court or family court often expects the criminal courts to deal with adults, and the system breakdown begins. To be sure, some communities have merged their family and criminal courts, and a small number have even merged juvenile, family, and criminal courts. Most of the merged approaches still seem to lack comprehensive service delivery models for helping children and adults at the same time.[22]

We Cannot Protect Children if We Do Not Protect Their Mothers

But even beyond some of the structural issues in the court system are profound philosophical issues. The abiding fundamental truth we have learned in recent years is that *you cannot protect children if you do not protect their mothers.* Lacking this fundamental belief, child protective systems have spent decades taking children away from battered women, blaming mothers for failing to protect their children, and universally failing to provide coordinated advocacy and support for battered women in the midst of dealing with child abuse issues in the family. Good people with good intentions have failed to help battered women in the name of child protection. Powerful, conscientious child advocates who did not understand the complex dynamics of battered women did not develop systems that wrap mothers in safety and support in the process of also working to protect their children.[23]

The reason for the Family Justice Center model, therefore, should be clear. We must have intervention systems that provide comprehensive support for adult victims of intimate partner violence in order to fully protect children in those homes. We must focus on dealing with domestic violence between the adults before we can fully address any violence going on between the parents and the children. Ironically, Lenore Walker identified this reality over 20 years ago. Dr. Walker found in 1984 that mothers were eight times more likely to abuse their children when they themselves were being battered than when they were safe from the violence. Sadly, however, as recently as 2004 domestic violence advocates in New York City were forced to sue the child welfare system for its policy of taking children away from battered women instead of focusing on supporting them, holding the batterer accountable, and working to ensure that mother and children could stay together in safety.[24]

Bringing Together Child Abuse and Domestic Violence Professionals

Tremendous work is now being done around the country in identifying ways to bring together two very separate and distinct movements—the child advocacy movement and the domestic violence movement.[25] The federal government's Greenbook Initiative and a host of other efforts have begun to create powerful and promising dialogue between professionals from these very separate movements. We talk more about these issues in Chapter 12.

Crucial, however, to the development of any successful Family Justice Center is the understanding that services for children will be central. We did not understand this reality when we opened the San Diego Family Justice Center. We had very little space for children's services and originally decided that we would provide little more than child care while adults received services. In Chapter 12, we discuss this journey in greater detail. But there is a more important point to be made in this chapter.

The relationship building that must take place between community agencies and criminal justice system domestic violence professionals must also take place between domestic violence and child abuse professionals. Centers must eventually provide a broad range of services to children. Before we can even begin to look at the details of this merger, as discussed later in the book, we need to be reminded of San Diego's journey towards a close working relationship between child advocacy professionals and domestic violence professionals. It did not happen one day because we decided to move in together at the Center. It evolved over many years as it formed the foundation for our working relationship today. Understanding how necessary this journey is becomes a central building block—a focus on adult intimate partner violence as a Center opens that later is able to expand to services for children. Let's briefly look at San Diego's experience.

San Diego: a Case Study

In 1989, when San Diego began its high-profile Task Force on Domestic Violence and started developing relationships with a host of agencies and disciplines related to domestic violence work, there was a major discipline missing from the room. The child protective services agency in San Diego County did not participate in our task force.[26] I have little doubt that they viewed it as irrelevant to their world. We already had a Child Abuse Coordinating Council in San Diego. The Council was strong, vibrant, and met regularly. No prior relationships had developed between the child advocacy movement and the battered women's movement in San Diego at that time. The result: Between 1989 and 1991, as the Task Force on Domestic Violence met, there was little input from child abuse professionals and no dialogue between them and domestic violence professionals.

As noted earlier, however, a new initiative developed at Children's Hospital through the official child advocacy center in San Diego, the Center for Child Protection. Dr. David Chadwick, the founder of the Child Protection Center, hired a domestic violence-trained advocate named Sandy Miller from Boston to develop a program designed to reduce foster care placements in the juvenile dependency courts. Sandy arrived in San Diego in 1989, conducted an assessment, and proceeded to develop a program that would become known as the Family Violence Program. Sandy's early assessment found that 49% of adult guardians of suspected child abuse victims brought to Children's Hospital reported a history of domestic violence between adults in the home. She also quickly determined that the large majority of foster care placements, where children were removed from the custody of a single mother, involved documented histories of domestic violence.

The stage was set—one of the largest reasons for foster care placements of children was a determination that the adult male in the home was violent and abusive toward both the mother and the children. Sandy Miller proceeded to develop a pioneering program that would assign trained domestic violence advocates to women who had lost or were at risk of losing custody of their children because of domestic violence. There was no dispute in the statistics. Women were not losing custody simply because their children had been abused. Women were losing custody because they too were victims of abuse and the *system* was concluding that the mothers had failed to protect their children.[27]

The Family Violence Program went on to become a powerful change agent and relationship builder between domestic violence professionals and child abuse professionals in San Diego. The journey was fraught with controversy, finger pointing, and tension, but the Program laid some of the crucial groundwork for powerful partnerships between child advocacy and domestic violence professionals.

Between 1989 and 1991, juvenile court judges agreed to allow domestic violence advocates from the Program to come into the confidential juvenile court proceedings and advocate on behalf of battered women who had lost or were at risk of losing custody of their children. For two years, advocates came out of those courtrooms with horror stories about how judges, attorneys, and CPS workers treated victims of domestic violence. Slowly, judges actually began allowing advocates to talk in the juvenile court proceedings and "failure-to-protect" cases and foster care placements began to decline.[28]

Family Violence Program advocates also began appearing in the family court and criminal court on behalf of battered women. Though many of the women had never reported the domestic violence to police up to this point, the City Attorney's Domestic Violence Unit assigned an investigator and prosecutor to assist the advocates in developing and filing criminal cases against the abusers. Since little was happening to adult male abusers in the juvenile court, the filing of misdemeanor criminal cases became the only vehicle for offender accountability once the domestic violence had been disclosed in the child advocacy proceedings.[29]

We quickly found what much research has now confirmed. When a battered woman has an advocate, her safety increases, the negative consequences of the system diminish, and the likelihood that she will get the necessary services dramatically improves.[30] We also enjoyed a good laugh now and then, finding that when an advocate was present in court in the criminal case, the sentence for the defendant always went up.[31] It became a joke that we probably didn't even need an advocate to be there in court. If our prosecutor just pointed to some woman in the courtroom and said to the judge, "The victim's advocate is present in the courtroom," the judge would then hammer the defendant at sentencing—more jail time, longer probation, and greater consequences for his violence! We never did that, but it would have worked!

The Family Violence Program, which existed long before the Greenbook Initiative or other collaborative work between the child advocacy and domestic violence world, taught us many lessons about the importance of building relationships. But the fireworks did not happen until 1991.

Karen's Story

In June 1991, the Task Force on Domestic Violence completed its two years of work. Ashley Walker and I were exhausted after our all-volunteer, effort. We planned a major wrap-up event with a press conference and luncheon. Every elected official and major policy maker in the county was invited and came! It was a party. Over 300 people attended the luncheon that day when our final report was released. However, we had a woman who decided, in consultation with Sandy Miller, that we needed to point out the work that remained to be done. Sandy's program was working with a client named Karen, who had lost custody of her four children based on the work of CPS. Karen was a victim of domestic violence. Working with Sandy's advocates, I had successfully prosecuted her husband John and put him in jail for four months. But our efforts to keep Karen with her kids failed and her parental rights were terminated by the juvenile court. Sandy wanted Karen's story to be told that day, and Karen was willing to tell it.

After an excellent luncheon, presentation of our report, and the obligatory slaps on the back for all elected officials and policy makers for supporting our grassroots task force, we brought Karen to the podium. She understood the consequences of what she was about to do. She knew the chances of getting the court to reconsider its decision after she went public with her story were slim. She was shaking and steadied herself by grabbing both sides of the lectern. As Karen began to tell her story of abuse, the room fell silent. She described being hit and kicked over the course of her 11-year marriage. She described bringing her children to the Center for Child Protection when she realized how severe her husband's abuse of the children had become. She explained the sick and twisted disciplinary tools that her husband had learned in his home growing up and went on to use on her children.

Karen described incidents where her husband placed raw chicken skin in her children's mouths and ordered them not to spit it out for hours at a time to punish them for talking back to him. She told of children being hit in the face. She told of times her youngest child, born with severe disabilities, was verbally and emotionally abused by her husband. She described one child being locked in a closet as punishment. Finally, she told of the juvenile court process, the involvement of CPS, and ultimately the termination of her parental rights. Then she told the final outcome that would never be forgotten by anyone in the room. Sobbing, she said that the court, on the recommendation of CPS, awarded custody of her four children to her husband's parents in Arizona. There was an audible gasp in the room. That night, Karen's story and the audible gasp played on every television and radio station in San Diego. No one missed the truth her story conveyed: Our CPS system was completely and miserably failing battered women and their children.

The next morning, I was at my desk in the City Attorney's Office when the phone rang. I picked it up and the voice on the other end of the phone said "Who the hell do you think you are?" Though I am not a profane person, my first thought was, "Who the hell is this?" I soon learned it was the Director of the Department of Social Services. He had not attended the luncheon and, in fact, his managers, including the supervisors of CPS, had never attended our task force meetings over the two years we struggled to improve the system. He made some veiled references to getting me fired for what I had done by allowing Karen to speak publicly and hung up on me. It was not the first time my career that I thought, this has been a good career, a short career, but a good career. It turned out, though he was wrong about getting me fired.

Six months later, he resigned as the head of the Department of Social Services and left San Diego. Within another six months, the County hired Cecil Steppe, the Chief Probation Officer, as the new Director of the Department of Social Services. It was the best thing that happened to battered women with children in the history of San Diego County. Cecil Steppe came in with the philosophy of a cop and the heart of a social worker and started listening to the domestic violence advocates about the need for system change. In less than a year, he tapped a CPS supervisor named Betsy Gross to help revamp the CPS system to build bridges between their child advocacy work and the domestic violence community.

Soon, Betsy Gross' leadership created a special Family Violence Project, which paired up probation officers and CPS workers whenever cases involved both child abuse and domestic violence. Within two years, the Domestic Violence Council created a Child Abuse/Domestic Violence Committee to facilitate dialogue between child advocacy social workers and domestic violence advocates. The meetings were often painful, even ugly. But the dialogue yielded a series of cross-trainings and conference workshops that played a role in slowly, over many years, building bridges between our child advocacy system and our domestic violence professionals in San Diego. Every unpleasant step of that process later yielded dividends, as we discuss in Chapter 12, when we proceeded to provide services for children at the San Diego Family Justice Center.

The journey was a long one with many ups and downs, but Karen will never be forgotten. She stood up, in the face of a system that was broken, and spoke the truth. Karen did not see her children again until they each turned 18, but her courage helped countless other children and battered women in San Diego in the years to follow. Her willingness to speak truth in front of the political leadership of San Diego helped shape the Center vision and laid the groundwork for bringing child advocacy professionals into the Family Justice Center.

Conclusion

Children growing up in domestic violence homes often abuse their own intimate partners as teenagers and adults. In America and around the world, we raise our criminals at home. The children of domestic violence homes go on to populate juvenile halls and state and federal prisons. The research is clear. The challenge is to understand the importance of providing services for children in Family Justice Centers. The child advocacy movement does excellent work in helping abused children but has historically done a very poor job of dealing with adult intimate partner violence, which also occurs in the context of child abuse.

Family Justice Centers should start with a focus on serving adult victims of domestic violence. But ultimately, they need to provide comprehensive services to children as well. Before this can happen, however, child advocacy professionals and domestic violence professionals in any community seeking to develop a Center must build relationships. They must find common ground. They must travel the long, painful journey of understanding each other and understanding that we will never be able to protect children if we do not learn how to protect their mothers.

Endnotes

1. Peter G. Jaffe et al., *Children of Battered Women,* Sage Publications. Thousand Oaks, CA, 1990.

2. The New York Society for Prevention of Cruelty to Children was one of the first cruelty societies formed in the country in 1874. By 1900, 161 cruelty societies existed in the United States. Many of the founders had strong connections to the developing animal rights movement.

3. Al Miles, *Violence in Families: What Every Christian Needs to Know,* Augsburg Books, Minneapolis, MN, 2002. [Rev. Miles does an excellent job of addressing the appropriate response of faith communities to domestic violence.]

4. To contact Rev. Ann Marie Hunter: Safe Havens Interfaith Partnership Against Domestic Violence, 31 St. James Avenue, Suite 730, Boston, MA 02116, or go to www.interfaithpartners.org.

   To contact Rev. Marie Fortune: Faith Trust Institute, 2400 N. 45th Street, #10, Seattle, WA 98103, or go to www.faithtrustinstitute.org.

   To contact Rev. Al Miles: The Queen's Medical Center, Hospital Ministry, 1301 Punchbowl Street, Honolulu, HI 96813, or go to www.queens.org.

5. Robin Karr-Morse and Meredith S. Wiley, *Ghosts from the Nursery: Tracing the Roots of Violence,* Atlantic Monthly Press, New York, 1997.

6. See www.ojp.usdoj.gov/bjs/cvict.htm for online data. Statistics accessed online on December 10, 2005.

7. <u>Nicholson v. Williams</u>, 203 F. Supp 2nd 153, 2002. In re Nicholson, 181 F. Supp 2nd 182, 188, 2002.

8. "A Guide to Research on Family Violence, Children in Violence Homes," in conference materials for *Courts and Communities: Confronting Violence in the Family*, State Justice Institute Conference, San Francisco, CA, March 1993, p. 27.

   See also Bonnie Carlson, "Children's Observations of Interpersonal Violence," in *Battered Women and Their Families*, A.R. Roberts (ed.), Springer, New York, 1984, p. 147-67.

9. M. I. Singer et al. *The Mental Health Consequences of Children's Exposure to Violence*, Cuyahoga Community Health Research Institute, Mandel School of Applied Social Sciences, Case Western Reserve University, Cleveland, OH, 1998.

10. C.S. Widom, *The Cycle of Violence*, research in brief, National Institute of Justice, U.S. Department of Justice, 1992.

11. J.A. Gazmararian et al., "Violence and Reproductive Health: Current Knowledge and Future Research Directions," *Maternal and Child Health Journal*, 2000, 146 (3), pp.309-10. See also G. Margolin. "Effects of Domestic Violence on Children," in *Violence Against Children in the Family and Community*, P.K. Trickett and C.J. Shellenbach (eds.), American Psychological Association, Washington, D.C., 1998, pp. 57-101.

12. *San Diego YWCA Battered Women's Services Study* (unpublished), available upon request at www.familyjusticecenter.org.

13. P. Salber and E. Taliaferro, *The Physician's Guide to Domestic Violence: How to Ask the Right Questions and Recognize Abuse*, Volcano Press, Volcano, CA., 1995, p. 9.

14. Murray A. Strauss et al., *Physical Violence in American Families: Risk Factors and Adaptations to Violence in 8,145 Families*, Transaction Publishers, New Brunswick, NJ, 1990.

15. Report downloaded on December 1, 2005, from the City of Seattle, Human Services Web site: www.seattle.gov/humanservices/director/ConsolidatedPlan/hsdomviolence-needsanalysis.htm. The report is an excellent overview of Seattle's review of the impact of family violence on children and the relationship between domestic violence and sexual assault in one community.

16. Casey Gwinn. *Children Caught in the Crossfire*, presentation to National College of District Attorneys National Domestic Violence Conference. Anaheim, CA, 1998.

17. *The Effects of Woman Abuse on Children: Psychological and Legal Authority*, 2nd edition, National Center on Women and Family Law, Inc., New York, 1994.

18. C. Dalton and E. Schneider, "Battered Women and the Law, the Impact on Children of Exposure to Partner Violence," introduction to *The Development of Research into Another Consequent of Family Violence*, George Holden, Foundation Press, New York, 2001, pp. 250-51.

19. The unpublished *San Diego Pregnant and Parenting Teen Study* was conducted by the San Diego City Attorney's Office in conjunction with the San Diego city schools, and statistics and results from the study are available upon request from the authors.

20. Statutory rape research has continued to focus on the power and control dynamic between older male aggressors and younger female victims. The power and control dynamic in statutory rape cases mirrors most teen relationship violence cases.

    See Sharon Elstein and Barbara E. Smith, *Victim Oriented Multidisciplinary Responses to Statutory Rape*, training guide, Office on Victims of Crime, 2000, NCJ178237.

21. Linda Spears, "Building Bridges Between Domestic Violence Organizations and Child Protective Services," unpublished paper, revised February 2000.

22. Some communities such as Dade County, FL, and Honolulu, HI, have reported success from a unified family court that combines criminal and civil matters related to family violence. San Diego experimented with this model from 2000-2003 and rejected it for a variety of reasons. The foremost reason was the slow decline in the approach of judges in treating the criminal conduct seriously when simultaneous family court issues such as visitation and child custody were being addressed by the judge.

23. Susan Schecter and Jeff Edleson, *In the Best Interest of Women and Children: A Call for Collaboration Between Child Welfare and Domestic Violence Constituencies*, briefing paper prepared for Domestic Violence and Child Welfare: Integrating Policy and Practice for Families, a conference sponsored by University of Iowa School of Social Work and Johnson Foundation with support from Ford Foundation, Wingspread, Racine, WI, 1994. Downloaded on December 1, 2005, from www.mincava.umn.edu/documents/wingsp/wingsp.html.

24. Leslie Kaufman, "Court Limits Removing Child When Mother is Abuse Victim," *New York Times*, October 27, 2004.

25. Susan Schecter and Jeffrey L. Edleson, *Effective Intervention in Domestic Violence and Child Maltreatment Cases: Guidelines for Policy and Practice*, recommendations by the National Council of Juvenile and Family Court Judges, Family Violence Department, 1999. [The Greenbook Initiative has clearly demonstrated that the child advocacy and domestic violence communities can come together if there is proper emphasis on building collaborative interaction between the two movements. The National Children's Advocacy Center approach, Huntsville, AL, also deserves to be recognized, where child advocacy and domestic violence services are provided in different buildings on the same campus.]

26. One child protective worker in San Diego, Linda Ostapinsky, participated in the San Diego Task Force on Domestic Violence. She played a powerful role in opening the eyes of the child protective system in San Diego to the importance of working with domestic violence advocates.

27. "Intervention and Prevention for Children and Youth," Chapter 9 in *Toolkit to End Violence Against Women*, United States Department of Justice, Office on Violence Against Women, 2001.

28. Sandy Miller became a pioneer with her Family Violence Program.

29. Our findings during this period (1989-1994) were reported regularly at the National College of District Attorneys' Annual Domestic Violence Conferences.

30. Nicole E. Allen et al., "Battered Women's Multitude of Needs: Evidence Supporting the Need for Comprehensive Advocacy," *Violence Against Women Journal*, September 2004, 10 (9), pp. 1015-35.

31. See note 29. Our regular reports included our analysis of all cases with a full-time advocate assigned and the impact this advocacy had on judges in the courtroom during sentencing proceedings.

9

Giving Hope and Healing Through Camping

Jasmine was only 11 years old. She had spent time doing what kids should do on a happy summer day. She went swimming in the lake, learned to kayak, tried a little tubing behind a ski boat, enjoyed a barbequed hamburger with some watermelon for dinner, and finished her day with a frog-catching adventure by the ramp to the boat dock at sunset. It was nothing unusual for a little girl from a healthy, middle-class family with supportive parents who had saved money over the course of the last year so Jasmine could go to camp for a week. But this was unusual—unique—even magical. In fact, it was nothing short of miraculous for Jasmine.

Jasmine's family didn't fit into those categories. She did not know how to swim, she'd never been to camp, she'd never been to a lake, her family could not afford to send her to such a place for a week, and she had never held a frog in her hand. Jasmine's dad was in jail. Her mom was in a battered women's shelter. Her parents drank often and usually yelled at her daily. She could not remember a time in her life when she was not afraid for herself and her mom, and angry at her dad. She had never ridden in a boat, could not remember the last time her dad had told her he loved her, and thought her family was like all others. Jasmine was caught in the nightmare of family violence. She lived most of her days in a desperate effort to not think about her family.

And in the midst of the nightmare, Jasmine went to camp for the first time in her life—a camp with a counselor for every three campers, a camp designed to teach children about healthy families, a camp where kids could have the most fun they have ever had in their lives. Jasmine laughed more that week than she had ever laughed in her life. She felt deeply loved, and she saw what loving family relationships are supposed to look like. It was an experience that changed her life forever.

The camp Jasmine attended last summer is called Camp Hope; it is one of the first dedicated camping operations in the country for victims of family violence and their children. It is one of the most exciting healing and therapeutic initiatives yet to grow out of the vision for the San Diego Family Justice Center.

I wish I could say Jasmine's experience and that of hundreds of other children like her started out with a consciously developed strategic plan right from the beginning of our vision for the San Diego Center. I wish I could say we systematically examined the issues, the challenges, and the available resources and developed the plan. But I can't. As is true with many great things in life, we stumbled onto the camping vision and only later developed the justifications and greater plan for its relationship to the Center. I believe in divine appointments, and Camp Hope became one of the those divine appointments born out of serendipity.

A Harley Ride Becomes a Divine Appointment

In February 2003, five months after the opening of the Center, I took a Harley ride one Saturday afternoon. It was a sunny San Diego day. As I drove into the mountains, I was reflecting on many of the challenges we had overcome and many we still had to face in developing the Center. Perhaps the most nagging issue on my mind was what we would offer clients and their children after the initial services. It had been bothering me for a number of months. Where would our clients and their children find hope? Where would they learn to laugh again and enjoy life? A high-rise office building in downtown San Diego might not be the best location to find affirmative answers to those questions.

City Councilwoman Toni Atkins and others shared my concerns. If all we were doing for victims and their children was providing professional services, we were doing a good thing. Life would go on, but who would be there for the victims and their children six months later? Who would have a connection to their lives a year later? Five years later? What opportunities were we offering for such long-term support, encouragement, and professional care?

As I climbed into the mountains of eastern San Diego County that February day, the nagging questions about long-term follow-up and healing for our clients did not go away.

Just west of the mountain town of Julian, I saw a sign for Lake Sutherland. I had never been there (hadn't even heard of it) but felt compelled to turn down the little two-lane road that pointed the way.

As I came around a bend in the road about two miles off Highway 78, I saw it! Sitting down in a beautiful valley surrounded by mountains, boulders, oak trees, and rolling hills was a small, serene lake. No houses surrounded the lake; no development was evident other than a launch ramp and a large concrete dam. As I traveled the three miles down to the lake's edge, a red-tailed hawk circled overhead, a wild turkey ran across the road, and rabbits scampered in every direction. It was a divine appointment.

As I pulled up at the closed gate of the reservoir, the sign explained the location: No Trespassing, City of San Diego, S.D. Municipal Code, Section 84.10. The reality quickly registered. Here in the remote, undeveloped, unincorporated area of San

Diego County sat one of the nine reservoirs owned by the City of San Diego. Open only three days a week, six months a year for fishing and a few weeks a year for wild turkey hunting, Lake Sutherland was one of the most beautiful spots I had ever seen in San Diego. I had grown up camping; the divine appointment was obvious.

This safe, serene spot should be the location of the first dedicated camp in America to serve the needs of victims of family violence and their children. This was the answer to the nagging concerns about hope, healing, and fun for our clients that my colleagues and I had struggled with for months. After an hour of soaking in the beauty, I headed home with hopes, prayers, and some pretty wild dreams about the future of this amazing place.

The next day I talked to my wife Beth into taking a Harley ride with me after church. I did not say a word to her about Lake Sutherland or the events of the day before. She climbed on the back of the motorcycle, and we ventured off into the mountains with no destination identified, as we often did on Sunday afternoon. When I got to the brown Lake Sutherland sign I turned and followed the two-lane road to the bend where the lake comes into view. I said nothing. As we came around the turn, Beth leaned forward and said, "We're going to build a camp at this lake for the Center, aren't we?" There was no need to answer.

The following Monday I called the head of the city's water department and asked for a breakfast meeting. Larry Gardner, the Director, was a dedicated public servant with over 20 years of city service. Larry and I were not close, but I knew he was a man of integrity. At breakfast that morning, I laid out my vision for a camp at Lake Sutherland. Larry listened intently and thoughtfully. After I had been talking for 20 minutes, Larry took another bite of his breakfast then said, "Casey, in the last 15 years, the Water Department has reviewed over 30 proposals for some type of development at city lakes. We have never supported any of them." My heart sank.

The dream seemed so right, but apparently short-lived, as I listened to Larry that morning. He paused and then began speaking again. "But I believe this is the right thing for us to support. It is consistent with the vision of the City Lakes Program. It creates a partnership between the Family Justice Center and the Water Department. And it will help thousands of children and families in the years to come." I was speechless, stunned, ecstatic, and filled with ideas all at the same time. Larry Gardner *got it*. Larry Gardner understood the power of the idea. He became our ally in one of the most exciting public/private partnerships the city has ever developed to help hurting families in our community.

A Camp Where Victims Can Be Safe and Free

In the days to come, the Camp Hope vision spread. The City Manager endorsed it. The Mayor endorsed it. Public officials and business leaders endorsed it. Momentum began to build. But major hurdles remained, including a lack of support from a key member of the City Council. Donna Frye, with strong ties to the environmental community and very little interest in development projects in general, had recently been elected. Her agenda focused on open government, better management of scarce city resources, and limited development.

I delayed meeting with Donna even as excitement for Camp Hope grew among the Center agencies. Perhaps it was fear—perhaps it was a lack of relationship with her, but I waited until after I had presented the concept of Camp Hope to all the other council members. Finally, in April 2003, Donna and I met for lunch at a deli near City Hall. We enjoyed sandwiches on an outdoor patio while I told her of our vision for Camp Hope and its key role in the future of the San Diego Family Justice Center.

After hearing the vision, Donna was silent for over 30 seconds. She took a bite of her sandwich, sipped her water, and sat quietly. I feared the worst. Camp Hope would have environmental impacts. Lake Sutherland was a pristine location that would be changed by the development of a camp. Finally, Donna began to speak. "Casey, you don't know me well. I was married once before." Donna's current husband Skip, a former professional surfer and well-known surfboard maker, was a bit of a legend in San Diego. I did not know it was her second marriage.

Donna continued, "My first husband abused me. When I left my husband for the last time, and carried my bags out the front door of our home, I remember only wanting two things in life—I wanted to be safe and I wanted to be free." For the rest of my life, I will not forget Donna's words. Then she said, "Casey, if you will promise to build a camp where battered women and their children can be safe and free, I will support Camp Hope." I made that promise to Donna Frye, and Camp Hope moved forward to become a reality.

The Mayor and Council authorized a 50-year lease for Camp Hope in June, 2003. Using a local nonprofit organization, we developed a partnership agreement with the City, and really started dreaming. Soon thereafter, we recruited a survivor of family violence who dreamed of helping to start a camp for abused and at-risk children. Tiffanie became our first Executive Director, and we began planning for camping operations to commence during the summer of 2003.

Maybe this won't seem important to you, but for the first time in my life, I got to go to camp! I left (camp) feeling hopeful. For the first time, I didn't feel so bad about myself, like a 'total loser' because I couldn't fix the trouble in my family.

—Jake, Age 9

On July 10, 2003, Camp Hope welcomed its first campers. Using volunteers and the generous donations of individuals and businesses in San Diego, we set up teepees and shade canvases, brought in temporary water, electricity, and portable toilets. With the support of the Water Department and a local state senator, we secured a permit from the state to use the lake Monday through Thursday for water body contact activities, using a boat donated by a local MasterCraft dealer.

Police Chief William Lansdowne helped recruit police officers to camp with our kids. Fire Chief Jeff Bowman helped recruit firefighters and lifeguards to volunteer their time at the lake. Parks and Recreation Department Director Ellie Oppenheim helped us set up a kitchen in the city's concession building to serve meals to kids that first summer. It was amazing to see how many city government leaders, department heads, and business owners donated supplies, and city staff members jumped in to help. We were underway. The dream had become a reality!

Why Choose Camping as Part of the Center Vision?

Why camping? Why did Center staff and partner agencies go down the road with me on this vision for camping as a core therapeutic initiative of a domestic violence service center? With so many challenges facing the movement in providing crisis intervention services to victims of domestic violence and their children, why focus on developing a camp? No battered women's shelter in America runs a full-time camping operation for victims of domestic violence. No specialized domestic violence law enforcement agency in the nation has created such a focus, so why did San Diego? And why should other communities pursuing development of a Center pursue San Diego's vision?

The answer is simple: Camping heals. Camping works. Camping takes people out of their routine, out of their day-to-day lives and places them in a safe, nature-oriented environment where they can focus on issues other than the everyday crises of life. Camping offers the opportunity to remove victims and their children from the terror, trauma, fear, and violence they are experiencing on a regular basis and places them in a safe, fun, and nurturing environment. Research consistently establishes the validity of the healing components of camping, scouting, and related opportunities for young people to be in nature and out of their daily environment.[1]

One of the most important driving forces behind Camp Hope, however, was my own life experience. I grew up at a camp where my dad was the director.[2] My dad invested much of his life in developing a camp where lives could be changed. I had seen firsthand the healing power of camping. For the first 18 years of my life, I was shaped by growing up in a camping environment. I visited camps with my dad in California, Oregon, Washington, Colorado, Texas, and a host of other states. I saw the magic of taking kids out of their own world, their own peer group, and their own unhealthy relationships, and giving them a totally different experience with new friends in a new place, out in the freedom of creation.

In our struggle to find some way to provide help beyond emergency services and the involvement of the criminal and civil justice systems, we had started out by talking about programs that exist all over society—sports teams, after-school programs, church youth groups. We agreed that all of these were important partnerships to develop with agencies that could serve as off-site partners of the Center. But we wanted more. We wanted to create a bond with our clients and their children that would last long after the three to six months of services at the Center.

With my background in camping and the shared experiences of many police officers, prosecutors, and other Center professionals who had gone to camp as children, our path slowly became clear. We would choose camping as one of the fundamental, long-term vehicles to promote healing from family violence. We would pursue camping as a way to offer hope for victims and their children. And we did not want to exclude those kids who had not yet been abused but might someday find themselves in trouble. We therefore included at-risk youth, those in danger of being victimized, of joining a gang in the future, of getting into trouble with the criminal justice system in the future, as candidates for Camp Hope.

Research Supports Camping

Among the many significant findings that have emerged from a hallmark study by Werner and Smith related to ways that children are saved from terrible experiences, most striking is the larger-than-anticipated number of individuals who adapt well as adults, despite having experienced serious coping problems as adolescents.[3] These individuals took advantage of "second-chance" opportunities that came their way during periods of transition in their lives. They had turning-point experiences that significantly improved the quality of their lives.

Turning-point experiences occur throughout our lifespan, yet young people have greater access to them than older adults.[4] Camping provides these experiences for victims of family violence and high-risk children. Camping takes advantage of the dynamic benefits of a small group gathering in a safe, fun location to offer children a positive setting for the recovery process to begin. The unique experiences of a simple camping excursion present a variety of life-changing lessons for each camper.

Since those early days, Camp Hope has now hosted more than 300 campers for day activities, two-day camps, and five-day camps. Children have come from local battered women's shelters, child abuse residential treatment facilities, and other social service agencies that work at the Center. We created a nonprofit foundation to support the San Diego Family Justice Center and Camp Hope and have raised nearly $4 million in cash and in-kind donations to help develop permanent facilities at the lake. Even as we process permits for construction of the permanent facilities, Camp Hope has become a beacon of hope, encouragement, joy, and support for hundreds of children. Though we have not yet developed comprehensive programming for battered women or families, the healing power of camp has been evident.

So many others have joined the vision as well. San Diego Police Chief Bill Lansdowne shares the vision and has helped facilitate "camp with a cop," encouraging San Diego police officers to share the camping experience with the kids. San Diego

Fire Chief Jeff Bowman shares the vision and has helped bring firefighters and city lifeguards to pilot boats, serve as lifeguards, and invest their lives in the children. Churches have provided volunteers. Other camps in the San Diego mountains have volunteered their expertise to help develop the camping operation consistent with the Western Camping Association accreditation standards. The power of *we* has produced results never thought possible when we chose to put our focus on camping just three years ago.

Jake, our nine-year-old camper, probably says it better than I ever could:

> *Camp HOPE is where kids like me—with lots of trouble—can go every summer and feel like other kids. There is lots to do and good food to eat, and all the adults really care about us. I'm not used to that cause in my home and neighborhood, people get real upset and angry a lot, and sometimes, even kids get hurt real bad. The camp people told me that it really didn't cost very much to open the camp last summer. They even picked me up and brought me home in a cool, new van. They told me any kid from a family where there's violence could stay for four nights and five days; enjoy all that good camp cooking, wakeboarding, and water-skiing; talk to counselors who help them feel better about themselves. I can see why they call it Camp HOPE—cause that's just what you get if you're a kid and you go there—hope.*[5]

Makes all the arguments about research and money seem less important, doesn't it?

The Camp Hope Program

The programming for Camp Hope will evolve in the years to come. During the first three years of operation, we have focused on camping only with children rather than adults. We need to develop different types of programs for women, men, and children. We hope to do camps for mothers and their children one day and, someday, camps for fathers and their children. But the initial programming has been extremely well received. Director Mickey Stone has developed a *family* philosophy to Camp Hope.

When the children arrive on the first day, after meeting at the Center for the ride to camp, they are welcomed to the *family meeting circle* and quickly learn that they are joining a *family* for the week. They are told some principles from healthy, happy, nonviolent families that will apply at camp, including: no physical aggression; no name-calling; rewards for encouraging each other; and rights and responsibilities. It is foreign to most of them at the beginning. They don't know how a healthy nonviolent family acts. But as the days go by they experience the Camp Hope family dynamic. The camp theme each year emphasizes the power of a loving family. Last year's theme was "Lean on Me," complete with a well-known theme song!

Activities include the chores of family life—preparing meals, setting up for and cleaning up after meals, cleaning up their teepees, caring for the family possessions (camp equipment), and maintaining toys and games. But there is so much more! The children spend time wakeboarding, waterskiing, tubing, kayaking, canoeing, hiking, and fishing. They rotate those activities with drama, arts and crafts, and music.

Interspersed in the fun and adventure are times around the *family meeting circle* where, as the week progresses, the conversation turns to experiences and tough times they have gone through with their families. Invariably, the conversation leads to sensitive and intimate discussions about violence and abuse. The children soon learn they are not alone in experiencing violence. The counselors become tremendous resources in affirming and encouraging the children. And the healing process begins through the loving investment of life into life. With one counselor for every three kids, the relationships become personal and meaningful between counselor and camper.

Who Else Will Pursue the Camp Hope Vision?

The standard has been set. The example has been proffered. We have special camps for children with cancer, children with multiple sclerosis, and children with disabilities. Why can't we have specialized camps for abused children and children who witness family violence?

As research continues to pour in about the effects of domestic violence on children, the need for such specialized services is clear. A 14-year-old boy who has grown up in an abusive home cannot simply be shipped off to a Y camp and have his life changed. Lost in a camp with 400 children, with one counselor for every eight to 10 campers, that angry, soon-to-be-violent 14-year-old needs special attention. He needs someone to passionately love him. He needs to know that God did not intend life to be lived like he is experiencing it. He needs a mentor and role model to show him what a healthy view of girls and women really looks like, what healthy families look like, and what kinds of choices he needs to make to break the cycle of family violence he is caught in.

Our current Executive Director, Mickey Stone, and many others stand ready to help others whose heart has beaten a little faster while reading this chapter. Many other communities pursuing the Center vision have not yet pursued the Camp Hope dream, but it promises to yield powerful results in the years to come in the lives of many victims and their children.[6]

Mentoring Must Be Included

Another key component that must evolve in a camping vision focused on abused, neglected, and at-risk children is personal relationships, often referred to as *men-*

toring. As we developed the Camp Hope vision in San Diego, we realized that a few days at camp would not change the world for abused and neglected children. It would not provide the long-term support that a single mom might need to put her life together again after violence and trauma in an intimate relationship. Mentoring offers one of the keys to such support.

A Camp Hope counselor began to teach us about mentoring just two years ago. Angela Smiley, a former child advocacy center case worker, came to Camp Hope as a summer counselor. She was young, energetic, and had a heart as big as a house. She wanted to do only one thing at Camp Hope all summer. She wanted to invest her life in the lives of hurting children. She led singing, organized the drama program, and spent her summer sleeping in a teepee with girls seven to 13 years old. But she wanted more for those children than a few days at camp. Each week as camp ended, the goodbyes were tearful and traumatic. We had tantalized the children with hope, fun, excitement, and adventure. We had given them a glimpse of a loving family, of respectful relationships between boys and girls, of what it means to live without profanity, fear, rage, and violence. But five days later we were sending them back to the same unhealthy home life we had just delivered them from.

Angela wanted to keep seeing those children. She wanted them to come back the following summer to Camp Hope. But she wanted even more than that. She wanted a relationship with them during the year. She longed to maintain relationships with them in the midst of their school year, in the midst of their moms trying to put their lives back together, and in the midst of the long journey of a domestic violence victim toward healing and health. Her vision should be a clarion call to all those who work in the field of family violence.

With the support of local philanthropists, foundations, and businesses, we began to develop a mentoring program, a special events program, and a family support program connected to Camp Hope and the Center. The first year it was simply special group events supported by volunteers—Sea World, the beach, Padres games, and a Christmas party. These fun activities began to create a bond and network between the children. As the special events program evolved, it supported not only the children but their mothers and fathers.

Now, the Center is developing a vision for long-term care and support for children and their families, working with other mentoring organizations in San Diego County. Families with children attending Camp Hope will be offered not only mentoring relationships for their children but family support programs for the whole family.

The Camp Hope vision offers an opportunity for any community to pursue a similar approach. How can we network faith-based organizations with domestic violence intervention initiatives? How can we couple mentoring programs and other outreach efforts to at-risk teens with child abuse advocacy and intervention initiatives? How can we build bridges between the silos (the child abuse movement, the domestic violence movement, the sexual assault movement, gang prevention work, human trafficking initiatives, and the like)? How can we connect violence prevention programs with domestic violence programs in order to touch the lives of abused and at-risk adults and children? What role can the domestic violence movement play in reaching out to victims with disabilities? Even as we develop Camp Hope, we are designing a camp that will be accessible to those with disabilities in order to share the unique healing environment with children in San Diego who might never experience a camping opportunity otherwise.[7]

Conclusion

The needs are great. The challenges are great. And the obstacles are enormous. But the threshold has been crossed. The thinking has gone outside the box. The opportunity to use camping, mentoring, and partnerships with faith-based organizations to offer hope and healing to hurting children and their families is possible. It works. It is viable. And the opportunity for a camp experience exists in virtually any community in America. How about a horse camp? An ATV camp? What about a sports camp? What about theme camps that include rope courses, rock climbing, and other safe but physically taxing adventures?

Camp Hope includes wakeboarding, waterskiing, fishing, tubing, kayaking, canoeing, arts and crafts, archery, drama, and a host of other activities coupled with therapeutic counseling, support group opportunities, and one-on-one sharing opportunities with loving staff for children. Why can't it happen across America if we dream big? Let's not say it's never been done before. Let's not say it is too complicated. Let's find a way. Let's expand the Center vision beyond cops, prosecutors, and advocates working out of an office building. In the *Family Justice Center Manual* to be published next year, we will include more practical steps on how to develop a camp as part of a Center. We have so much to do. Let's pursue the healing promise of camping along with the services of a Center!

Endnotes

1. A number of national and international organizations, both secular and faith-based, have developed tremendous resources on the impact of camping in the lives of young people and adults. See www.acacamps.org for a host of resources.

2. My dad, Rev. William D. Gwinn, served as the Executive Director of Mount Hermon Christian Conference Center for over 20 years until 1978. Mount Hermon is a large, nondenominational conference center located in the Santa Cruz Mountains approximately one hour south of San Francisco.

3. Margaret McGrath, D.N.Sc., R.N., *"Journeys from Childhood to Midlife: Risk, Resilience and Recovery," Journal of Developmental & Behavioral Pediatrics*, December 2005, 23, 6, p. 456. Emmy Werner and Ruth Smith conducted on of the most thorough child resiliency studies in history on the island of Kauai from 1955-1995. Early childhood

experiences of trauma, child abuse, and poverty were risk factors for adolescent and adult criminal behavior in the children studied. However, having just one positive, long-term relationship with a parent, family member, or community member (e.g., a friend, neighbor, minister, teacher, or mentor) to whom one could talk about stress could override the risk factors. Werner and Smith identified feeling loved by parents and being able to communicate with and confide in an adult about difficult topics as protective factors that can outweigh risk factors and help at-risk youth. It is this reality that formed the basis for the philosophy of Camp Hope. For more information, see www.preventionworksct.org/infostats/resresearch.html.

4. Ibid.

5. Quoted from Mickey Stone, "Camp Hope—a Reality," *Camping Magazine*, July/August 2005, 78 (4).

6. Ibid.

7. For more information on Camp Hope, go to www.camphopesandiego.org.

10

Making the Family Justice Center Work

By Casey Gwinn and Gael Strack

It was about 4:00 p.m. and I was just finishing a meeting in my office as the City Attorney of San Diego. The San Diego Family Justice Center had been open for over a year. The phone rang. It was Gael Strack, the Center Director. Her voice was frantic. "We have a big problem," she said. My mind raced. Then she dropped the bomb: Someone with red shoes used the bathroom on the police floor at the Center without permission. I pondered her statement for a few seconds and then burst out laughing. Was this a joke? Gael was not laughing.

Within hours, the story became clear. The day before, a female detective in the Police Department's Domestic Violence Unit at the Center went to the restroom. Both stalls were being used. She noted the person in one of the stalls was wearing red shoes. Feeling put out, she used the stairwell to go to another floor and used that restroom. She returned to her desk and continued to fume. Had someone else used the Police Department bathroom without permission?

The detective got up from her desk and did a quick survey of the 6th floor. None of the detectives were wearing red shoes that day! It took astute detectives less than a day to get to the bottom of the red shoe mystery. The suspect was a victim advocate from the 7th floor; she had delivered a police report to a detective and had to use the bathroom before she returned to the community service floor where she worked. Within an hour of the conclusion of the manhunt—well, woman hunt—the inconvenienced detective had complained to her supervisor, and within days nearly 20 detectives were contemplating signing a grievance against the city, which would be forwarded to the Police Chief.

By the time Gael called me, the detectives wanted a formal apology from the city, and the whole idea of moving in together to help violent families seemed like one very bad idea. everywhere. It took a few days to get to the bottom of the Hunt for Red (Shoes) October. But at the core of it all were small problems that had festered into big problems with some very angry police officers at the center of it all. Though laughable at first glance, this incident was much more complicated at its core than anyone could have imagined. And it was no laughing matter.

The grievance letter laid out the whole story. It had been nearly 18 months since the Center had opened. As already discussed, exposure on the Oprah Winfrey Show had brought site visitors from 50 states and 37 countries. Every day, strangers without identification and visitors without background checks streamed through the Center. No advance notice of tours was given. They were conducted morning, noon, and night. On one visit, the lockers in the police officer area were fair game for tour members. Guests from another tour dined on food left in the kitchen area of the law enforcement floor. The grievance letter exposed a lack of security, violated privacy, and compromised work areas. In our excitement and exuberance to show off our innovative Center, we had violated the space of police officers and possibly others. It had little to do with the red shoes. It had everything to do with learning how to make a Center work.

Two weeks later, at a community partners meeting, I stood before a large group of very angry detectives and apologized to them all. We had violated their work space, we had disrespected their values, and we needed to ensure that we would not do it again. One sincere apology from the guy in charge and the temperature in the room went down by 20 degrees. It was a lesson we would need to learn over and over again. When you make a mistake, apologize. When you need forgiveness, ask for it. When you have wronged somebody you live with, fess up to it! True in life, true in Family Justice Centers!

The red shoes have become famous in the lore of the San Diego Family Justice Center. In fact, merely invoking the phrase *red shoes* is still a reminder to us all of the need to communicate, show grace and mercy, and address problems sooner rather than later. They were an unanticipated object lesson for anyone interested in taking coordinated community response strategies and collaboration to the level of moving in together in a specialized service facility. They will forever be the link between the concept and the reality of the Family Justice Center.

The Family Justice Center concept is straightforward. It calls for co-locating professionals and volunteers from public and private agencies in one location in order to provide more effective and efficient services to victims of family violence and their children. As we have seen over and over in this book, the reality is far more difficult than the concept.

The *Family Justice Center Manual*[1] will focus in detail on the practical steps and processes for opening and operating a Center. In the absence of the manual, however, we must introduce the complex realities faced by any community that wants to relocate competing, diverse public and private agencies into a single location. This chapter will touch lightly on the basic challenges in birthing a Center but focuses primarily on the challenges of keeping a Center fresh, innovative, and alive after it opens. It touches on sustainability issues but is more focused on the necessary foundation for maintaining a Center and the change process that must occur in order for it to thrive.

As Family Justice Centers are opening[2] in San Diego, California; Brooklyn, New York; Nampa, Idaho; Tacoma, Washington; Waterloo, Ontario; St. Louis, Missouri; Collins County, Texas; Calgary, Alberta; Monterrey, Mexico; Riverside, California; San Antonio, Texas; Oakland, California; Tulsa, Oklahoma; Ouachita Parish, Louisiana; and Croyden, England, we are quickly finding that opening such a facility is only the beginning of a long, long journey.

Change is The Highest Priority

Bringing people together and moving in together is not the end. Once this new community is created, once this new, living organism is brought to life, the fundamental mission becomes constant change and adaptation. Facilitated strategic planning and problem solving become almost daily activities. Enhanced communication, honesty, information sharing, grace, and mercy must become staples if new Centers are to overcome the challenges of bringing such diverse cultures together in one place.

Not unlike a healthy interpersonal relationship, a Center requires constant maintenance, nurturing, and support. Not unlike healthy children, staff members need a balance of affirmation and accountability. Problems must be dealt with quickly before small issues erupt into large issues. Apologies for real and perceived wrongs must be offered sincerely and freely. Power and control tactics don't facilitate good working relationships between individuals or organizations. Power and control breeds abuse and unhealthy interactions in individual relationships, and it breeds destruction in Centers.

How do you learn to get along? How do you build strong working relationships? How do you bring together people with differing value systems, ideologies, world views, and approaches to service delivery? One organization might provide all services in complete confidentiality. Another might have mandatory reporting responsibilities.

One organization may have a faith-based value system that does not support the core mission of another organization—providing social services to gay and lesbian couples. One organization may have pro-life tendencies; another may have pro-choice beliefs. One organization may be a law enforcement agency that sees criminal justice system intervention as central to any long-term successful outcomes. Another may see the criminal justice system as an obstacle to long-term positive outcomes for the victim and his or her children.

Putting all these folks together may create a fascinating melting pot or it may produce a nuclear reaction that results in toxic gases being emitted all over a community! What makes the difference? How can we lay the foundation for a healthy effective Center from the beginning, and how can we nurture it into a healthy, viable long-term entity for meeting the needs of victims and their children for years to come?

> The proof that a Family Justice Center is successful is when cops and prosecutors can work together while still respecting their different roles. Success is when gay and lesbian-identified staff and pro-choice feminist advocates can work alongside pro-life, conservative evangelical chaplains and stay focused on the mission of helping those in need. No matter what our beliefs and values, we choose to respect each other. The San Diego Family Justice Center is not successful because of political correctness; it is successful because of a shared value to let everybody be who they are while staying focused on the mission of providing the best possible services to victims in need.
>
> —*William Lansdowne, Chief of Police, San Diego Police Department*

This chapter will focus on two key phases to making a Family Justice Center work. The first critical process starts long before the Center opens; the second must be constant, ongoing, interactive, and transparent throughout the life of the Center. Let's think of building a Center just like we think of building a house. You need a plan and then you need to follow the plan.

Much of the philosophy and many of the practical concepts in this book focus on the construction process, the decorating process, and the ultimate moving in and living-together process, but we have touched only briefly on a key piece of building a solid, well-constructed Center. When you build a home, you want to pick the right community. You want to pick the right location. And you want to make sure the soil is good. Jesus said it over 2,000 years ago: Don't build your house on the sand; build it on solid ground. Why? If you build it on sand, bad things will happen, right? Storms will come and wash away the sand. Tough times will destroy that house. The three little pigs learned that lesson, too, didn't they? The object lesson is simple but applicable to developing Centers.

A portion of Highway 52 in San Diego is built over the old city dump. Imagine what has happened! The ground emits terrible odors of methane gas, the road keeps settling and buckling, and the highway has to be repaved every year or two. It is entertaining to ride on but not a place you would want to build your dream home. So it is with Family Justice Centers.

The Center concept developed throughout this book and in the rapidly developing movement across the country is simple: Services for victims are often best provided from one location for the most effective, efficient, and coordinated services possible based on the needs of victims and their children[3]. But what if the soil is bad? What if the city dump is underneath the ground? Translated, what if agencies don't get along? What if the prosecutor does not trust the police officer? What if the shelter community is alienated from other social service agencies? What if there is no history of working together? What if there is no commitment to the fundamental principles that can form the foundation for a Center?

The result will not be a cohesive living organism that grows and adapts to meet the needs of victims and their children. The result may endanger battered women and may make getting help more difficult rather than easier. How do you determine whether you have the right foundation? And if you have it or can cultivate it, how do you then adapt, grow, change, and even remodel soon after you open?

Learning to Live Together

A long journey is the best path to a Center, not a quick formula or checking the boxes on a simple checklist. But even if communities are able to go forward, apply the principles in this book, follow the *how-to* ideas, and make a Center viable, the journey is not over. It is only beginning. Personality conflicts, turf issues, conflicts over offices, disagreements over breakfast snacks for clients, disputes over responsibilities among participating agencies, and a host of other problems will immediately appear. There will be red shoes. There will be hurt feelings. There will be resource shortages. The list of tensions, challenges, and problems is endless.

> At first, the cops were dragging their feet and they didn't want to leave the security of headquarters. We didn't want the City Attorney's Office trying to tell us what to do. We needed to have assurances that our autonomy would be respected. We spent a lot of time working out the issues up front and developing protocols. It was all about relationship building and it paid off.
>
> —*Lt. Jim Barker (Ret.), San Diego Police Department*

So how do these Centers thrive? You figure it out as you go. You commit yourself and don't leave. How can we make Centers work? Get partners to come together and commit to stay together for the long haul, to work through issues and solve them no matter what.

Even if we have the right foundation, the necessary prerequisites, and the key elements in place, what then?

> I've had countless opportunities to witness Family Justice Center volunteers, staff, and community partners all come together to provide everything a victim needed. When clients come to the Family Justice Center they feel the warmth right away…and know that their care and safety is our first priority. For me, it's extra rewarding to have the resources to relocate a family to safety in another city or state. It's beautiful to see everyone working so hard to get the job done. It is an honor to work with such amazing compassionate people. We are a team. We are a family.
>
> —*Mina Moody, Traveler's Aid*

After we opened the San Diego Family Justice Center, the issues came down like rain. Who is in charge? Where does the buck stop? Who makes the final decisions about policies and procedures? What if an agency has a staff member assigned to the Center who cannot get along with other partners? Indeed, there was no end to the questions, the issues, and the problems to be addressed.

We began to address the issues systematically, keeping our sense of humor in the process. Four major components have formed the basis for making the San Diego Family Justice Center work. Each component deserves discussion here. Each component can point the way for other Centers in the future.

First, we identified a governance structure with clear processes for who was in charge. A Center cannot be healthy if it is not clear who has the ultimate responsibility for how it functions. Second, though the governance structure was clear at the outset, we also created processes for significant input from and dialogue with all partnering agencies. Third, we created events, activities, and special opportunities to build community together. By helping the Center develop an identity, helping staff create memories together, and providing conflict resolution processes, we facilitated the most fundamental element of a Center: positive, healthy personal relationships.

Finally, we implemented policies, procedures, and protocols that continually attempted to re-focus all participants on the mission—meeting the needs of victims and their children. If everyone stays focused on the mission, many things fade to insignificance. Many conflicts become less important when everyone involved is constantly reminded of what the Center is all about.

Each of these components can and must receive focused attention if Centers are to become successful and stay successful. Each of these components, therefore, deserves focused attention here.

Governance

To be sure, there is no single governance approach that is appropriate for running a Center. In reality, there is no single model that is right for all communities.

All Centers should support the fundamental goal of multidisciplinary, co-located services for victims of family violence. Services should come from a variety of community partner agencies that bring staff to a single location, while maintaining autonomy as local agencies. Any governance approach must provide for this fundamental element. In addition, each model should be supplemented by a strong volunteer component. Beyond that, the likelihood is strong that each community has unique strengths and challenges that may lead them to one model over another.

Drawing on experiences of the San Diego Family Justice Center and the models of existing child advocacy centers, the approaches listed here identify core models that every community should consider. Each model's potential strengths and weaknesses should be analyzed in the context of a particular community.

Public Agency Driven-Host Agency Model

In this model, one existing public government agency acts as the host of the Center and provides broad leadership for planning and implementation. Leadership is typically provided by a visionary who believes in the model. This model was used to create the San Diego Family Justice Center. We recruited the support of the Mayor, City Council and Police Chief. While the San Diego Domestic Violence Council was important in the development process, an individual elected official, the City Attorney, led the way.

When local government funds underwrite the Center, there is a clear, long-term buy-in that draws outside community organizations to the table. The risk comes when the Center is linked to a specific elected official, and a political successor does not support this vision. There may also be conflicts down the road when the public agency vision does not match with that of the community board created to help support the Center. This model may work best if only a small number of management employees are hired by the public agency while most on-site service provider staff remain employed by their own individual partnering agencies.

Local Government Department Model

Under this model, the Center is established as a separate, unique department within city or county government with an appointed department head, and core governance and fiscal responsibilities managed by city or county employees assigned to the department. In this model the entire Center is the responsibility of the governing entity, including that of building relationships with service providers.

This structure will work well if the executive management team provides freedom and autonomy as necessary to community-based, nonprofit organizations that place staff at the Center. It may tend to overemphasize prosecution and law enforcement services unless precautions are taken to prioritize community-based input.

In San Diego, this model was adopted after the initial success of following the public agency driven-host agency model, and the San Diego Family Justice Center Foundation 501(c)(3) was established in order to provide financial support to the Center and Camp Hope. In this model, the Center is managed by public agency employees in collaboration with community partners. However, most service providers remain under the authority of their own organizations, even while working at the Center. In the absence of strong, collaborative strategic planning, this model may lead to confusion among the roles of the public agency, the foundation, and the community partners unless clear roles and responsibilities are worked out in advance.

Independent City or County Agency/Corporation Model

In this model, a legal entity with quasi-government powers and authority is formed to oversee the Center. This model has not been used with an existing Family Justice Center and has only rarely been used by a child advocacy center, but many local governments develop joint powers authority entities to collaborate on any number of specific projects. It is a potential model for long-term sustainability and for establishing multiples sites within one region. The model allows for multi-government leadership structures and financing options such as a bond measure or special tax to support operations. Tulsa, Oklahoma, is considering this model in order to have regional power as a major public safety initiative.

This approach ties the Center closely to public safety funding from many cities in a region, although it may take a very long buildup of political will to support such an entity. But it focuses on what should be true—stopping domestic violence should be as important as stopping drunk drivers or gang bangers or bank robbers. It should be part of the highest priority of government—public safety.

Independent Nonprofit Agency Model

This approach involves sponsorship by an existing private, nonprofit entity or creation of a new 501(c)(3) organization to manage the Center. This new entity assumes responsibility for governance and philanthropic outreach, as well as future public and private funding, under an independent board of directors with an appointed executive director. This is the most common governance of child advocacy centers.

In this model, decision making is in the hands of a community board of directors, which may create conflicts with law enforcement and prosecution public agencies that normally provide funds and benefits for employees. In addition, there may be a perception of competition for fund-raising and private underwriting for existing agencies. Concerns about the identity of the Center, the separate mission of the sponsoring agency, and the use of public funds to support a single nonprofit enterprise may develop.

If your eyes are glazing over, don't fret. There are many in your local government who can assist in sorting out these options if your community gets excited about creating a Center!

There is little doubt that this movement will chart new territory in developing workable governance structures for each Center as it develops. Every community will need to evolve just as the San Diego Family Justice Center has. San Diego was the first truly comprehensive multidisciplinary family violence service center of its kind in the country when it opened in 2002. Yet in the first three years, it has moved through three of the models described above. The lesson from San Diego is applicable to all communities seeking to develop a Center. Each community must be willing to pursue a particular governance approach, but also be willing to reevaluate, change, and adapt, depending on issues and challenges that arise as a Center develops over time.

Ten Important Steps to Making a Center Work

Before actually moving into the Center, our transition team began looking at core issues to ensure a successful grand opening. Below are the important steps we recommend in making a Center work.

Use a Strategic Planning Process to Operate

A good strategic plan and a dynamic facilitator can help any organization stay focused and accomplish its goals. Our strategic planner, Judi Adams, funded by the California Wellness Foundation, was the difference between success and failure. However, the community must be willing to invest in the process and commit to the action plans. The strategic planning process is an opportunity for all of the partners to become involved in the design and share their varied expertise. During the process, community partners can develop a vision for effective service delivery, cultural competency, and community outreach. The vision can be compared to the day-to-day operation of the Center. By including the day-to-day service providers in the strategic planning process, the Center will have an effective reality check while "vision casting." The strategic planning process can then become a road map for day-to-day operations instead of simply being a set of long-term goals.

As each Center develops its own unique operational plan, soliciting the help of a qualified strategic planner can be a wise investment of time and money. Each part of your Center will be better thought out with the aid of a strategic planner. The day-to-day working relationship among on-site and off-site community partners will be far stronger if they have worked through the issues involved in developing a workable strategic plan together.

> After working in human service systems for close to 30 years, I finally have found a program that has accomplished "second order change." For me, it's like going on a diet, losing 30 pounds and keeping it off for life.
>
> —*Judi Adams, Family Justice Center Strategic Planner*

One strategic planning process may not be enough to cover all the demands and needs of a Center. Designing the model may take multiple phases and even multiple plans. For example, in San Diego we developed the initial model, then a one-year strategic plan, and then a five-year strategic plan. Each plan changes the model for providing services. Never underestimate the importance of ongoing planning. Your strategic plan also needs to be flexible enough to capture new ideas that were not included in the original plan and a way to orient and educate new players on how your process works. Many of your partners may not be accustomed to strategic planning and find it uncomfortable and threatening.

Share Leadership and Development of an Infrastructure

Although a Center is a community partnership, a leadership team needs to be clearly identified to maintain continuity and direction. A Center needs a management team to provide the day-to-day management. For San Diego, our management team included a director, a manager of operations, a manager of client services, a budget/grants analyst, and administrative support. This management team works together to provide leadership, supervision, and oversight of day-to-day operations. You may want to research collaborative leadership models to help you design a model that will work best for your community partners. Developing an organizational structure to manage operations is crucial to a Center's success. This structure will vary, depending on the lead agency, the community partners, and the available resources.

After all necessary positions for supervision and management have been identified, it is important to define each person's roles and responsibilities. Likewise, when selecting the actual staff assignments, consider the strengths of each individual assigned to that position. Working at the Center requires, among other things, the ability to work well with others, the ability to handle a high-stress environment, and flexibility in addressing unanticipated day-to-day challenges.

Below is an overview of the duties your leadership, management or administrative team will likely be responsible for. Each Center's structure may vary, and position titles and particular needs therefore will vary, but this list provides a basis for developing a management structure. The individuals chosen to lead the Center must work together closely and will often need to act as a team in addressing many issues:

- Providing overall direction and vision for the Center.

- Providing leadership to ensure the mission and the philosophy are maintained.

- Identifying new partners when needed.

- Developing partnership agreements.

- Managing Center funding.

- Developing primary and secondary liaisons with community partners.

- Managing the facility.

- Providing liaison with building management/ownership if the office space is leased or rented.

- Coordinating site visits.

- Supplying liaison with providers of information technology services to the Center.

- Developing policies and procedures related to Center operations.

- Developing, modifying, and updating an operations manual.

- Developing and overseeing a volunteer program.

- Finalizing systems installation, including furniture, computer systems, etc.

- Coordinating events.

- Overseeing and developing training.

- Scheduling, coordinating, and conducting site visits to other centers even after the Center is operational.

- Coordinating communication and disseminating information such as a newsletter.

- Gathering statistics.

- Answering requests for information via the phone, mail, e-mail, or in person.

- Facilitating intake of clients and service delivery.

- Addressing confidentiality issues and sharing information in order to evaluate the program.

- Arranging and overseeing security.

- Furnishing orientation for new partners, staff, and/or volunteers.

- Arranging staff recognition and awards.

- Developing shared sustained funding.

- Participating in strategic planning.

- Supplying community outreach.

Ongoing communication and problem solving is critical, but everybody at the Center comes to the problem solving with their own approach! We discovered early on that each of our community partners has its own problem-solving strategies. Crucial to our success is not taking ourselves too seriously and keeping our sense of humor. When things heat up at the Center and conflict finally erupts among partners—which is normal and expected—we joke that everybody's own "stuff" comes out.

The police officers usually want to separate the parties, take statements, and ultimately arrest someone!

The prosecutors want to air grievances in open court, take testimony from witnesses, and introduce evidence. They want to argue! They demand a ruling, and any unfavorable rulings will automatically be appealed.

Therapists and advocates, on the other hand, want to slow everything down to find out *how everyone feels*! They are intent on revisiting those feelings over and over again until they are satisfied everyone is happy again.

The chaplains are secretly praying for us!

The medical professionals simply want to spike the water cooler with Prozac. Actually, they really do start talking about medication when things get hot!

Judi, our strategic planner, wants us to stop everything and develop an action plan.

Imagine when these different styles and approaches all gather in the same room to solve a problem. Understanding everyone's different approach, which is based on training and beliefs, goes a long way toward understanding, resolving, and preventing future problems among partners.

Needless to say, it is imperative that processes be set up to address personality conflicts, agency conflicts, and the impacts of change and innovation on the established practices of the disparate community partners. A good rule for problem solving comes from our good friend Phil Keith, former Police Chief from Knoxville, Tennessee. He encouraged me to apologize quickly. He said, "It's better to eat crow while it's still warm; it goes down smoother."

Provide Access to a Multidisciplinary Team of Professionals and Services

Each Center needs to provide as many services for victims and their children as possible and in the easiest way possible. The following are just some of the services that should be considered to be part of the one-stop shop approach:

+ Prosecution.

+ Law enforcement.

+ Civil legal services (temporary restraining orders, court representation for contested hearings related to custody support, protective orders or contempt hearings, and immigration).

+ Crisis and/or individual counseling as well as support groups in various languages.

+ Forensic documentation of injuries.

+ Limited medical services.

- Spiritual support from faith-based organizations.

- Military advocacy.

- Access to child protective service professionals.

- Access to adult protective service professionals.

- Access to victim witness services and restitution recovery.

- Child care.

- Parenting programs.

- Sexual assault advocacy.

- Access to mental health and substance abuse professionals.

- Access to emergency shelter and housing.

- Transportation assistance.

- Food and clothing.

- Access to workforce partnership/job training programs.

Give Careful Consideration to the Location

The location of a Center is critical to its success. The location should be easily accessible to clients, should be close to the courts and public transportation, and should have adequate parking for the clients, site visitors, and staff. For safety reasons, the location and the building should be somewhat anonymous so it does not attract any unnecessary attention. In San Diego, for example, victims told us during our focus group process that they wanted to come to an anonymous location. They did not need to come to a secret location, but they did not want a clearly identified social service building.

In identifying a location, plan for the inevitable growth that will occur as awareness about your Center grows. New partners will approach you and want to be a part of your Center after you are underway. You will also identify needs that require additional partners to be added after the Center is operational. In San Diego, we have added more services for children, more agencies, and prevention programs, which were not part of the original operation.

Give Careful Consideration to Space Planning

The design of the space needs to be victim-centered, friendly, and accessible. During the space planning process, make sure you have enough space to meet the needs of the partners, such as sufficient offices/cubicles for staff and volunteers, adequate interview and waiting rooms for adults and children, exam rooms, storage space, and training and conference rooms. In San Diego, we dramatically underestimated the necessary storage space for donations and needed supplies. In planning your Center, consider the following:

- How will clients move through the Center?

- How will you maintain a safe, yet friendly, environment for victims in the reception area and at all entrances and exits?

- What will your interview rooms look like?

- Will they have your existing "early government garage sale" furniture? Or will you consider nice living room furniture with soft lighting and artwork?

- Will you have a kitchen where food can be provided to victims and their children?

- Will you have a children's play area that is visible to parents and where children can easily be supervised by staff?

- How much room do you need for the most popular services you will deliver, such as legal services?

- Where will your bathrooms for clients be located?

- Will you have separate restroom facilities for victims, children, and/or staff? How will you decorate—same as you always have—or will you be bold enough to try something new?

- Will Center staff need a place to get away and relax, such as a kitchen or a lounge that is exclusively their own? Consider involving your staff in the design of their work space, meeting areas, and training rooms. Bringing the staff into the process will pay dividends down the road, even in such matters as picking out the furniture for work areas. You may also want to consider where various partners should be located in order to protect and promote confidentiality and agency autonomy.

Perhaps one of the most important lessons learned in San Diego is that you will always need more space than you have available. At the onset, we had an opportunity to lease an additional floor in the building we had chosen. We decided against the lease because the cost was significant and, at the time, we had no need for additional space.

I was one of the first partners to move into the Family Justice Center. Even though I was the only one representing our agency, I didn't feel alone. I would soon be joined by many other professionals and discover how empowering it is to be here with them. It makes my job easier.

—Jan Maiden, Civil Attorney, San Diego Volunteer Lawyer Program

Think Safety at Every Level of the Operation

As a Center is developed, safety for the clients and staff must be a top priority. To maintain a safe environment, client screening policies were critical to San Diego's Center and must be developed for any Center. Determining who should receive services and who cannot receive services is a complex task. Criminal defendants with pending cases should not receive services at the Center. Such potential clients should be referred to private social service agencies. The more complex issues arise when a current victim has previously been arrested or convicted for a domestic violence offense. The San Diego Family Justice Center intake staff members address these issues on a case-by-case basis. Some current victims with previous arrests or convictions are provided services while others are referred to off-site social service agencies.

> The lines of communication between the criminal justice system and the medical community have been open like I've never seen before. There's mutual respect for the expertise that we each bring to the Center. I'm thrilled to see so many diverse professionals there.
>
> —*Diane McGrogan, Licensed Clinical Social Worker*

For all potential clients a simple computer check when they first come in can assist in deciding whether services should be provided. The Center's receptionist can conduct this first screening process before a client is allowed into a secured area. Be prepared to offer other services and referrals to anyone who is determined to be ineligible to receive services at the Center. Care should be given in determining who will inform clients that they are not eligible for services. Realize that not everyone will welcome the decision to exclude them from services.

All staff should be trained in responding to security breaches, emergency procedures and protocols that deal with emergency evacuation, and emergency response to potentially dangerous or hazardous situations—similar to a fire drill!

Respect Confidentiality Issues

Each client should be assured that her case and the services she receives while at the Center will remain confidential. Partners and staff work together in a concerted effort to ensure client confidentiality is maintained by each agency providing services.[4] Each client, however, should be informed of mandatory reporting laws that may cover certain community partners. In San Diego, for example, the Forensic Medical Unit operates under California's Medical Mandated Reporting Statute.[5] All patients are advised that injuries resulting from a criminal offense must be reported to the Police Department's Domestic Violence Unit located at the Center.

Though great controversy continues to swirl around medical mandated reporting, such informed consent has not been a major issue at the San Diego Family Justice Center.[6] When the client feels safe and is wrapped in services, confidentiality concerns and the sharing of information do not become major issues. *Only a handful of the approximately 500 clients referred for forensic medical examinations have declined medical services* after being advised about the legal requirements of medical mandated reporting.

Agencies such as the Police Department, the District Attorney's Office, and the City Attorney's Office all have reporting obligations as well as discovery obligations to criminal defense attorneys in pending cases. Such legal obligations do not allow these agencies to provide all services in confidence. But a clearly worded consent form and a clear advisory to clients about the limits of confidentiality at the Center can alleviate most client concerns. Notably, since the opening of the Center only a few clients have declined to sign a consent form to authorize the sharing of information among agencies for the benefit of the client being served.

To avoid potential legal issues, each client should sign a confidentiality agreement to keep confidential what they see and hear at the Center. This agreement should be one of the forms the client receives when checking in with the receptionist. It is also important for staff to participate in this agreement. Confidential conversations between staff and clients should never occur in any public location at the Center. Oftentimes a simple question-and-answer session in a hallway can quickly turn into a longer discussion of the specific issues involving the client. On-site staff should be regularly reminded to share confidential information in a confidential setting. The issue of confidentiality should be part of regular discussions among staff at the Center.

Create a Client-Centered Flow Process Throughout the Center

Advocates and survivors should play a central role in designing the intake process. Advocates have the background in assessing clients' needs and providing services. Survivors have the perspective of those most in need of the Center's assistance. Ongoing feedback from clients will help to refine the intake form as the Center evolves.[7] Each Center needs to find a simple and efficient way to provide services.

In San Diego, we started with a reception form for all arriving clients. We added a specialized intake form to determine which service partners clients wanted to

---

I love working here. It's so rewarding. I get to see the difference the people and the services from the Family Justice Center mean to victims. You can see it on their faces. They walk in upset and scared but walk out looking different. They seem more confident and less afraid. They know we're all here to help and they're not alone.

—*Brenda Lugo, Receptionist*

see and an exit survey. Part of the intake process should collect relevant demographic information that will assist with program evaluation. Clients should also be asked to complete an evaluation of their visit prior to leaving. This feedback will be invaluable as the Center changes over time.

In San Diego, regular focus groups with clients provide meaningful feedback used to keep the intake system client-centered. The commitment to a client-centered approach must be constantly reiterated. "It is the responsibility of justice personnel and victim service providers to facilitate victim safety planning, utilize available safety planning tools and conduct risk and lethality assessments."[8] Many large bureaucratic organizations tend to move more and more toward staff-centered service approaches over time. Don't let it happen!

Estoy muy agradesida por la ayuda que e resivido pues nunca imagine que algien podria interesarse en alludarme gracias. (I am very grateful for the help I was given. I had never imagined that so many would show an interest in me and be willing to help. Thank you.)

—Veronica, Family Justice Center Client, 2005

In San Diego, we started out using a paper system but quickly realized that an automated system was needed because of the number of clients. The use of an intake management system assists with maintaining a constant flow of clients receiving services from community partner to community partner. Volunteer case managers are assigned to oversee the flow of clients and ensure that each receives the personal touch by escorting them from community partner to community partner. Volunteer case managers also pay close attention to time, knowing that every minute counts. They will monitor and manipulate the intake system to ensure clients do not have to wait unnecessarily for services. In many ways, they operate as air traffic controllers to accomplish a proper flow.

It is recommended that the initial system be as simple as possible while each Center studies how its system will work best. Be aware that the system may change several times before you develop one that does work best for you. Be careful to allow a sufficient amount of time to assess progress before making changes.

Consider the Funding Needs of Community Partners

Financial issues can become very touchy. On one hand, each agency moving into the Center must be responsible for its own funding for assigned staff. On the other hand, the Center does not want to begin operations and then regularly lose valuable partners. In San Diego, we often chose not to pursue a certain funding source in order to increase a community partner agency's chance of receiving a grant necessary to help them stay at the Center.

We try to avoid competing for funds. But it does happen. No matter how hard all agencies work to support each other, some competition for limited funds will occur. One agency will lose the funding source for its Center staff, and another agency may have to replace it. Each partnering agency must be challenged to support the vision with or without funding from the Center financial team.

> The Family Justice Center is an amazing concept! When any city is thinking about opening a Family Justice Center, it is important to remember that victims of domestic/family violence are walking through the door in crisis. Volunteers may be available to meet and greet the client; however, it is imperative that mental health professionals are available to conduct intakes and mental health assessments. A one-stop shop must include mental health professionals that are trained to assess for and respond to high-risk factors, such as suicidal and homicidal ideation, as well as being skilled and trained to work with children who have witnessed the violence. The San Diego Family Justice Center has worked hard at taking those steps and including the mental health professionals every step of the way.
>
> —*Cindy Grossman, President, San Diego Domestic Violence Council*

To survive the challenges of limited resources and funding, be brave and address the *F* word (funding) head-on. Anticipate that the Center's on-site partners will likely suffer some funding challenges and even lose funding for their staff to be on-site. Recognize that their funding challenges will ultimately become the Center's funding challenges. Challenge your financial team to look beyond the general operating costs of your Center. Take the time to learn about the financial needs of each community partner, try to create an agreed-upon funding plan, and support their efforts to seek funding.

Develop a Volunteer Program and a Meaningful Sustainability Plan as Soon as You Open

Developing the perfect sustainability plan, how to pay the bills in the long run, is not a simple assignment. If it were simple, someone would have written a book by now called *Sustainability for Dummies*. Instead, in this section we offer a few guiding principles to consider when it comes to developing a viable sustainability plan.

Volunteers are the lifeblood of a Center. If you focus on them, recruit them, and develop a program around them intentionally and thoughtfully, you can come close to doubling your workload capacity with volunteers. Today the San Diego Family Justice Center has over 100 active volunteers who commit a minimum of 12 hours per month to the Center. Like other aspects of the Center, the volunteer program has been hailed as a model for Centers everywhere.

> The Family Justice Center has engaged the community. We have over 100 volunteers from all walks of life. We have seniors, retired executives, college students, survivors, chaplains, nurses, lawyers, and therapists all donating their personal time and experiences to helping others. Everyone here at the Family Justice Center feels a sense of ownership in making our dream a reality and making a difference in people's lives.
>
> *—Sgt. Robert Keetch, San Diego Police Department*

The Center's approach to developing and using volunteers was a dramatic shift from the approach of most of the other agencies before they moved to the Center. Historically, if a person had a pulse, brain waves, and had not been recently released from prison, we were willing to have them join our agencies as a volunteer! But we decided to create a top-notch program and require volunteers to pass a police background check, attend a 40-hour academy, pass a final exam, and graduate before serving at the Center. Sgt. Robert Keetch was tasked to develop a program based on the highly successful San Diego Police Department Retired Senior Volunteer Patrol Program. In the upcoming manual, a step-by-step process for developing a volunteer program will be laid out, but for now we must acknowledge the powerful role that volunteers fill at the Center.

When we say "sustainability," we are talking about how a facility will pay for itself down the road—after the first grant runs out or after the first major donor stops giving you money. How do you plan for the financial future at a Center? First, develop a "Community Curriculum Vitae." When it comes to funding a community project, funding agencies will want to know about a community's commitment to the issue of domestic violence prevention and intervention. Don't be bashful about telling them about your vision for the future and about the organizations or individuals who have already invested in your community efforts. Rural communities may need to be creative in identifying every possible resource they can to show some level of commitment to helping victims. Many poor, rural communities must go after state or federal dollars rather than seeking significant money at the local level, but even then community curriculum vitae can be helpful.

Second, write your community's Domestic Violence Movement history now. Often, the detailed history of collaboration in a community is not documented. It's time-consuming and takes a lot of work. You may need to do a lot of digging to find out the history of your community's response to domestic violence. Often, this

> When I first learned the Family Justice Center had a critical need for volunteers, I jumped at the chance. I knew I could help them get started developing a volunteer program and also bring all my friends. Three years later, I'm still volunteering and love it! Everyone really makes us feel appreciated, which makes all of us want to help even more."
>
> *—Carolyn Wilson, First Family Justice Center Volunteer*

history is not written down; it is stored in someone's memory files, which means someone will likely need to interview many of the original movers and shakers to recreate the community's historical response to domestic violence. If you can show a long-term commitment from your local government and civic leaders, this will likely impress donors and convince them that the community is definitely committed for the long haul.

Third, think about starting a foundation dedicated to the Center. By doing so, you are saying to donors that you are committed to the project for the long haul. You are announcing to your community that this issue matters. But most importantly, you are developing a long-term funding source. You are also creating a team, made up of foundation staff and board members, to work on long-term sustainability. In San Diego, we hired a professional fund-raiser to lead our foundation.[9]

Conclusion

Though the concept of a Family Justice Center is straightforward and grounded in common sense, achieving the reality can be a painful and often frustrating journey. Agencies don't want to cooperate all the time. Many staff may enjoy the new culture for a time but then will slowly begin reverting back to their own organization's norms, values, and culture.

Don't forget the importance of volunteers and "people power." Volunteers can be a great resource, in the form of money and community support, when seeking grants or pursuing sustainability. Often, volunteers are willing to help with the day-to-day needs of running a Center, administration, community outreach, special events, and aiding your foundation with fun raisers and fund-raisers.

The biggest lesson learned, as touched on over and over in this book, is that the operation of the Center is an evolving process. People of varied backgrounds and talents moving in together for a common purpose will have challenges, but the struggles will be worth the result—*effective help for hurting families.*

Endnotes

1. For more information, go to www.volcanopress.com.

2. For more information, go to www.familyjusticecenter.org.

3. Del Martin, *Battered Wives*, Volcano Press, Volcano, CA, 1983, p. 123.

4. *Promising Practices, Improving the Criminal Justice System's Response to Violence Against Women*, Stop Violence Against Women Grants Technical Assistance Project, NCJ-172217, p. 8.

5. California Penal Code, Section 11160.

6. Mia McFarlane, "Mandatory Reporting of Domestic Violence: an Inappropriate Response for New York Health Care Professionals," *Buff. Pub. Interest L. J.*, 1998-99, 11, pp. 20-32.

7. Melanie Shepard, "Evaluating a Coordinated Community Response," Chapter 9 in *Coordinated Community Responses to Domestic Violence, Lessons from Duluth and Beyond,* Sage Publications, Thousand Oaks, CA, 1999, p. 169.

   See also "Coordinated Community Response," *Promising Practices*, Chapter 7, p. 251.

   Ibid., "Ongoing Evaluation."

8. *Promising Practices*, "Victim Safety Planning," Chapter 1, p. 15

   See also Jill Davies, *Safety Planning with Battered Women, Complex Lives/Difficult Choices,* Sage Publications, Thousand Oaks, CA, 1998, p. 113.

9. The San Diego Family Justice Center Foundation is a private, nonprofit 501(c)(3) corporation with a 15 member Board of Trustees.

11

Measuring Success and Evaluating What Works

By Gael Strack

What Took You So Long?

We were in the middle of our first focus group of 20 clients who had received services at the Center. The conversation covered the expected range of personal experiences, including which services were utilized and which were not. At the end of our focus group, the most remarkable question came from a client named Della. "What took you so long?" It stopped us in our tracks. I glanced at the other professionals with me—Judi Adams, our Strategic Planner and Kimberly Pearce, our Director of Client Services. I could tell that we all understood the implications of Della's question. It reached far beyond the walls of San Diego's Family Justice Center. Della simply wanted to know what took so long to open the Center. She continued, "If only this place had been here just five years ago, my life would be so different. And my children's lives would have been different."

Della said that five years earlier she did not know where to turn. She had no place to go. She didn't want to testify in court. In fact, she actively avoided testifying in court. She ignored our calls and dodged our subpoenas. She wanted help from social service agencies but had lost the sheet of paper the police officer gave her. She tried to call 411 to find those agencies, but they kept referring her to the wrong place. Nobody answered at some numbers and others were disconnected. She became frustrated and gave up. Her husband was threatening her on a daily basis. He said if she dared to show up in court to testify against him, he would get even with her. He promised to make her life miserable and do everything he could to take her children away. Della felt she had no options. She had to go back for the sake of her children. She was tired of trying to figure it all out.

When she returned, she knew nothing had changed despite her husband's promises and tears. Della told us, "He continued to make my life miserable. I'm tired of him getting away with it. That's why I'm back here with another case. But this time, it's different. You're all here at one place. It's much easier now. And I just want to

You guys are very great people, thank you, and god bless you! The people here are the only people that seemed to care and understand my situation. I can't thank them enough for listening to me and believing in me. Domestic abuse in the gay community is just as painful and serious as any other form of domestic violence, but usually no one cares.

—*Todd, Family Justice Center Client, 2004*

know what took you so long to figure this out? Don't you know we've all been waiting for a long time for something like the Family Justice Center?"

Della's question still sends chills up my spine and it energizes our efforts to continue expanding the Center. It's that one question that repeatedly came up in the early focus groups: What took San Diego so long to co-locate all the professionals under one roof to make it easier for victims and families struggling with domestic violence? From that moment forward, we were humbled by the realization that there were thousands of hurting families that needed us to figure it out and get it right.

There were other questions as well as we spread the word about the most comprehensive Center in America for victims of family violence and their children. The professionals in the community frequently asked "How do you know this is going to work? How are you going to measure success? How will you know when you're successful?" It didn't take us long to figure out that what everyone really wanted was proof that the Center concept really works. It also became clear that neither our years of experience nor thousands of anecdotal stories from victims, police officers, and advocates were going to satisfy their inquiries or their curious minds.

Soon after our opening in October 2002, we needed to provide clear evidence whether the Center concept was working. We needed concrete answers and we didn't have them. My philosophy has always been, when in doubt, form a committee. If you don't have the answers, someone else will. So we started yet another committee, but this time we invited professionals who really knew how to evaluate programs.

We started by inviting colleagues with whom we had previously worked on research projects. They were well recognized and respected in the research community and quite curious themselves about the concept of co-location of multidisciplinary professionals. We discovered they too wanted to know if it could work and how it would work. And, they wanted to know if we could get along with the new living arrangement—25 agencies with staff in one place, 120 professionals, and 100 volunteers working together every day in a high-pressure, high-stress working environment where life and death hung in the balance in every case.

Starting with No Money

At our first evaluation committee meeting, we shamelessly picked their brains about how to get started, who to invite, what could be studied, how long it would take, how much money it would cost. We quickly discovered we had a problem. We had no money to pay them for their time and expertise. Fortunately, we were advised that the researchers would come if we made good use of their time, stayed focused on the purpose of the committee, and were willing to share information and data for use in future studies that could be funded and/or articles that could be published.

To make good use of their time, we enlisted the help of Judi Adams, our grant-funded professional facilitator/strategic planner to develop a stated purpose for the committee. The purpose was to design a practical evaluation strategy for the Center that "will *identify practical outcomes* that can be used *to shape policy and improve our community response* to domestic violence." We also decided to include professionals from the Center on the committee. We all needed assurance that if we invested our time and energy in this evaluation process, the results would be practical. I knew I would not be able to get anyone at the Center—the police, prosecutors and advocates in particular—to read anything the evaluators wrote unless is was useful in day-to-day operations and useful to the on-site professionals. It also had to be in plain language, not "researcheze," as we grew to affectionately call the strange language of researchers.

Getting to Know Each Other

It took a full year. At the first committee meeting it became painfully clear that we were coming at this from two very different perspectives. Those of us working at the Center were the practitioners. Our new friends were scholarly researchers and academics. We had no prior working relationship as a group, which meant we first needed to get to know one another. And we quickly discovered we knew very little about research and the researchers knew very little about the criminal justice system or the Center. So we started at the beginning. We explained who was on-site and what services were being provided. We explained (in excruciating detail) our mission, our vision, our strategic plan, and each and every goal ever articulated

---

In law school, it's all about academics. Working at the Family Justice Center has helped me put a face on domestic violence. I now realize it could happen to anyone. I'm amazed how many people care about victims of domestic violence here. The Center makes every effort to ensure the victims won't feel betrayed in seeking help . . . an important experience for these victims, who have already been betrayed by their partners or spouse. I can't even imagine what it was like before the Center.

—*Kate Lyon, Legal Intern/Law Student*

in our grants. It turned out to be a worthwhile exercise for several reasons. Quite frankly, we had never taken the time to chart all these articulated goals and figure out how they all connected to the vision. The researchers gave us homework assignments at the end of every meeting. This was going to be hard work.

The next step was to show the evaluators everything that had been created at the Center thus far so they could develop a design tool to evaluate success. We showed them our operations manual, our grant proposals, our consent forms to protect confidentiality and share information with other partners, the forms we used to conduct client intakes, the statistics we were collecting to demonstrate how the services at the Center were being used, and the automated intake system. The evaluators quickly saw things we hadn't seen. They pointed out data we should be gathering. They pointed out how information should be collected. We responded by modifying our forms and computer systems to improve our ability to collect data and analyze our programs.

In turn, we had to learn the ABCs of research and evaluation. We also needed to understand their terminology and ultimately develop a glossary for the work group to help us stay focused. During our early meetings, we had huge philosophical discussions and disagreements about evaluation and what to evaluate. They wanted to study quality-of-life impacts, the qualitative impacts on clients of utilizing services, as well as to dissect the impact of each service on clients. To the professionals working at the Center this seemed over the top, especially considering the day-to-day struggles of running the center.

Defining and Measuring Success

Prior to creation of the evaluation committee, Jackie, the Center receptionist, measured success by the number of calls she could answer within an hour without having to put a victim on hold. She measured success by whether we had access to translation services for our clients within 15 minutes or less. And, having enough staff on-site would mean she could take breaks and go to lunch on time. That was nirvana to Jackie. To our police detectives and prosecutors nirvana meant having enough staff to be able to devote quality time to the cases that were sitting on their desks. To the advocates, nirvana meant increased victim empowerment, victim autonomy, and economic justice. To me, as the director of the Center, nirvana was just having happy, well-trained, and experienced staff; sustained funding' and harmony among the 25 on-site partner agencies, none of whom reported directly to me.

To meet our researchers halfway, we quickly educated ourselves about research and evaluation. I purchased Jeffrey L. Edleson's book, *Evaluating Domestic Violence Programs*, and read it from cover to cover.[1] I shared what I learned with others. Then it hit me—success means different things to different people. There will always be disagreement about how to measure success. Even if our distinguished evaluation team figured it out, there would always be someone from another agency somewhere who would see things differently. And ultimately, who gets to decide if the work we do in San Diego is successful? For us, it became quite simple: Our victims would decide. If we were going to be a *victim-centered* facility, we must let our victims/clients tell us if we are being successful. They must help us with focus groups and client surveys. Our academic/research friends would play the foundational role, but our clients would prove to be the best compass of all.

In the process of developing client surveys and focus groups with victims and on-site partners we also discovered another issue—what to call victims. Police, prosecutors, judges, and probation officers work with *victims*. However, advocates work with *survivors*.[2] Doctors have *patients* and therapist have *clients*. While recognizing the movement's reluctance to call battered women cases or clients, we had a unique situation as we began to develop our own Center vocabulary. There wasn't one word that worked for everyone, but by consensus and with the guidance of our focus groups, we agreed to use the word *client*. People seeking help did not want to be called *victims* or *battered women* or *battered men*. Everyone understood that we needed to maintain a customer service approach, but in order to recognize many of the confidentiality issues we would regularly encounter, *clients* became the best choice for our Center.

> I felt very insecure and frightened about the decision to come here, but everyone I met with today reassured me. They were on my side. I have hope!
>
> —*Elizabeth, Family Justice Center Client, 2004*

Ultimately, our evaluation committee decided we would start the evaluation process by analyzing who was coming to the Center, finding out what services our clients were utilizing, and identifying the services that still needed to be provided. We devised a plan to review the data in our existing database, approximately 2,000 clients. We also developed focus groups and survey questions for our clients. All this information would be reviewed and summarized by our evaluation team.

The Client Profile Study

Dr. John Landsverk, one of our volunteer researchers, took the lead in profiling the clients and the services they used. He recruited staff from his Child and Adolescent Services Research Center (funded by the National Institutes of Mental Health) and members from the Family Justice Center's evaluation team to develop a client profile.[3] The Child and Adolescent Services Research Center is affiliated with Children's Hospital, with strong ties to San Diego State University. The profile was completed in August 2004 from information derived from the Family Justice Center's intake system thanks to the help of our research scientists Andrea Hazen and Cynthia Connelly. It covered the period from October 2002 through April 2004. Our team studied a total of 2,226 random client intakes.

One of the first things we learned was that many intakes were not being electronically logged due to constraints on staffing levels at the Center. Many clients coming in to see certain agencies were not having their visits documented, particularly during high-volume intake periods. When there was sufficient staff at the Center, electronic logging was consistent and complete. However, when it was busy, electronic logging stopped, and staff directed their efforts to helping clients. From manually prepared daily records, we knew that Center staff had seen steady growth and increase in clients from October 2002 through April 2004. The first month the Center was open, staff recorded 87 walk-in clients. By April 2004, the number of clients had grown to 500 per month. But the profile told us much more.

We learned that many of our clients would return to the Center for additional services—the range was from one to 11 visits. Our clients were referred to the Center by police (44%), prosecutors (9%), shelters (9%), on-site community partner agencies (8%), friends (6%), family members (1%), media (1%) and other (22%). Our clients were primarily seeking civil legal assistance (42%), as well as help from detectives (6%), city attorney advocates (9%), transportation (12%), military advocates (3%), and other help such as chaplain services, counseling, or medical/forensic documentation (22%).[4]

Out of 1,570 unduplicated (not counted twice even though they may have come back) clients in the profile study, we learned that 91% were female and 9% were male. They ranged in age from 15 to 89 years old, with the average client being 34.8 years old. They represented all races and ethnicities: White (38%), Hispanic (33%), African American (15%), Asian (7%), American Indian (1%), and other (7%). English was the primary language spoken, followed by Spanish (22%) and other (3%). However, anecdotally, Center staff still reported that up to 40% of our clients speak Spanish. Our clients were single (40%), married (38%), divorced (11%), separated (7%), and cohabiting (5%). Given San Diego's proximity to military bases, we saw many clients with a military affiliation (12%). Annual family income ranged from under $10,000 per year (47%) to over $100,000 (1%). Our clients had anywhere from one to eight children, with the average being two. Most of our clients came from within the San Diego city limits: central San Diego (57%), east county (5%), north central (22%), north coastal (1%), north inland (5%), south (7%), outside San Diego County (4%).

Client Focus Groups

We initially conducted five focus groups with a randomly selected set of clients between April and July 2004. A summary of the results was prepared by the Child and Adolescent Services Research Center in July 2004. Three English-speaking groups were conducted with a total of 17 women participating, one group was made up of seven Spanish-speaking women and one group consisted of three men, for an overall total of 27 participants. Participants commented on the range of services received at the Center. The researchers discovered primary themes related to (a) helpful aspects of services, (b) benefits of services and perceived changes resulting from services, and (c) recommendations made by participants. The actual statements from clients in the focus groups (in italics) always grabbed us! Here's what the researchers reported:

Helpful Aspects of Family Justice Center Services

Caring personnel

- Staff members were described as friendly, helpful, patient, comforting, and reassuring.
- Staff was available when needed and took the time to listen.
- Contact with staff left clients feeling respected and safe.

Safe environment

- Clients reported feeling safe at the Center.
- They described the Center as a warm, comfortable place in a good location where they could go for respite and access to services.

For the first time in months, for the first few months of my experiences, I felt safe here. I was here from opening to closing because I felt so safe here and this was really important to me.

Professional organization

- The services were provided in a quick and efficient manner.
- The services were also seen as being very responsive to addressing problems and meeting needs (such as legal assistance to obtain restraining orders).

Helpful services provided

- In addition to the main services offered, clients appreciated getting information on next steps, referrals for other services and help in communicating with others in the system.
- Clients also commented over and over on the convenience of having needed services under one roof.

Having all the services together in one place was so nice, I can't even tell you!

Benefits of Services/Perceived Changes Resulting from Services

. . . they helped me here . . . . My life is much better now than it was before. I feel more able to take care of myself and stronger. Before I came here I was scared of everything. It has changed me a lot. I can stand up for myself more. I'm not as afraid.

- Participants reported feeling stronger and more independent, better able to care for themselves, and not as afraid.
- They reported having improved relationships with others.
- They described themselves as being able to make better/stronger decisions and to pursue goals again (e.g., return to school).
- They felt that they were able to make changes that resulted in obtaining visitation with their children or regaining custody.
- Clients indicated that they were comforted by the recognition that they are not alone and could see that others were going through the same thing.

It made me feel like I was not alone; other people have experienced what I went through. The people here who I talked with understood my situation and validated my experience. That made me stronger.

Concerns Expressed in Focus Groups

General

- Concerns were expressed about police or legal system response:
  - police handling of cases
  - delays in legal proceedings
  - lack of knowledge about what is occurring with the offender in regard to the criminal justice system
  - follow-through to ensure guns are taken from offenders
- Concerns were expressed about the impact of exposure to violence on their children; most of the participants who had children stated that the children were in counseling or needed counseling.

I would like to be in the loop of what happens with my offender. . . . I continue to file police reports. But not knowing what happens when I file, and where he is, is a big concern for me.

I feel really guilty because for years my children lived in a home full of domestic violence. Because they suffered, they need to go to therapy for a long time. I hope they will continue to go to therapy and will continue to heal. I want them to understand that they do not need to live that way.

- Some concerns were also expressed about the quality of shelter/housing currently available for victims of domestic violence.

Specific to the Center

- Being turned away from services because not eligible or service wasn't available.
- Negative encounters with some staff members.

Recommendations Suggested by Participants

Fine-tuning existing services

- Importance of having staff and volunteers who are well-trained, compassionate, and knowledgeable about services and resources available within and outside the Center.
- Importance of being able to speak to a person when calling rather than a message or recording.
- Speeding up intake on busy days.
- Improved communication regarding services available on-site when people first come in.

Find ways to make sure people are more aware of all the services that are available. Not just that the Center exists, but what it has to offer.

- Conduct intakes in a private area, not the waiting room.
- Offer male-friendly services (e.g., provide written materials that are gender neutral, include more men on staff).

If there had been more males working here, that would have helped me open up. If a male would help me or I saw more males here I might feel more comfortable.

Additional services

- Support groups that meet monthly
- Monthly lunches with presentations on topics such as housing
- Additional legal clinic lawyers to decrease waiting time

- Safe place to meet with other clients/coffee shop

- Employment assistance

- Financial support, temporary financial assistance

- Counseling for children affected by the violence

- Childcare

- On-site phone banks to make and receive calls

- Help with moving; storage assistance (for personal possessions such as furniture)

Daily Client Exit Surveys

We also developed a daily client exit survey tool to solicit feedback from clients and evaluate the delivery of services as quickly as possible. Comments from the client surveys have been included throughout the book. Using a scale from 1 to 5, we asked each client the following questions:

- How was your experience checking in with the reception?

- How was your experience in hospitality while you waited?

- How was your experience with the intake specialist?

- Were services explained and offered to you?

- How would you rate the overall services provided to you?

- How would you rate your overall experience?

- What is your feedback on your visit?

Overall, the evaluations were extremely positive, heartfelt, and inspirational. They were also practical. Through these surveys we learned what food and beverages to provide clients and children. We learned about room temperature. We learned whether staff members were caring and nurturing, and we learned which staff members from which agencies should never work at a Center again!

The direct feedback from our clients through focus groups and client surveys continues to inspire and motivate our evaluation committee and our agency part-

---

As a researcher, I know it's too soon to conclude whether the Family Justice Center works, but the early signs are very promising.

—Dr. Andrea Hazen, Family Justice Center Researcher

ners. Such statements should challenge every interested community to move down the Center vision road:

The most helpful were legal services, chaplains (spiritual support), and counseling. All services were helpful. Legal was really helpful. With legal, my abuser was convicted, got a restraining order (which I would have never gotten on my own). The chaplain was good for my soul. The chaplain was the one who referred me here initially and helped with my immigration services. All the services were here. Every time I walked in here—there was always somebody there with something nice and comforting to say. I felt thankful for the people here and their helpful (and positive) attitudes.

Socorro was an angel for me. Seven months ago Socorro told me that she'd bring food to me. I was in desperate need and had no support or help. Socorro brought me diapers, food, and other goods—nobody else has taken the time after work to help. Jan Maiden is excellent as my attorney. She feels more like a friend, not just like an attorney. Marta has helped a lot, too. So has Juan Gonzales. Everyone at the Family Justice Center has helped me to save my marriage. My husband is in therapy and in counseling, too.

I had a phone call from my husband (he's not supposed to call me, but he did) when I was here. I had a three-year restraining order. The detective made a report for me and answered the call from my husband while I was here in his office.

For the first time in months, for the first few months of my bad experiences, I felt safe here. I was here from open to closing because I felt so safe, and this was really important to me. The nurse examined me and I was able to get a real exam, not just looked at but touched and really examined. The nurse was wonderful.

This was such a handy, peaceful, safe, and professional building. I didn't feel like I had to go to a bad part of town, and that made me more comfortable to come in and receive services. The building provides a sense of home and security. It had a good location. My only suggestion is to have a phone bank here to receive messages for victims that people could access if they ever have the need. My attacker is in prison now and I'm safe.

There's such a sense of security here. After experiencing what we go through, you can become desensitized to the whole thing. Coming here provided me with a backbone. Here I was seeing other people who were here; all kinds of people, professional, from the street, people you would walk by everyday form all walks of life and have no idea they were going through the same thing that you were going through, too. It made me feel like I was not alone; other people have experienced what I went through, too. The people here who I talked with understood my situation and validated my experience. That made me stronger.

A lot has changed. It's been a positive change. I'm still here and I'm not just running away and fleeing back to Germany. I still have the opportunity to be here. I feel at home here (in this country). My offender finally had his hand slapped. I found out I was not his first victim, there was another woman before me. But each time he violated his restraining order I put him in jail. The Family Justice Center was very helpful in that. You don't walk around and hear about domestic violence. It's helpful to learn more, hear more and grow.

I'm more secure and more independent. I'm going back to my studies. I'm especially much more secure about the issue that I don't have my papers here yet. We're working on it together. Now, I feel better. I'm not afraid any more. Thank you for the Family Justice Center.

Current Research Pending

The evaluation committee is currently engaged in its first comprehensive evaluation. The project is small but will point the way forward. The National Institute of Justice assisted in reviewing our research design. The initial project will give us our first comparative data on victims of domestic violence in San Diego that do not access a Center and victims that do obtain comprehensive Center services. The research should be available for publication within a year.[5]

Homicide Reduction Data

The evaluation committee will also focus on additional analysis of the impressive homicide reduction numbers being reported by the San Diego Police Department and the San Diego Domestic Violence Council since the beginning of collaborative efforts toward a coordinated community response in 1986. San Diego's domestic violence homicide reduction data garnered national attention both before and after the opening of the Center.

In 1988, led by Lt. Leslie Lord of the San Diego Police Department, the fledgling San Diego County Task Force on Domestic Violence planning team participated in a homicide file review of domestic violence-related homicides in the City of San Diego in 1985. Lt. Lord, assisted by Homicide Unit detectives, identified 30 domestic violence homicides in San Diego in 1985.[6] In 1992, Sgt. Anne O'Dell conducted a similar analysis with the assistance of Homicide Unit detectives, identified 22 domestic violence homicides in 1991 in San Diego.[7] Between 1985 and 1991, the San Diego Task Force on Domestic Violence implemented a series of coordinated community response initiatives including the creation of specialized intervention services throughout the criminal justice system.[8]

In 1991, the City Attorney's Office began to pursue co-located, multidisciplinary services following the theme of the Center vision. The vision started small with professionals from the YWCA Battered Women's Services and the Center for Community Solutions first co-locating with prosecutors in the City Attorney's Domestic Violence Unit. By 1994, detectives from the Police Department's Domestic Violence Unit and prosecutors from the City Attorney's Domestic Violence Unit began to rotate between their agencies two to three days per week. This early approach to co-location clearly laid the groundwork for future development of the Family Justice Center in San Diego. It also played a central role in continuing the consistent decline in domestic violence homicides over a period of years.

In 1991, San Diego reported 22 domestic violence homicides. In 1995, a similar review identified 13 such homicides. In 2002, the year the Center opened, the Police Department reported nine domestic violence homicides.[9] In 2003 San Diego reported seven such homicides, in 2004, six,, and in 2005 only five.[10]

The evaluation committee intends to conduct further analysis on the readily identifiable data related to domestic homicide from over 16,000 client visits since the opening of the Center. At the time of publication of this book, no client who has participated in the Center intake process, danger assessment evaluation, and clinical assessment has been killed by his or her partner. During the last four years, however, the City of San Diego has experienced a total of 27 domestic violence homicides (24 women, 3 men). None of the victims participated in the full array of services available at the Center.[11]

Conclusion

Without question, there is much to be learned about the effectiveness of the San Diego Family Justice Center model. Early data, however, suggests only powerful positive effects from the co-located, multidisciplinary service delivery approach. While such results are clearly limited in extrapolation only to the San Diego experience, they point the way for other communities. Perhaps most importantly, San Diego's focus on client feedback and client service effectiveness evaluation reminds all communities pursuing the Center vision that no measurement of success is more important than the satisfaction of victims of family violence accessing available services.

Though additional evaluation will be critical, a great deal of national attention has focused on the reduction in domestic violence homicides during San Diego's journey to and since establishment of the Center. The domestic violence homicide reduction numbers between 1985 and 2005 place San Diego with a small number of major U.S. cities that have experienced domestic violence homicide reduction rates in excess of 90%.

Endnotes

1. Jeffrey Edleson, , Ph.D., *Evaluating Domestic Violence Programs*, Domestic Abuse Project, Minneapolis, MN, 1997.

2. Susan Schecter. *Women and Male Violence: the Visions and Struggles of the Battered Women's Movement*, South End Press, Cambridge, MA, 1982, p. 63.

3. Jim Barker, San Diego Police Department; Elizabeth Becker, UCSD; Jennifer Bodine, Crime Victims Fund; Cynthia Burke, San Diego Association of Governments; Amy Carney, Family Justice Center, Forensic Medical Unit; Cynthia Connelly, Child and Adolescent Research Center; Ted Ganiats, UCSD; Casey Gwinn, City Attorney; Rusty Kallenberg, UCSD; Sgt. Robert Keetch, SDPD; Diane Lass, Student; Sandy Liles, SDSU; Suzie Pennell, retired researcher; Renee Sievert, Consultant; Mary Ann Stepnowsky, Family Justice Center; Gael Strack, Family Justice Center; Dr. Ellen Taliaferro, Family Justice Center, Forensic Medical Unit.

4. San Diego Family Justice Center, Evaluation Committee Client Profile Study, Charts.

5. San Diego Family Justice Center, Evaluation Committee Initial Comparison Study, Research Design.

6. Lt. Leslie Lord reported on her homicide review project in 1988 at the San Diego Task Force on Domestic Violence Planning Team Community Needs Assessment Meeting. Lt. Lord reported that she categorized homicides based on the definition of domestic violence found in California Penal Code, Section 13700. In addition, she included a number of unsolved homicides where the primary suspect was identified as a domestic partner as defined in Penal Code, Section 13700. She reported that 26% of all homicides identified by Homicide Unit detectives in 1985 were domestic violence-related.

7. Sgt. O'Dell presented her findings in her feasibility study for the creation of the San Diego Police Department Domestic Violence Unit requested by Chief of Police Robert Burgreen. She also utilized the definition of domestic violence from California Penal Code, Section 13700, for her review.

8. See San Diego Task Force on Domestic Violence Final Report, June 1991, available upon request at www.familyjusticecenter.org.

9. Critics of the San Diego homicide reduction data acknowledge the reduction but question causation. During the development of the Family Justice Center, we recognized the validity of the criticism. Given the difficulties in controlling for all variables, it is impossible to point to any single cause. Instead, we believe the consistent reduction in homicides over the last 20 years is the result of a host of initiatives and efforts from many different agencies working together. Few, however, can question the overall decline that, to our knowledge, gives the City of San Diego the lowest domestic violence homi-

cide rate of any major city in America. Today, San Diego has a population of 1.3 million people, with evidence of consistent population increase each year since 1985; yet domestic homicides have continued their 20-year decline.

10. The San Diego Police Department identifies domestic violence homicides based on the definition of domestic violence contained in Penal Code, Section 13700. This approach maintains consistency with the homicide study conducted by Lt. Lord in 1986 for purposes of data comparison. The Penal Code definition does not include suicides or the death of children. These deaths have not been included in San Diego's reported domestic homicide numbers at any time since 1985.

11. In 2005 the City of San Diego experienced one domestic violence homicide where the perpetrator had been prosecuted by the City Attorney's Domestic Violence Unit. The victim did come to the City Attorney's Domestic Violence Unit, housed at the Center, to meet with an advocate. Sadly, she did not access any other Center services. A fatality review process related to this case is underway.

12

Helping Kids, the Elderly, and Rape Victims

Monica came to the San Diego Family Justice Center to get a restraining order. She could not take any more verbal, emotional, and physical abuse. She needed to get out. She arrived about 9:00 a.m. with her four children in tow. Her children were 13, 9, 7, and 4. Monica went through the cafeteria-style intake menu with an advocate but chose only to work with the Center for Community Solutions. As her children were being fed and cared for in the kitchen and playroom, Monica met with a lawyer to file for a domestic violence restraining order against her boyfriend. It was an appropriate place for her to come for that need. The Center's focus is on violence between adults in intimate relationships. But there was more to Monica's story, and we were not equipped to deal with the rest of it.

Thirty minutes into her meeting with the civil attorney to obtain a restraining order, Monica made a stunning disclosure. She was listing all the reasons why she needed a restraining order, including experiencing emotional, physical, and sexual abuse. Then she paused and said that she also feared for the safety of her children. She told the attorney that she worried that her boyfriend had been sexually assaulting her 9-year-old daughter. When asked why, she said her daughter had made a few comments and had blood in her underwear. In fact, she believed her daughter was bleeding from the rectum. Immediately, the case was no longer simply about domestic violence between the adults in the relationship. The San Diego Police Department was immediately notified of the disclosure of child sexual abuse. The 9-year-old daughter was in the playroom of the Center when her mother disclosed her suspicions.

But then it got very, very messy. Under the San Diego Police Department's child abuse protocol, a report of molestation triggers a patrol officer response. The patrol officer was required to respond and screen the case before calling a child abuse detective. After a child abuse detective responded and confirmed reasonable suspicion for a report, the officer was then required to transport the child to the child advocacy center for an initial screening.

Once notified, I was upset. The mother was safe at the Center. All four children had been there for hours by now. They had become accustomed to the facility and had been welcomed by our volunteers with open arms. But according to the child abuse protocol, we needed to take the child (alone) from her siblings and mother and transport her across town to the child advocacy center. It made no sense. I called Lt. Jim Barker, then-head of the San Diego Police Department Domestic Violence Unit. Jim confirmed that was the policy and they had to follow it.

But it got worse. A patrol officer was not available to come to the Center to take a report. Finally, three hours later, an officer responded. Then the child abuse detective was not available for over an hour. By now, it had been six hours since the mother first disclosed the suspected anal intercourse. By the time the child abuse detective authorized the girl's transfer from the Family Justice Center to the Chadwick Center for Children and Families (our local child advocacy center), it had been seven hours. The girl now refused to talk. Days later, the 9-year-old victim was finally transported in a police car to the Chadwick Center for a forensic interview and examination.

Two days after that, charges were filed and a warrant was issued for the boyfriend. Within a week, he was in custody. Today, he is serving over 20 years in state prison for sexual assault on a 9-year-old girl. Our system held an abuser accountable, but the process was shameful.

In Monica's case, we got the bad guy, but her story reminds us how far we still have to go in providing services where domestic violence and child abuse overlap. Yes, we got him, but in the process we exposed the glaring dysfunction of a system with large, separate, often impenetrable "silos" known as the *child advocacy movement* and the *domestic violence movement*—silos designed not for the benefit of families as much as for the benefit of the system. We touched on this in Chapter 8 when looking at the impacts of family violence on children, but the issue is much broader when we look closely at the domestic violence, child abuse, sexual assault, and elder abuse movements in our culture. The bottom line is clear: We need to provide the same type of services to children, the elderly, victims with disabilities, and rape victims that we are providing to domestic violence victims through the Family Justice Center model.

We have separate and distinct social change movements going on in this country. They share some foundational elements, but they are different social change movements in many ways and have resulted in different laws, policies, procedures, and protocols throughout the criminal and civil justice systems. I refer to them as silos. Silos, of course, usually hold grain in the Midwest. They are extremely tall and stand out proudly across the countryside. But the silos I am referring to here are systems. We have the child abuse silo, the domestic violence silo, the sexual assault silo, and now, most recently, the elder abuse silo. In this chapter, we need to look briefly at the genesis of each of these important intervention and prevention systems and then look at how the Center vision can and should open the doors of the silos and help build connections for the sake of women, men, and children who need their services brought together, not separated.

The core focus of any new Family Justice Center should be providing services to victims of domestic violence and their children. First, from the beginning meeting the needs of battered women has been the reason for the creation of Family Justice Centers. Second, Centers must address the needs of the children of domestic violence homes. Why? Because no one else is doing it well, because the need is so great, and because battered women bring their children with them when they come to a Center for services. We cannot allow Family Justice Centers to develop but allow their children to be carted off to a child advocacy center or to five separate agencies where services can be provided to them. Finally, Family Justice Centers provide the best hope for comprehensive services to battered women anywhere in the national and international domestic violence movement. Based on the constant feedback from clients using operating Centers in San Diego and around the country today, it would be difficult for anyone to argue there is a better model for comprehensive services to victims.

The Family Justice Center concept offers the best approach to bringing together not only agencies helping domestic violence victims but bringing together services for elder abuse, child abuse, and sexual assault victims as well. We cannot continue to do business in this country in separate movements. We must become one movement, with everyone working well together and completely focused on meeting the needs of victims instead of meeting the needs of the system.

—Bonnie M. Dumanis, San Diego County District Attorney

But Family Justice Centers cannot stop with services to victims of domestic violence and their children. We already know too much about the positive impacts of bringing committed professionals to one location to provide domestic violence services to not conclude that the co-located services model is the right model for elder abuse and sexual assault systems. We know it is the right thing for the child abuse movement because they are already doing it with the creation of 500 child advocacy centers in the last 25 years.

As we look at the major social change movements related to interpersonal violence over the last 30 years, we find essentially the four major movements mentioned earlier These movements are all intimately related, as we will discuss later in this chapter. But these movements are quite separate sociological phenomena. Understanding the development of each movement will help inform our ultimate efforts to bring them together under the Center vision.

A Short History on Separate but Related Movements

In the early 1900s the child advocacy movement was born. It grew out of the animal rights movement. The first laws on the books related to child abuse were modeled after laws related to animal abuse.[1] The American Humane Association first called for the elimination of child abuse.[2] It is a sad commentary that our culture cared for abused animals before it cared for abused children. But that would be a separate book!

As the movement developed and laws were passed, the child advocacy movement evolved into a formidable social change initiative in the 1960s and 1970s. Specialized centers to serve the needs of children began to develop in the late 1970s and early 1980s. Child Advocacy Centers now number more than 400 across America.[3]

The sexual assault movement developed with multiple influences from the civil rights movement, the women's movement, and the child abuse movement. The first enforced laws and specialized policies on sexual assault developed during the 1960s and 1970s. Specialized sexual assault investigation and prosecution teams emerged in the early 1980s. Fueled by support from the women's movement and the growing political power of women, Sexual Assault Response Teams began to emerge with specialized protocols and policies for investigating and prosecuting sexual assault in the late 1980s.[4]

The domestic violence movement grew out of the women's movement, but it developed its own evolutionary path as the battered women's movement emerged in the mid-1970s. The domestic violence movement evolved with distinct connections to the sexual assault movement in the advocacy arena. This was facilitated by the reality that many domestic violence victims were also being sexually assaulted by their partners.[5]

But as specialized services were created, protocols for domestic violence and sexual assault interventions diverged. Sexual assault response teams developed with a hospital focus. By definition, most sexual assault cases could not be proved unless the victim alleged forced sexual activity. In contrast, as feminist ideology about domestic violence mainstreamed itself into the criminal and civil justice systems, the focus was not on victim participation or cooperation but on offender accountability. Indeed, the primary criminal justice intervention innovation in domestic violence over the last 20 years has been evidence-based prosecution.[6] The notion became that we could and should prove domestic violence cases even if the victim was unable or unwilling to participate.

On the contrary, no approach similar to evidence-based prosecution evolved in the sexual assault movement. Even today, if a rape victim does not want to testify, cases generally do not go forward. The Kobe Bryant case taught us that in living color on national television.[7] Kobe Bryant got off not because he was innocent but because his victim could not survive the terrible revictimization of a very broken criminal justice system.[8] The domestic violence movement, however, driven by the call to hold batterers accountable, did indeed develop prosecution strategies to go after batterers even if the victim refused to prosecute. This profound difference has separated the two movements in significant ways that complicate the need to bring them together.

The elder abuse area developed as the population aged and we began seeing seniors being abused. While some of the abuse was by an elderly mate (domestic violence), other abuse being identified was in residential care facilities or at the hands of a grown child now caring for a disabled parent. And the abuse was not all physical. Gradually, neglect, financial exploitation, and other forms of verbal and emotional abuse were identified.

The response from AARP and other major national organizations advocating for the elderly was to develop specialized responses to victims of all forms of elder abuse.[9] Task forces were formed. Laws were passed. Specialized police officers, prosecutors, and advocates developed across the country. In San Diego, a deputy district attorney named Paul Greenwood invested his life in elder abuse work and quickly became a national and international expert in the prosecution of elder abuse cases.[10] Conferences developed, protocols and policies emerged, and elder abuse was here to stay as an important part of the movement to stop violence and abuse against vulnerable human beings.

Though each of these dynamics in the social change process deserves more attention, the point is clear: Domestic violence, child abuse, sexual assault, and elder abuse have quite separate etiologies. Each of them has a different genesis and each arena has developed in somewhat different patterns. The effort to bring them together, however, is not new. For many years, some have called for the coordination of all such efforts in an "anti-violence" or "anti-abuse" movement.[11] Others have focused on patriarchy and a feminist analysis of violence that points to power and control behaviors as the link between each of the movements. Prosecutors' offices have created Family Protection Divisions or Family Violence Projects with the goal of bringing together all such cases under one roof in the prosecutor's office. But a brief review of the literature, conferences, research, and the reports of specialized professionals focused in each area makes the reality clear: These intervention areas have remained distinct and not terribly well coordinated.

The research, as noted earlier, confirms the overlap between the separate movements and the related *silos* that have evolved to provide the resources for victims in each arena. Between 50% and 75% of all children growing up in homes where violence occurs between adults are also being physically or sexually abused, depending on the study you read.[12] Depending on the study, between 20% and 50% of all reported elder abuse is actually perpetrated by an intimate partner.[13] It is "domestic violence grown old."

The majority of battered women in shelters do not describe themselves as victims of sexual assault when they first disclose domestic violence. But when asked if they have ever been forced to engage in sex acts against their will, the majority say *yes.*[14] Indeed, the majority of victims of sexual assault in this country are assaulted by someone they know.[15] The majority of children molested in this country are not assaulted by a stranger but by someone in their own home.[16] The intimate connections between domestic violence, child abuse, elder abuse, and sexual assault cannot be ignored.

The Family Justice Center vision offers a new paradigm for bringing the silos together. The evolving model described in this book promises to give us an opportunity to bring professionals from each of these movements to one place so victims can come to one place for most of their services.

As noted earlier, we are still advocating for starting the co-location process with only domestic violence professionals. It keeps the focus on addressing violence and abuse issues with the parents or adults in the home first. It allows us to work closely with the battered women's movement in developing intervention strategies that protect battered women while acknowledging the gender-specific nature of the large majority of domestic violence—that most domestic violence is perpetrated by men against women.

At the San Diego Family Justice Center, we started with our focus on adult victims of intimate partner violence. It was the correct approach. This has been confirmed by focus groups conducted regularly with Center clients who have praised our focus on meeting their needs with specificity. Sadly, entities that try to be everything to everyone and to do everything for everyone are far more likely to create chaos and, in the process, meet very few needs of those they are seeking to help. Thus, the logical progression: Start with victims of domestic violence and then add services for children. After meeting the needs of women, men, and children, then start using the growing power and synergies of your facility to meet the needs of victims of sexual assault and elder abuse.

Bringing in Child Abuse Professionals

In San Diego, we began the Center with very little focus on children. In fact, our children's room on the first community services floor was less than 120 square feet. We were focused on the adult victims. We wanted to *do domestic violence work* well. Though we remain happy that we started with a focus on adult victims, we soon realized the need to adapt. Women were coming to get help with their children! Children were arriving in large numbers—as many as 100 children a month in the early months of the Center. And we quickly learned that children in a safe setting will begin to disclose their own "stuff." If the research is accurate, then approximately half of those children coming in have been physically or sexually abused. Imagine 50 children a month at the San Diego Family Justice Center who were physically or sexually abused and we had no on-site services available to them!

We quickly went into high gear in looking at the options for how to meet the needs of children. We talked to a number of national organizations about possible partnerships. We looked at the research literature. And we asked our clients what they needed. Finally, we settled on our own child advocacy team in San Diego at the Children's Hospital, Chadwick Center for Children and Families. To be sure, we had been working collaboratively with the Chadwick Center (formerly The Center for Child Protection at Children's Hospital) for many years. In fact, Dr. David Chadwick, the founder, helped us begin to work on the overlap between child abuse and domestic violence in 1988-89. But we had certainly never thought about moving in together!

What would normally take us a week to get accomplished now takes us a day. We can also assist multiple clients without ever having to leave the Center—one client may be at the legal clinic, another at the Forensic Medical Unit, and yet another meeting with a detective. It's made a huge difference for our clients and their children.

—Jackie Dietz, Children's Hospital

The discussion with the Chadwick Center for Children and Families was the culmination of all of those years of relationship building. As discussed in detail in Chapter 8, in 1989 the Chadwick Center had created the Family Violence Program in order to attempt to reduce foster care placements for children. By creating specialized advocacy for mothers of children with suspected child abuse injuries, the Chadwick Center had found the majority of such mothers were victims of domestic violence and sexual assault. The Family Violence Program then sought to provide specialized domestic violence advocacy to mothers in the dependency court process while also providing specialized counseling and support groups to children witnessing family violence. This program, now a national model, had grown to 11 staff members—six child trauma therapists and five support staff members.

In 2003, a little over a year after opening the Center, we made the decision to bring the Family Violence Program team from the Chadwick Center to the Family Justice Center. We designed a new community floor, leased another 12,000 square feet in the building, and moved all our community agencies and the Family Violence Program onto the new community floor. Now, clients *and their children* could come to one place for services. But the journey was not over.

In the months that followed, we continued the dialogue on how to resolve the problems created by Monica's story. Monica's daughter had to be carted off to the Chadwick Center for interviews. Why? We had a Forensic Medical Unit at the Family Justice Center. We had interview rooms. Well, we had "dens" and "living rooms," but they were certainly adequate for interviewing children. So the planning continues.

Now we have a dedicated forensic interview room for non-acute child abuse cases complete with concealed videotaping equipment and microphones. We have an office for child abuse detectives when they need to come to the Center to work with a client and her children. And we are now aiming to bring the entire San Diego Police Department Child Abuse Unit to the Center in the future.

> It makes perfect sense for Children's Hospital to be here. The professionals from both the child abuse and domestic violence communities are seeing the same families. The lessons we've learned from working with children traumatized by abuse apply to children who witness domestic violence and vice versa. We learn from both systems and we apply them broadly. It's a win and win situation.
>
> —*Charles Wilson, Director*
> *Chadwick Center for Children and Families*
> *Former Director, National Child Advocacy Center*

Whether the entire child advocacy center of Children's Hospital will ever fully co-locate with the San Diego Family Justice Center is unclear, but it is an item of discussion. And communities are going down that road. In Ouachita Parish, Louisiana, the Child Advocacy Center and the new Family Justice Center have moved into buildings right next to each other with a connected hallway.[17] The idea is not new. The National Child Advocacy Center in Huntsville, Alabama, has the domestic violence team in a nearby building on the same campus where the Child Advocacy Center is located. The notion of co-location with child abuse and domestic violence services has been evolving for a number of years, but it is clearly gaining steam. The underlying goal, however, can be accomplished with even portions of these entities moving in together—bridges are being built between the silos. Lines of communication are developing, and relationships are being forged that can help in providing more effective and efficient services to victims and their children.

We should note, before moving on to other partnership opportunities, that bringing together child abuse and domestic violence professionals is not without its challenges. As noted earlier in the book, there are major tensions in many places between child abuse and domestic violence professionals. Many battered women have lost custody of their children in family and juvenile court systems that focus on the safety of the child exclusively without understanding the complex impacts of intimate partner violence on a parent's ability to protect her children.

On the other side, child abuse professionals often view shelters as entities that will not protect abused children in their efforts to advocate for mothers and the mother's ability to make her own decisions about the welfare of her children even in the face of violence and abuse. Historically, these issues have created tension, finger-pointing and name-calling. The result has been a great deal of animosity and distrust between child abuse and domestic violence professionals.

Without belaboring the issue here, however, we need to deal with it. We need to work through the problems and figure out how to work together. As we have brought services to our clients from different disciplines, the overwhelming response of the clients at the Family Justice Center has been "What took you so long?" The answer is not very satisfying: We did not want to work together. Turf issues were more important than best practices. Egos drove our work, not what was in the best interests of our clients and children. Personality conflicts and philosophical differences mattered more to us than meeting needs in the best possible way.

The better answer to the question of what took us so long to open Centers should be: We didn't *get I,*" but we do now! We now realize that we need to solve our system and silo issues with each other. We need to figure out how to find common ground and how to work together in the best interests of our clients instead of ourselves and our agencies.

> First, let me say 45 years ago there was nothing like the Family Justice Center. I'm very glad to see this is here. Although I didn't use all the services, because I didn't know about them, it seems there's so many services here and available. I would have liked to have known more about what was here.
>
> —*Anonymous, Elder Abuse Victim*

Bringing in Elder Abuse Professionals

The Family Justice Center vision is not only big enough to call for co-location of domestic violence and child abuse professionals; it is big enough to call for the participation of elder abuse professionals. If the statistics cited earlier are accurate, then we need a similar model for working with elder abuse victims. In fact, it makes more sense for elder abuse victims. Not only should the agencies working with the elderly get together for the sake of efficiency, but ambulatory elder abuse victims should not have to go from agency to agency to agency to get help. They too should be able to come to one place to get the help they need. I recently learned of an Elder Abuse Forensic Center in California, and I was so excited. Finally, someone had figured this out. But I was wrong. Upon visiting the center, I found no co-located agencies providing services—in fact, there were no services available to clients at all! The facility is essentially a case conferencing process for staff from agencies to come together to talk about cases they are working together to prosecute. To be sure, this is an exciting and positive idea, but this is not what our elder abuse victims need.[18] They need one place to go for help! At the San Diego Family Justice Center, we have started down this road. In January 2005 we moved the Police Department's Elder Abuse Unit (one sergeant, six detectives) into the Center. We are now focusing on providing all necessary services for ambulatory elder abuse victims by bringing in our specialized elder abuse advocates and prosecutors from the District Attorney's Office. The wraparound model makes as much sense for elder abuse victims as it does for domestic violence victims.[19]

> The Police Department's Elder Abuse Unit moved into the Family Justice Center in January 2005, almost two years after it opened. Seniors in particular do not have the time or energy to go from place to place. Not only do they need a central location to go, they also need a safe and comfortable place to go. Our victims feel comfortable in the dining room and the quiet room that has been especially set aside for seniors.
>
> —*Detective Nancy Kulinski, San Diego Police Department*

We already have the City Attorney's specialized elder abuse prosecutor on-site. In addition, many of the 25 agencies with staff at the Center have the ability to also assist elder abuse victims in some way. The Forensic Medical Unit is on-site and it can be available for forensic examinations of elderly victims. The chaplain's program can likewise offer services to victims of elder abuse.

Replicating this model will not be easy; just as with the child abuse movement, folks will want to protect turf, avoid competition for funds, and desire to maintain their separate identity. But again, why should those issues rise higher on the priority list than meeting the needs of those in need? *Why should our warped sense of significance in this work trump the opportunity to work well together, irrespective of who gets the credit?*

Without question, services for elderly victims of abuse should be available at a Center. If a community already has a child advocacy center and an elder abuse center, perhaps they need to sit down and start talking about partnerships and synergies to be gained from co-location. If a community already has a child advocacy center and a battered women's shelter, maybe it is time to at least start a dialogue and build a relationship, even if they are not ready to move in together!

Bringing in Sexual Assault Professionals

Rape crisis centers and sexual assault response teams (SART) do tremendous work today all over America. They are the culmination of 20 years of advocacy, political action, and determination from many impassioned change agents in the women's movement. Thankfully, in recent years, men have added their voices to the sexual assault movement as well. But when we start talking about the future and the best ways to meet the needs of victims of sexual assault in the years to come, I hope the Center vision will be an option for many in the sexual assault movement.

At the San Diego Family Justice Center, we have just recently begun moving toward the actual co-location of sexual assault professionals. When we opened the Forensic Medical Unit, we did envision this reality one day. We created the Unit to operate consistently with the SART protocol. We enlisted the services of sexual assault nurse examiners and other forensic nurse practitioners to ensure that our Forensic Medical Unit could one day perform rape exams. Within a year it is should become a reality.

Our Center medical director, Dr. George McClane, has worked closely with SART nurses for years. Most recently, he helped facilitate small group discussions with current SART nurses to get their feedback on the pending proposal to shift rape examinations from area hospitals to the Center. There is strong support.

Though the idea of a multidisciplinary team coming to a hospital to assist a rape victim has been innovative over the last 10 years, the question remains: How can we keep moving forward in providing better and better services to victims? How we can build critical mass to prevent the rape instead of intervening after the rape has occurred? How can we use the power and political strength of the Center to help move the sexual assault movement forward in our community?

The Alameda County Family Justice Center has already chosen to bring the sexual assault community into their Center. They have realized that rape victims deserve the best possible services. The Family Justice Center, not some room at a hospital, provides the best approach to helping rape victims.

Stay tuned for the outcome in our community. The hospitals currently conducting such examinations have made clear that they do not want to give up the income they receive from contracts with the city for such examinations. Ironically, they are asking for even more money, claiming that the current contracts are inadequate to compensate them for their costs. The Center, on the other hand, has little of the overhead of traditional hospitals and may be ideally suited to provide the exams at even less expense than currently being incurred at local hospitals.

The Center vision is big enough to build alliances with rape crisis centers, sexual assault response teams, and medical facilities. A Center-based Forensic Medical Unit, if operated as a private doctor's office, has far less overhead than a hospital. Though such a unit is unable to provide acute care, protocols can be established with the ire department or other contracted emergency medical responders to deal with the acute care patient in the appropriate circumstances.

Beyond the medical component, bringing in sexual assault agencies also makes services available to domestic violence victims who may not initially disclose sexual assault. Often, after domestic violence victims are safe and supported, they will disclose prior incidences of forced sexual contact and violent sexual assault. Such services should then be available on-site instead of having to refer the victim to some off-site location once disclosure has been made. We cannot properly address the needs of domestic violence victims if we do not provide co-located services for them when they disclose sexual assault. When a woman is raped by a total stranger she lives with incredible trauma and terror, when she is raped by her husband, she lives with the rapist. We cannot provide a "referral" off to another system or set of agencies in providing healing services from such a violation.

Conclusion

The Family Justice Center vision must ultimately include child abuse, sexual assault, and elder abuse professionals. Though domestic violence victims will be the primary focus at the initial development stages of a Center, efforts should be made early in the planning process to engage representatives from the other *silos*.

As we said at the beginning of this book, Family Justice Centers are about *relationships*. Building bridges to child abuse, sexual assault, and elder abuse professionals will also be about building relationships. If there is a history of mistrust between disciplines, relationship building may have to start with baby steps. Relationship building may take years before any form of co-located services is appropriate. But the effort needs to start now if we are going to bring together disparate movements that have far more in common than what separates them. The story of Monica and her children should always be a reminder that we must come together for the sake of those we hope to help.

Endnotes

1. The American Humane Association identified the link between child abuse and animal abuse more than 125 years ago. In 1894, a speaker at their convention noted, "A man who is cruel to his beast would be unkind to his wife and child." See www.americanhumane.org for the history of one of the leading animal rights organizations in America and the development of their journey in advocating for victims of child abuse.

2. Ibid.

3. See www.nationalcac.org for an excellent overview of the National Children's Advocacy Center. The National Children's Alliance now connects more than 500 child advocacy centers across the United States.

4. Susan Schecter, *Women and Male Violence: the Visions and Struggles of the Battered Women's Movement*, South End Press, Cambridge, MA, 1982. [An excellent discussion of the history of the sexual assault movement.]

5. Diana Russell, Rape in Marriage, Macmillan Press, New York, 1990. [Diana Russell, a prominent rape researcher, interviewed over 900 randomly selected women and found that, while 3% had experienced completed rape by a stranger, 8% had experienced completed rape by a husband. Russell's finding that more than one in every seven women who have ever been married have been raped in marriage must continue to be a wake-up call to everyone working with domestic violence victims regarding the need for co-located sexual assault services.]

6. Sarah Buel, "Effective Prosecution of Domestic Violence Cases," available at www.safestate.org/documents [An excellent overview of the elements involved in so-called evidence-based prosecution, referring to prosecuting domestic violence cases even without the participation of the victim.] See also Casey Gwinn, "Evidence-Based Prosecu-

tion in the Aftermath of Crawford v. Washington," *NOTICE,* (Vol. II, No. 2), newsletter of the National Center on Domestic and Sexual Violence, Austin, TX, Fall 2004, II(2).

7. The criminal charges were dropped against Koby Bryant when the victim in the case declined to cooperate with the prosecution. In the context of a domestic violence case, the victim's willingness to cooperate with the prosecution is not a relevant consideration now that prosecutors regularly go forward without victim participation in domestic violence cases.

8. Dr. George McClane, Director, Forensic Medical Unit, San Diego Family Justice Center, would likely have served as an expert witness for the prosecution in the Koby Bryant case after examining the medical records based on his expertise as a national forensic/ strangulation expert.

9. The fifth White House Conference on Aging, held December 11-14, 2005, included a review of the history of the slowly developing elder abuse national movement. For more information, go to www.whcoa.gov. The National Center on Elder Abuse (www. elderabusecenter.org) is also an excellent resource on the history of the elder abuse movement.

10. Deputy District Attorney Paul Greenwood trains across the United States and around the world on elder abuse issues. He argues that the elder abuse movement is "30 years behind the child abuse and domestic violence movements."

11. *Not for Sale, Feminists Resisting Prostitution and Pornography,* Christine Stark and Rebecca Whisnant (eds.), Spinifex Press, North Melbourne, Australia, 2004. [An articulate view of the need to include the anti-pornography movement in the wider anti-violence movement.

    Writer and speaker Angela Davis has provided an excellent critique of the domestic violence movement and its failure to address violence against women of color. See her keynote remarks at the 2005 Color of Violence Conference in Santa Cruz, California, available from http://www.arc.org/C_Lines/CLArchive/story3_3_02.html on January 29, 2006.

    The Lesbian, Gay, Bi-sexual, and Transgendered community has also advocated for inclusion in the larger focus on violence and abuse rather than the narrow focus on violence against women in the traditional feminist movement. Some writers and advocates in the anti-violence movement seek to develop an umbrella that includes sexual assault, child abuse, pornography, violence against women of color, and elder abuse in a very broad coalition that often has competing value systems. These clashes are nowhere more evident than in the issues that arise when male victimization is included in the face of feminist views of family violence, which seek to minimize the existence of female perpetrators.

12. See Chapter 8 for an extensive discussion of the research on co-occurrence of child abuse and domestic violence.

13. V. Drake and P. Freed, "Research Applications: Domestic Violence in the Elderly, " *Geriatric Nursing*, 1998, 19 (3), pp. 165-67. [One of the earliest articles overviewing the relationship between elder abuse and domestic violence.]

14. In one study, 45.9% of the battered women who reported abuse also reported being forced into sex by their intimate partners. See Jacqueline Campbell and K. Soeken, "Forced Sex and Intimate Partner Violence: Effects on Women's Risk and Women's Health," *Violence Against Women*, 1999, 5, pp. 1017-35. Most battered women's shelters report that battered women report levels of sexual assault at far higher rates once they are safe and allowed to speak confidentially.

15. Most research confirms that 80-90% of all sexual assaults are committed by someone the victim knows.

16. A not-yet-published study at McMaster University in Canada confirmed that 80% of the child victims knew their abuser.

17. For additional information on the Ouachita Parish Family Justice Center and its work with the local child advocacy center contact the Center at Family Justice Center of Ouachita Parish , 620 Riverside Drive, Monroe, LA, 71201, (318) 998-6030, fax (318) 998-6034, Or e-mail the Center at ehobson@wellspringalliance.org

18. For additional information about the Orange County Elder Abuse Forensic Center, contact the Center at P.O. Box 22006, Santa Ana, CA 92702-2006, (714) 825-3087, fax (714) 825-3001, or go to their Web site at www.elderabuseforensiccenter.com. Dr. Laura Mosqueda serves as the director of the Center.

19. In January 2006 the San Diego County District Attorney's Office, in partnership with the Family Justice Center, implemented a "wraparound service delivery approach" for elderly victims of financial exploitation, physical abuse, and neglect. The initiative is funded by one of the leading innovators in elder abuse services in America, the Archstone Foundation. See www.archstone.org.

13

Joining Hands Across America–the National Network

On October 8, 2003, President George W. Bush helped to launch what is now a bipartisan effort to begin connecting newly developing Family Justice Center's across America. The text of his speech that day included these words:

First, I've directed $20 million in 2004 to help communities create family justice centers, where victims of domestic violence can find the services they need in one place, one central location. Too often, the services designed to help victims are uncoordinated and scattered throughout communities.

Imagine what it would be like if you were an abused person trying to find help and you went from one place to another. . . . The victim has been so traumatized, and then she has to tell her story over and over again, which repeats the trauma. There's a better way to do this. There's a better way to help people who need help in our society.

San Diego figured it out. They've got a city attorney . . . who recognized that there's a more compassionate way to help people who have been abused. And so he did something about it. He created what's called the San Diego Family Justice Center. It's a full-service center for domestic violence victims, where police officers and prosecutors and probation officers and civil attorneys and counselors and doctors and victims advocates and chaplains all come together to help somebody. The runaround is over in San Diego. There's a central location where somebody who desperately needs help can find compassion and help.

Victims can pick up food vouchers; they can get help with transportation; they can file for a temporary restraining order against their abusers; they can sign up for supervised visitation programs to keep their children safe; they can get their cell phone there. They can find help.

The San Diego Family Justice Center opened a year ago. It has already served thousands of victims. They tell me the story of Caitlin Effgen, who is a brave woman who lives in San Diego. It's probably, unfortunately, a typical story I'm about to tell you. What's atypical is that she found help in a brand new way of helping victims of domestic violence. Her boyfriend started hitting her. She tried to break up with him and he began to stalk her. In other words, he was not only abusing her one way, he decided to abuse her in another way, as well. And she went to the authorities and got a restraining order, which, as the experts will tell you, sometimes it works and sometimes it didn't—because, in her case, the boyfriend continued to harass her, just wouldn't leave her alone.

You can imagine the fear she felt. He pled guilty to charges, but he still stalked and haunted her mind. And then she discovered the center. They helped her get counseling. They got another restraining order. A victim's advocate joined her and her dad in court. She got all the help she needed. I can imagine the relief that she must have felt when somebody who heard the call to love a neighbor did just that.

The guy ended up...behind bars, which is the right thing to do. I congratulate the San Diego law enforcement officers. But more important, she got to remember what life was like without her misery. Those are her words, not mine. She found compassion. The funding I've set aside will help begin a national movement toward more of these centers. Twelve will be funded through this initiative.[1] When they work, there's another 12, and maybe even more. Maybe we can escalate the request. But the point is, we have found what can work in order to provide efficient help to channel the compassion so somebody can get their life back together. . . ."[2]

Today, just a few years later, there are 10 operating Family Justice Centers in the United States, including the nationally and internationally recognized San Diego Family Justice Center. By the end of 2006, we estimate there will be 25 to 30 operating Centers in the United States, including the 15 created in the President's Initiative.

But Centers are not just coming online in the United States, as discussed throughout the book; they are coming online all over the world. There is a Center in Croyden, England, one in Waterloo, Ontario, and as many as five others in planning stages in other parts of Canada. The first Mexican Center has opened in Monterrey, Mexico, with the support of President Vicente Fox. There are another 25 to 30 communities moving toward such Centers across the United States and many more beginning to discuss the concept. It is an idea whose time has come.

Oprah Winfrey's profile on the Center concept in early 2003 and the President's focus on the San Diego Family Justice Center in his speech in October 2003 clearly helped draw national attention to this budding movement. But with new Centers coming online, major challenges await. How will they maintain a unified approach? Should there be fundamental elements at each Center? Should they all use the same name? Can there be some type of branding that will allow them to be consistent in their general approach even while providing different services in different communities? How will such Centers sustain themselves? How can they learn from each other?

Though the issues are complex, the answer is crystal clear. If Centers are to play an important role in the struggle to stop family violence and bring hope to violent families, we must connect them as they develop. We must generate strength in numbers and power in shared passion. The potential synergy and capacity that can be developed by networking the new Centers has already been learned from the child advocacy movement.

Battered women's shelters have taught us the lesson of organizing through the leadership of Rita Smith at the National Coalition Against Domestic Violence. State domestic violence coalitions have banded together at the national level through Lynn Rosenthal's leadership at the National Network to End Domestic Violence. We have also seen the power of coalition building by the National Domestic Violence Hotline, led by Cheryl Cates. So too, Family Justice Centers must come together and build a national and international coalition.

How To Build A National Network Of Centers

The question remains: How do we build a network of Family Justice Centers?

Over the last year, representatives from developing Centers across the country have begun a dialogue on the issues. The result? A fledgling plan…a modest beginning. This chapter seeks to flesh out the basics of the plan for the benefit of anyone interested in developing such Centers and then joining hands with other Centers. The world steps aside to let anyone pass who knows where they are going. So we need to figure out where we are going in order to take this movement forward. Three primary avenues will be pursued initially: creation of a national initiative, including coordinated, national fundraising efforts; development of an international conference/forum to discuss the issues in this fledgling movement; and publication of a specialized, practical "how-to" manual on developing a Center in your community. Let's look at each piece of this budding plan.

The National Family Justice Center Initiative

Soon after the creation of the Department-of-Justice-funded President's Family Justice Center Initiative, it became clear that structures would need to be developed far beyond the President's Initiative. To be sure, President George W. Bush saw it coming when he declared on October 8, 2003, that "...this funding will help launch a national movement toward the creation of these Centers across the country."[3] But the initiative, as developed by the Department of Justice, was not intended to evolve into a formal program of the Office on Violence Against Women (OVW). Instead, OVW chose to see it only as a demonstration initiative with funding for the general concept to become available in subsequent years through the Violence Against Women Act's Grants to Encourage Arrest Program.[4]

If the Department of Justice is not going to oversee the development of a long-term, sustainable program at the national level, then this task is left to the communities moving forward with this exciting vision. In many ways, it may be better for this effort to evolve outside the confines of the federal government. The flexibility and creativity necessary to make such a national initiative work may be more readily accessible with committed, local public and private sector individuals working together, in relationship, and free of the plethora of rules and regulations that necessarily come with federal funding. And at its core, these Centers need to be organic and grow out of local communities rather than face a "top down" management approach.

With these ideas in mind, it is time to launch the privately developed National Family Justice Center Initiative. Though in its infancy, concept ideas for the national initiative are evolving quickly. To understand the vision, let's look at key elements of the concept that have moved around the country and are now forming the basis for a national initiative.

This initiative should be a national public/private partnership between currently developing or existing Centers and national foundations, corporations, businesses, and philanthropists. This effort should not be created with federal money from any existing initiative. At the time of publication of this book, it is rapidly developing as a private, charitable venture by the San Diego Family Justice Center Foundation, doing business as the National Family Justice Center Foundation, with volunteer participants from a group of federally funded and other locally funded Centers across the country. Eventually, this initiative will assist other developing and operating Centers nationally and internationally that maintain compliance with the fundamental elements as defined in the National Family Justice Center Initiative.

The long-term vision of this initiative includes developing a national funding mechanism to support the burgeoning movement of co-located, multidisciplinary service centers for victims of domestic violence. The Centers, commonly referred to as *Family Justice Centers* and based on the San Diego model, are designed to reduce the number of places victims of domestic violence and sexual assault must go to receive needed services. After a reduction of nearly 95% in domestic violence homicides over the last 15 years, the San Diego Family Justice Center has rightly been hailed as a national model. As we have described throughout this book, using a "wraparound" service delivery model, the Center concept seeks to marshal all available resources in a community into a coordinated, centralized service delivery system with accountability to victims and survivors for the effectiveness of the model.

While not intended to replace or compete with existing, independent nonprofit social service organizations in a community, the Center offers the opportunity to provide effective, efficient services to victims and their children using staff from existing government and community-based organizations. Developed using the child advocacy center model, the vision for this National Family Justice Center Initiative includes such Centers one day providing services to victims of child abuse, sexual assault, elder abuse, stalking, and domestic violence. The philosophical basis for the movement includes a commitment to accountability for offenders, prevention initiatives, comprehensive intervention services, and long-term healing and restoration for hurting and violent families across America.

The San Diego Family Justice Center Foundation, doing business as the National Family Justice Center Foundation, will oversee this Initiative. A national board, made up of selected representatives from the existing Centers across the country, corporate sponsors, domestic violence advocates, and survivors, will be developed to provide leadership, guidance, and oversight. All financial activities will be documented in annual audited financial statements and detailed in a published annual report on the Initiative.

This Initiative is designed to provide $50,000 to $100,000 per year over the first three years to the first participating Centers to join. Funding will come from corporate and individual philanthropic support and sponsorships through a National Founders Circle and major corporations developed in partnership with the Corporate Alliance to End Partner Violence. After funding the first participating Centers over a three-year period, the National Foundation hopes to create an endowment, to be known as The Family Justice Center Trust Fund, for future funding.

Fundamental Elements of a Center in the National Initiative

The required fundamental elements for a local Center for purposes of receiving funding from the National Family Justice Center Foundation include the following:

- Co-located police and prosecutors: Law enforcement officers investigating domestic violence cases and prosecutors specially trained to handle domestic violence cases must be geographically co-located on a full-time basis at the Center.

- Co-located local domestic violence/sexual assault programs: Community-based advocacy programs must provide full-time, on-site advocacy services, including safety planning, to clients at the Center

- Partnerships: The Center must have active partnerships, including on-site or on-call victim services, with probation, military advocacy/liaison services (if applicable), and services from diverse community-based organizations, including a non-sectarian chaplain's program.

- Comprehensive legal services: Comprehensive legal services must be available to clients of the Center, including access to protection orders; representation in divorce, child custody, child support, and supervised visitation matters; and assistance with immigration, housing, employment, public benefits, and other legal services needed by victims.

- Central intake system: A central intake system must protect victim confidentiality but allow for information sharing between agencies when agreed to by the client.

- Culturally and linguistically competent services: Culturally and linguistically competent services appropriate to the community served are essential, including, providing impartial interpreters for victims, ensuring the service providers have culturally appropriate and diverse staff, and ensuring physical environments that respond to the unique needs of all victims.

- On-site medical services: On-site medical services should include forensic medical examinations and links to medical and mental health providers in the community.

- Child care: On-site free child care should be provided for the children of clients while clients are receiving services.

- Transportation assistance/accessibility: Assistance with transportation should be provided by a public or private entity on an as-needed basis.

- Volunteer program: A volunteer component should include a comprehensive, mandatory training program for volunteers on the dynamics of domestic violence and complete background checks on all volunteers.

- Pro-arrest/pro-prosecution policies: Each site should have law enforcement and prosecutorial agencies that emphasize the importance of arrest, prosecution, and long-term accountability for domestic violence offenders.

- Security plan: A security plan should be in place to ensure the safety of clients and staff at the Center.

- Prohibitions against offenders on-site: No criminal defendants should be provided services at the Center. Domestic violence victims with a previous history of violence or with a current incident in which the victim is the alleged perpetrator should be assessed on a case-by-case basis for eligibility for services at a Center. Identifiable procedures should be created to ensure availability of off-site services for victims in the event a current or prior criminal conviction prevents receiving services at the Center.

- Sustainability/strategic planning/local funding commitments: Any Center receiving funding from the National Family Justice Center Foundation must develop and implement a strategic planning process to ensure sustainability and development of the program and local funding options to assist operations.

The National Family Justice Center Initiative will form the basis for the first comprehensive national effort toward co-located multidisciplinary services for victims of domestic violence and their children. The new movement promises to develop innovative approaches to meeting the needs of victims and their children through specialized Centers across America and throughout the world in the next 20 years. The National Founders Circle and national board outreach effort is the vehicle to enlist the support of major national corporations that will commit significant resources to underwriting this developing national and international movement.

Opportunities should also be explored with major foundations and national corporations that may wish to offer in-kind services or products to support this Initiative. As this effort evolves, all avenues for expanding and developing this Initiative should be explored.

Communities across the United States and North America have been moving toward greater collaboration and coordination in the delivery of intervention and prevention services to victims of family violence and their children. Now the National Family Justice Center Initiative offers the vehicle for a coordinated, supported, accountable national movement working in collaboration with the original participating Centers.

An International Forum to Develop the Vision and the Network

Beyond reaching out to major donors and creating a grant funding entity, some of the most important work to be done in this movement is philosophical. We must develop a far-ranging discussion about how co-located services should operate. What is the model if the facility is hospital-based? What is the best approach if the facility is shelter-based? Can the San Diego model be replicated in any community, or do unique organic factors impact whether a community can pursue such an approach to service delivery? How will the model look in a tribal community in Alaska as opposed to a large metropolitan city in the Midwest?

Toward this end, the San Diego Family Justice Center has created an international forum to move the effort forward. Each April in San Diego, California, domestic violence professionals and caring community members from all across the country will gather to debate, discuss, and evolve the Center vision. In the years to come, annual conference information will be available at the Center's award-winning website: www.familyjusticecenter.org.

Indeed, with the movement gaining momentum in Canada, Mexico, and Great Britain, there will doubtless be attendees from all over the world. Since being profiled on the Oprah Winfrey Show in February 2003, the Center has hosted visitors from over 37 countries and all 50 states. The challenge now becomes how to structure national and international discussions. This annual three-day forum promises to be an important vehicle for moving the debate forward on the effectiveness, the challenges, and the hope of the Center vision.

As the conference evolves, researchers too will play a critical role in evaluating communities before and after the creation of multidisciplinary service centers for victims and their children. While the research in San Diego, including the focus groups with clients, has been touched on throughout this book, particularly in Chapter 11, more work needs to be done in evaluating Centers in different geographic, ethnic, and socioeconomic settings. The effectiveness of individual Centers will likely vary based on their philosophy, policies and procedures, and staffing levels. As discussed in Chapter 6, the effectiveness of Centers will hinge on the resources invested in individual communities. Lip service to the vision without the investment of substantial resources may yield a poor imitation of a fully funded, fully staffed Center.

Developing a "How-To" Manual to Guide Communities

This book is intended to whet your appetite. We want it to help you start dreaming big for your community. We have included a host of tips and insights throughout the book to help get people thinking about the possibilities and the challenges. But we have agreed with our publisher to write a detailed Family Justice Center Handbook or "how-to" manual in the next year. This manual, complete with CD-Rom resources, will include sample protocols, policies, and procedures. It will include the details that can so often determine the outcome of major community initiatives.

Without question, however, a practical how-to manual will evolve as time goes by. Many of the tips and insights included in this book were learned during the first three years after the San Diego Family Justice Center opened. Today we are learning very different things as the Center continues to evolve. Though the tips included here are extremely helpful and effective, based on three years of operating a Center, it is already clear that the manual we hope to produce next year will have many new and different insights. The Center, as we have discussed throughout this book, is a living organism. It must change and grow constantly in order to remain healthy, viable, and effective. The manual published next year as a companion to this book will reflect the long journey that our community has embarked upon in moving staff from 25 agencies into the same building along with another 20 off-site agency partners who come on an as-needed basis.

Conclusion

The National Family Justice Center Initiative will become the organizing structure for this developing movement of Centers across America and around the world. Staff exchanges, compliance with fundamental elements, joint fundraising efforts, and regular national and international forums can all play a role in moving this vision forward. For more information about the National Family Justice Center Initiative, go to www.familyjusticecenter.org and open the door to the professional visitors' site.

Endnotes

1. Ultimately, the President's $20 million Initiative funded the creation of 15 Family Justice Centers across the country. The San Diego Family Justice Center served as the coordinator of the Technical Assistance Project for the Office on Violence Against Women, which is overseeing the Initiative. While the current Initiative is not expected to continue, it is likely that communities will be able to seek federal grants through the federal Grants to Encourage Arrest Program under Title I of the Violence Against Women Act in order to develop Centers in the years to come.

2. Downloaded at www.whitehouse.gov/news/releases/2003/10/20031008-5.html on December 5, 2005.

3. See www.familyjusticecenter.org/library for a link to streaming video and transcript of the President's speech on October 8, 2003.

4. The Violence Against Women Act will likely continue to serve as the primary funding vehicle for Family Justice Centers on the federal level. However, most funding for local Centers can and should come from local monies in local communities where a Center is identified as a public safety initiative and given high priority by local elected officials. In many poor rural communities, funding mechanisms will need to be developed through state and federal funding strategies.

14

A Call to Action

*W*e are sending ambulances to the bottom of the cliff instead of building a fence *at the top.* And we are building faster and more efficient ambulances as the years go by! We now give priority to family violence-related 911 calls. We train police officers on how to respond. We have specialized cops, prosecutors, advocates, probation officers, therapists, and judges who focus on family violence cases once they come to the attention of the system.

We have dramatically expanded resources and multiplied programs for domestic violence victims over the last 30 years. Yet we fail to spend the much lesser amounts of money necessary to focus all our service providers on stopping the escalating violence at early stages and stopping domestic violence homicide before it happens. We are content to go after the children of domestic violence homes when they join a gang, use drugs, or bully a fellow student. We are content to prosecute the murderer after the homicide. Then our community can say we are tough on crime and we can lament the terrible decline in the social mores of our society.

Domestic violence and domestic violence homicide are preventable crimes. There is a reason we call our work at the Family Justice Center *homicide prevention* work. We can stop the violence and break the cycle of family violence that preys upon one generation after another.

We know that collaboration breeds efficiency. We know that victims feel empowered and experience greater safety and support when we offer them comprehensive services from a single location. We know that people working together from a single location are far more effective that people working separately. We know that when information is properly shared among agencies, we can increase safety for victims and accountability for offenders. We know that professionals working together have a much higher work satisfaction rate than those isolated in separate agencies. We know that professionals working in the same location with other professionals create powerful synergies and efficiencies. We see the possibilities of coordination, collaboration, and co-location. No one can argue with the evidence that victims of violence and abuse are more likely to live if we wrap them in services and support. The testimonies of the Center clients throughout this book provide irrefutable proof of the success of the vision.

But now comes the big question—*will* we do something about it? *Will* we stand up and become the change we desire? *Will* we pull together key folks in our communities and start pushing for change until something happens? *Will* we engage in the local, state, national, and international discussion into the appropriateness of co-located, multidisciplinary services for victims and their children? It sounds easy enough but it is *not* easy. Turf issues come crashing in. Egos of elected officials are often the size of Alaska and Texas combined. Agencies don't trust each other. People in the various agencies have offended one another. Agencies are viewed as a threat to one another. The list of excuses is a mile long. but we know that caring people who rise above all this can change lives.

The ladies that helped me—Maggy, Teresa, Jean and Helen—were so compassionate and caring. Excellent service! Juan was also very compassionate. Everyone is and was very professional at their jobs. I wish there were more caring people in this world like all of you. God bless all of you. Thank you.

—*R.E., Family Justice Center Client, 2005*

Women, men, and children are still dying. Families are still being torn apart. Children live with the memories of their trauma for a lifetime. Violent families don't even know there is another way.

Well, let's get down to business. Are you willing to make a difference? Are you willing to help change the world? How about if you just help change your little corner of it? The poster in the doctor's office was indelibly imprinted on my mind after one viewing: One hundred years from now it will not matter what kind of home you lived in, what kind of car you drove, or how much money you made. But the world may be a different place because you made a difference in the life of a child. Are you willing to make the difference in the life of a child? Because that is exactly what this book is all about. It is about breaking the cycle of family violence that visits generation after generation until caring community leaders and others try to stop it. It is about delivering the child from that black hole in the domestic violence poster a child survivor created for us 10 years ago. Children raised with domestic violence raise children with domestic violence—*unless* we stop it—*unless* we help those kids get out—*unless* we help victims find safety—*unless* we hold offenders accountable for their behavior!

Let's look at the possible steps we can each take. It does not matter what your profession, what your level of influence in the community, or what your income. Everyone can do something. People in the family violence movement may know more about where to start than others, but there are so many options.

Write a Letter

Everyone reading this book can put the idea of a Family Justice Center on the radar screen of elected officials and policy makers in their communities. It is simple, it is easy, and it takes little time. Write a letter! In straightforward language, ask them to support a process to study the possibility of co-locating staff from agencies in your community to help hurting families.

> I was not there very long before I wondered why we had not done this a long time ago. It was the best thing that has ever happened to our Police Department's Domestic Violence Unit.
>
> —*Sgt. Jim Arthur, San Diego Police Department*

During my eight years as an elected official, I never received a letter from a constituent that I did not at least scan. Perhaps the only exceptions, in the later years of my career, were anonymous letters or hate mail. Even in the seventh largest city in the country, letters from constituents got my attention. And if the subject matter was not something that I personally worked on, I would forward the letter to someone else in my office for a response. When I got four or five letters on a single subject, it definitely got my attention. So write a letter!

Go on the Internet, use a search engine and pull up five web sites about Family Justice Centers. Use the information in this book and write three paragraphs to your mayor, a city council member, a county commissioner, or the police chief; ask them to evaluate the creation of a Center in your community. You will be amazed at the possible impact of one single letter.

Create a Forum or Go to a Meeting

If you are in the domestic violence world professionally, maybe you should get more sophisticated. Bring the idea before your local coordinating council or domestic violence task force. Send it up your chain of command. Even if you are a social worker or a receptionist, you can do something to cultivate the seeds of this dream in your community.

Organize five folks that work in the field, create a little letterhead, make up a name for your group, and send some letters to people in positions of power. I learned the power of letterhead many years ago. When we started our domestic violence task force in San Diego, we had no power. We were trench workers—police officers, prosecutors, advocates with no power—so we created stationery and put our names down the side. Suddenly, the The San Diego County Task Force on Domestic Violence existed, and we quickly came to matter to elected officials, business leaders, and policy makers. We had no organizational structure when we began, we had no money, and we had no power; but we had stationary, and it was amazing how quickly we mattered. Stationary can help change the world.

So how about "Mothers Against Family Violence" or "Parents Against Abuse" or "Church Leaders Against Domestic Terrorism"? Pick a name, any name! And write a letter with your Bible study group, service club, soccer moms in your neighborhood, Little League parents, whomever! You have everything you need in this book, including testimonials from victims and staff at a Center to help light the fire of this vision somewhere.

The San Diego Teen Court is located now at the Family Justice Center. Whether on school campuses or in their homes, a significant number of Teen Court clients are exposed to domestic violence. We are extremely grateful to be in a facility where, under one roof, the families who come through our program can obtain assistance and learn about the resources that can help break the cycle of violence and improve their lives.

—*Heather Dugdale, Executive Director, San Diego Teen Court*

The first great challenge is to start the dialogue about the need for a better service delivery model for families in need. Call for policy makers to study how many places victims in your community must go to get help. Organize a meeting of your service club and figure out what your number is! My wife and I just bought a sleep-number bed. This company has done a great job of marketing its beds by having commercials where everyone is asking, "What is your number?" Wouldn't it be great if we were that successful with the Center vision? What if every community had many people asking, "What is our number—the number of agencies victims have to travel to for the help they need?" Okay, so you think I've been smoking something? Come on, dream big!

Maybe the number is not 32 agencies like it was in San Diego. Maybe it is only seven agencies or 10 agencies, but whatever the number, it is too many! Why should victims of the most intimate forms of violence and abuse have to go even five or six places when they are in need? Why can't we get our act together enough to bring services to one place? We provide *one-stop shops* in the aftermath of earthquakes, hurricanes, tornadoes, fires, and airline crashes. Why can't we do it for victims of family violence? The simple act of writing a letter, organizing a meeting, or calling for a discussion of the issues may be enough to start the long journey toward a Center in your community.

Make a Phone Call

Ditto on getting the attention of elected officials by calling their offices and leaving a message about the need to help coordinate services for hurting families! If a letter may get someone's attention, so will a phone call. Small-town elected officials return their own phone calls. Big-city elected officials have staff members who field constituent calls. But either way, a simple phone call can often get an idea or issue on the radar screen of an elected official at the local, state, or federal level.

Ask Community Leaders and Elected Officials Questions

Whether you work in the field of family violence or not, there are clearly some very simple questions that need to be answered as we start probing whether a community might be ready to move toward a Center. We saw those factors earlier when we talked about the fundamental elements that should exist in a Center. The next time you see your mayor, city council member, sheriff, DA, head of the Chamber of Commerce, or anybody else in any position of power, ask some questions! Be bold—families you know are still being torn apart—for some reading this book, it is your family too. Asking questions gets us all thinking. People that make noise get attention. Let's take a two-week break from complaining to City Hall about pot holes and focus on violence in the family!

Is there a family violence task force or coordinating council in your community? If not, why not? Is there a history of some agencies working together cooperatively? What is the level of communication and interaction between law enforcement (police officers, state troopers, deputy sheriffs) and the domestic violence shelter that supports your community? Do they hate each other? Do they respect each other? If you don't have a shelter, why not? Do you have an animal shelter in your community? If so, why do you have a shelter for animals but not one for people being abused?

Even if you have no one to ask, do your own mental review of the issues you have learned about in this book. Can elected officials get along? Is there someone or even more than one person in a position of power you know who might be willing to focus on the issue of family violence? Is there a minister, priest, or rabbi that *gets it* when it comes to domestic violence? Have you ever heard your minister preach on it? Are there any specialized police officers or detectives who handle family violence? Buy them the book! Is there a hospital or doctor in town with some particular interest in the issue? Buy them the book!

It will not take long to figure out whether your community has some history of specialized work in the area of domestic violence that can form the foundation for greater partnership, collaboration, and cooperation. If there isn't that kind of history, what then? I remain convinced that the answer still must be to start where you can!

Develop One Relationship to Help Change the World

What is the history of the domestic violence movement? It took battered women and allied friends organizing to create safe places for women to hide. Then, it became women and allied men advocating for laws that would make a statement about family violence and define intolerance for it in the criminal justice system. Battered women's advocates built relationships with people in the system. When laws were not followed, lawyers had to bring lawsuits, citizens had to stand up and publicly criticize elected officials who were not doing enough. But most of the best work was about *relationships*. It was about organizing. It was about alliances and building on what came before. And so it is with the Family Justice Center vision. Communities need to figure out where they are and then figure out how to get from where they are to where they need to be.

> History is being made at the San Diego Family Justice Center. Services for domestic violence victims and their families will now be changed forever. The San Diego Family Justice Center is the gold standard. Having personally experienced the loss of a bright light in my life because of a domestic violence-related murder, I benefited from the support and services of the Center. Now, as a volunteer, I want to do all I can to prevent violence in the lives of others.
>
> —*Larry Lima, Volunteer*

If you can't do anything else, invest your self in one relationship. Ashley Walker did when she invested her life in me, and San Diego will never be the same. Gael Strack has invested her life in countless others, recruiting them to the cause, and it has changed the world. If you are a survivor of family violence, your story may help someone else care. Take the time to tell your story if it is safe to do so and let it be a vehicle to build a relationship with someone that can make this vision a reality in your community.

If you are a system professional, you have an enormous ability to make a difference. If a community has a shelter director and a police chief who hate each other, they should probably not move in together and bring their staff members to one location in order to provide better services to victims. What if you can help heal such a relationship? What if the shelter director can build a bridge with the prosecutor's office or the sheriff's department? What if the shelter can reach out to the local hospital emergency room? What if there is a local bar association that could consider having its lawyers come to the shelter three days a week? Isn't that how most legal clinics for battered women started?

Today, most shelters have some version of co-located, multidisciplinary services. They offer legal services, schools, child care, limited medical help, art therapy, play therapy, housing, and a host of other support options. How did they get this far? They built alliances. They kept listening to clients and asking them what they needed and then worked to provide it. At the core of it all, somebody helped heal or start a relationship.

The journey cannot stop now! Clearly, there is power in the criminal and civil justice systems. The legal system is where the law keeps its promise. The business community is where we see the powerful engine of capitalism produce wealth and opportunities for people. The faith community is where we feed people's souls—especially those who consciously long for spiritual encouragement. So why not challenge your community to go beyond the basic services for most battered women's shelters? Why not seek to pull in more partners? Why not at least consider the Family Justice Center model?

If you have a shelter, does it have to run the Center? Maybe, maybe not. What if the most powerful community force in the domestic violence field is the local hospital? Maybe it could take the lead in bringing agencies together. Perhaps it could be the district attorney or police chief. Each community will likely be different.

Existing Resources to Point the Way

There are many questions worth asking if you can start a dialogue. And there are now many resources evolving across the country—communities that have created Centers. They have learned lessons and come to understand how different the process is in diverse types of communities. Different communities have evolved different approaches. One size does not fit all. The San Diego journey may not be similar to that of other communities. Victims of family violence in one community may not ask for the same kinds of services that victims in other communities are seeking. But there are now models out there for other communities to study.

The dynamic, committed Director of the federal Office on Violence Against Women, Diane Stuart, recently recognized the importance of San Diego's journey to the Center. "I was present at the ribbon cutting when the doors of your Center first opened. I recall that even during the ceremony, domestic violence victims were lining up for services. It was achingly evident that the family justice center concept was an idea whose time had truly come. You are all true pioneers. It was your Center that inspired President Bush to create the President's Family Justice Center Initiative. Family justice centers are now sprouting up all across the country, committed to the concept of co-locating vital services for victims of domestic violence."[11] Will you join us? Will you find even a small way to help? There are many who will help you if you want to become a change agent in your community.

In California, we are beginning a three-year project to evaluate communities to see who is ready to move down the road toward a Center. Some communities in California, like Riverside, have evolved a model for three Centers in their county to cover each defined geographic area under the leadership of their innovative District Attorney, Grover Trask. Other communities have found a close, positive working relationship between domestic violence professionals and child abuse professionals and have decided to co-locate the child advocacy team and staff from agencies that specialize in domestic violence.

But at every turn, experts are being created. People are figuring out what works and what doesn't. All of these resources will evolve and become available to communities that have the courage to look at co-located services as an option for better meeting the needs of victims.

Let's Not Forget—Some Communities May Not Be Ready

On the other hand, as we assess more communities, we are also finding that some are not even close to being ready for a Center. Perhaps some communities will never be ready. They are too spread out, too rural, or too unique for a variety of reasons. Communities without a history of collaboration and cooperation should probably start with some basic coalition building and relationship development before they even think about the Center vision.

Communities with great hostility between the child abuse and domestic violence communities should not try to move those folks in together. If the criminal justice system is routinely arresting battered women or revictimizing victims with inappropriate policies and procedures, it should not be leading the way to start a Center. Discernment is necessary. Patient, careful analysis is crucial. Slow, thoughtful review and discussion is important. Help start asking the questions! What communities like ours have gone down this road? Is our community ready to talk about it? Should we go visit that similar community with a Center and see how it works?

It has always been so. Dedicated, passionate individuals change the world—not necessarily big or powerful people, but people with big hearts and the guts to step out and do something that others have not done—people who are willing to recruit allies and then move forward together. Moms can make this vision happen. Dads can make it happen. Doctors or nurses can lead the way. Judges can push the movement forward. Business leaders…attorneys…therapists…police officers…probation officers…church leaders…the list is endless. But without question, the need is great and the laborers are still too few.

Conclusion

If you have made it to the end of this book, you have a role to play. If you have trudged through the mundane and the complex here, you need to do something now. There is hope for hurting families. There are hundreds of programs that can provide help, but we can do more together than separately. There are laws, policies, and procedures in public and private agencies. There are thousands of caring professionals available to help.

But if the Center vision is going to be part of the solution to family violence in America and around the world, we need people to take it forward and help to make it a reality in more communities. If our book has proven its point—that hope for hurting families is available through the Center vision—then only one more thing needs to happen. We need *you* to help us give victims and their children hope. Will you help?

Endnotes

1. Letter from Diane Stuart to the San Diego Family Justice Center staff dated October 14, 2005. Available upon request at www.familyjusticecenter.org.

BOOKS FROM VOLCANO PRESS

FAMILY AND FRIENDS' GUIDE TO DOMESTIC VIOLENCE: How to Listen,
Talk and Take Action When Someone You Care About is Being Abused
by Elaine Weiss, Ed.D. $17.95

SURVIVING DOMESTIC VIOLENCE: *Voices of Women Who Broke Free*
by Elaine Weiss, Ed.D. $17.95

CHILD ABUSE AND NEGLECT: *Guidelines for Identification, Assessment*
and Case Management
co-edited by Marilyn Peterson, M.P.A., M.S.W and Michael Durfee, MD $60.00

LEARNING TO LIVE WITHOUT VIOLENCE: *A Handbook For Men*
by Daniel Jay Sonkin, Ph.D. and Michael Durphy, MD $15.95

LEARNING TO LIVE WITHOUT VIOLENCE (Work tape: Two C-60 Minute Cassettes)
by Daniel Jay Sonkin, Ph.D. and Michael Durphy, MD $15.95

APRENDER A VIVIR SIN VIOLENCIA (*Learning To Live Without Violence* in Spanish)
Adaptation by Dr. Jorge Corsi $14.95

THE COUNSELOR'S GUIDE TO LEARNING TO LIVE WITHOUT VIOLENCE
by Daniel Jay Sonkin, Ph.D. $29.95

FAMILY VIOLENCE AND RELIGION: *An Interfaith Resource Guide*
compiled by the staff of Volcano Press $29.95

THE PHYSICIAN'S GUIDE TO INTIMATE PARTNER VIOLENCE AND ABUSE:
How to Ask the Right Questions and Recognize Abuse (Another Way to Save a Life)
by Ellen Taliaferro, MD and Patricia Salber, MD $34.95

BATTERED WIVES by Del Martin. $12.95

CONSPIRACY OF SILENCE: *The Trauma of Incest*
by Sandra Butler $13.95

THE WOMEN WE BECOME: *Myths, Folktales, and Stories About Growing Older*
by Ann G. Thomas, Ed.D. $17.95

TESTIFYING UNDER OATH: *How to be an Effective Witness*
by James M. Vukelic. $18.95

HOPE FOR HURTING FAMILIES: *Creating Family Justice Centers Across America*
by Casey Gwinn, JD and Gael Strack, JD $26.95

Volcano press continously updates its website for our own and other fine books.
volcanopress.com

TO ORDER

ONLINE	E-MAIL	TELEPHONE	FAX	BY MAIL
www.volcanopress.com	sales@volcanopress.com	800.879.9636	209.296.4995	Volcano Press Box 270 Volcano, CA 95689

Please send check or money order for the price of the book(s) plus $6.95 shipping charge for the
first book and $1.75 for each additional book. California residents please add appropriate sales tax.

Volcano Press books are available at quantity discounts for bulk purchases, professional counseling,
educational, fund-raising or premium use. Please write or call for details.

VOLCANO
· PRESS ·

Box 270, Volcano, CA 95689